EASY CHINESE

PHRASEBOOK & DICTIONARY

Wendy Tung

PASSPORT BOOKS
NTC/Contemporary Publishing Company

Library of Congress Cataloging-in-Publication Data
is available from the United States Library of Congress.

$12.95 new 5/12/98 (8D)

Published by Passport Books
An imprint of NTC/Contemporary Publishing Company
4255 West Touhy Avenue, Lincolnwood (Chicago), Illinois 60646-1975 U.S.A.
Originally published by Foreign Languages Press,
24 Baiwanzhuang Road, Beijing 100037, China.
Copyright © 1991 by Foreign Languages Press
Printed in the United States of America
International Standard Book Number: 0-8442-8526-9

18   17   16   15   14   13   12   11   10   9   8   7   6

Contents

Introduction   1
Discovering China   3
Pronunciation Guide   7

1. The Basics   9

Meeting and Greeting / Requests / Expressing Thanks / Polite
Remarks / Questions / Exclamations / On the Phone / Apologies
/ Help / Good-byes
Key Words / What You May Hear / Signs

2. Travel   25

At Customs / Money in China / Booking an Air Ticket / Planes /
Trains
Key Words / What You May Hear / Signs

3. Health   37

Seeing a Doctor / In the Hospital / Taking Medicine, Having an
Injection
Key Words / What You May Hear / Signs

4. Transportation   45

Buses and Trolley Buses / Subways / Taxis / Renting a Car /
Bikes / On Foot
Key Words / What You May Hear / Signs

5. Hotel   57

Check In / Check Out / Service / Problems / Laundry / Mail /
Phone Calls / Telegrams, Telexes and Telefaxes /
Barbershops
Key Words / What You May Hear / Signs

6. Eating   69

Breakfast in a Hotel / Eating in a Restaurant / Making a
Reservation / Looking for a Restaurant / During the Meal / Cold
Drinks / A Quick Lunch
Key Words / What You May Hear / Signs

7. Shopping 83

Shopping in a Department Store / At an Arts and Crafts Store / Buying Books and Newspapers / Buying Clothes and Shoes / Shopping in a Free Market / Printing Film
Key Words / What You May Hear / Signs

8. Making Friends 99

Meeting for the First Time / Introductory Remarks / Invitation / Calling on Someone / Calling a Friend by Phone / Talking About Hobbies
Key Words / What You May Hear / Signs

9. Sightseeing 113

Preparing for a Trip / Visiting a Tourist Site / Visiting a Factory / Visiting the Countryside / Taking Photos / Talking with Chinese Tourists
Key Words / What You May Hear / Signs

10. Entertainment 127

Watching a Performance / Getting Tickets / Getting Seated / Discussing the Show / Watching a Sports Event
Key Words / What You May Hear / Signs

English-Chinese Dictionary 135

Chinese-English Dictionary 208

Appendices 241

1. A Table of Chinese History
2. Time Around the World
3. Chinese Measures and Weights
4. Measure Words
5. Week Days
6. Months
7. Figures
8. Directions
9. Chinese Horoscope
10. Family Relations
11. Traditional Chinese Festivals
12. Chinese Idioms
13. China's Provinces, Autonomous Regions and Municipalities
14. Common Flowers
15. Common Trees
16. Temperatures (C) in Ten Major Chinese Cities

TIPS

Pronunciation   **7**

Chinese phonetic system / Pronunciation

1. The Basics   **9**

Chinese names / We, you and they / Pronouns / Verbs / "To be" / Did it, is it, or will it? / Questions / Courteous phrases / What to say when you're sure / Negatives / What one? / Is it better or best?

2. Travel   **25**

Customs and money exchange / Chinese currency / Exchange / International airlines / Flights / Trains / Boats / The opposite of . . . is

3. Health   **37**

Good medical care / Chinese medicine / Acupuncture / Qigong / Medicine / Ordinal numbers

4. Transportation   **45**

Buses / Bus fare / Bus routes and operating hours / Minibuses / Taxis / Subway / Bicycles / Rent a bike / On foot / Toilets

5. Hotel   **57**

Tipping / Don't drink the tap water / Safety / Toiletries / Laundry / Postage / Using the phone / Electric appliances / Long-distance phone calls / Telexes and telefaxes

6. Eating   **69**

Fried crullers and beancurd milk / Two musts / Four major regional cuisines / Chopsticks / Wait, there's more / It's called what? / "Dry the cup" / Pigs, snakes and frogs / Rice, steamed buns and boiled dumplings / Small restaurants

7. Shopping   **83**

Ordinary stores / Foreign articles / Friendship stores / Antiques / Newspapers, books and maps / English books on Chinese

topics / English language reading materials / Recommended
articles / Chops (seals) / Other gift items available in all cities /
Buying and printing film / Batteries and their sizes

8. Making Friends 99

Hello, comrade / Old Wang and Little Li / Unique greeting /
Invitation to a meal / That's Mrs. who? / Age and salary /
Jasmine or green tea / Chinese idioms / What to wear on formal
occasions / Holidays / Festivals

9. Sightseeing 113

How big is China? / *Putonghua*—standard Chinese / The four
seasons / Smoking / Dialects / Common flowers / Common
trees / Taking photos / Two slangs / Telephone service /
Measure words

10. Entertainment 127

Peking opera / Chinese musical instruments / Table tennis and
other sports

Introduction

Mandarin Chinese (or *pǔtōnghuà*) seems impenetrable, but the wonderful truth is that it is not. Hiding within Chinese characters (*hànzì*) is an elegantly simple grammar. After mastering a few basic patterns, you won't sound quite like a Chinese scholar, but you will be able to communicate effectively and easily with the average Chinese. The *Easy Chinese Phrasebook and Dictionary* is designed to get you started and to be a convenient guide for you on your trip to China.

We have spelled out the *hànzì* in this book in order to put the emphasis on actually communicating with people. The system used, known as *hànyǔ pīnyīn* (the Chinese phonetic alphabet), was developed in China in the late 1950s. The spelling popular in the West until recently is the Wade-Giles system, developed by two Englishmen in the 19th century. Their system was meant to be understood by speakers of all the European languages—which led to the assignment of odd consonants to sounds in Chinese, as in *p* instead of *b* for the English *b*-sound (*p'* was to stand for *p*), and *t* instead of *d*. The new *pīnyīn* system is based on English pronunciation, and so, besides a few unusual sounds, for an English speaker what you see written is what you say. (By the way, the *j* in Beijing is said like "jingle," not with a French accent as in *bon jour*.)

Most Westerners have the impression that Chinese speak many dialects that are mutually unintelligible, and that *putonghua* doesn't work too far outside of the north. To a certain extent this is true. There are eight major regional dialects in China. Seven of these, however, are found in the southeast ranging along the South China Sea, between Shanghai and Guangxi. In most other areas—including two-thirds of China's population and over three-quarters of its territory—*pǔtōnghuà*, or a regional variant that is similar to it, is spoken. And the popularity of national and local TV programs in the standard dialect, as well as the requirement that *pǔtonghuà* be taught to all school children, means that even in the areas with regional dialects you can find people that can understand you.

Chinese, you'll find as you learn it, is based on monosyllables. This makes it easy to substitute words. One of the helpful features of this book is that the variable words in the sample sentences are bracketed so that you can identify them and substitute an alternative from the lists provided.

In this book, however, we've sometimes put two or even three syllables together when giving *pīnyīn* forms. This is because Chinese

1

has a growing group of compound words—expressions similar to the English words "airplane" and "handball." The word "*pǔtōnghuà*," which literally means "common speech," is one. Some of the many other words that are formed like this are *fànguǎn* (restaurant, literally "food place"), *qìchē* (car, "steam vehicle"), and *tuōlājī* (tractor, "pulling machine"). In many compound words the second syllable is *zi*. This *zi* has no meaning itself; it functions simply as a noun marker. Similar to *zi* is the *r* sound that Beijingers add to the end of nouns. These aren't added to all nouns, though, so be careful to follow the form given in the sample vocabulary. There's an easy way to remember how to pronounce compounds: Chinese words almost always begin with a consonant and end with a vowel. *Zhūròu* (pork), for instance, would never be said "*zhūr-òu*." (Cantonese, on the other hand, being a more ancient form of Chinese, has many consonant endings.)

Besides the initial consonant sound and the final vowel sound, every Chinese word has a third component—one of the four tones or a neutral tone. This is an important part of the meaning of the word, as there are many homophones in Chinese; the entire language, in fact, has less than 1,000 "words" if tone differences are ignored. The tones are the most difficult part of Chinese. It will take some practice to get mastery over them. For one, it will take some practice to avoid using the fourth tone for every word—a mistake natural to English speakers. And you'll need to get used to the fact that statements in Chinese sometimes end with a word that takes the first, second, or third tone. The best way to guide yourself through the tones is to get familiar with how Chinese speakers use them.

You'll find that in everyday spoken Chinese not every tone is spoken clearly. Some tones are difficult to say together, or, if said with emphasis, would bring attention to a less important part of the phrase. For example, *bù* (not), a fourth-tone word, is pronounced *bú* if it comes before another fourth-tone word, as in *Wǒ búqù* (Meaning "I'm not going.") In addition, *yī* (the number "one") often becomes *yí* in colloquial speech. These changes in the "official" tone have been marked in the sample sentences of the book.

Still, Chinese as a whole is very accessible to beginners. The more arcane aspects of the complicated Chinese poetry and essay styles, which some consider the best parts of the language, need not be studied at all to grasp ordinary spoken Chinese. If you start with a few of the simple sentences in this book and use them in everyday situations, you'll find that soon you are speaking quite passable Chinese!

Discovering China

China can be an overload for tourists. It's so big and there's so much to see. To get the most out of your trip, you might do some reading ahead of time, though this doesn't have to be a lot. For instance, you could read up on Xian—a place most tourists like to stop. This ancient city is known for, among other things, the spectacular legions of terra-cotta warriors unearthed in the 2,000-year-old tomb of the Emperor of Qin. But if you're not ready to concentrate on just one place, then you might consider one of a few other approaches.

The traditional approach is the **DYNASTY MODEL**, which gives you the dates of the rulers and their major achievements.

The prehistoric **Xia Dynasty** (21st-16th cent. B.C.), founded on the northern plains, is said by the ancient historians to have seen the invention of agriculture, writing, and flood-control, and to have started what were to become Taoism and Confucianism. The **Shang** and **Zhou** dynasties (16th cent.-221 B.C.) that followed are known as a feudal period when the emperor, competing for power with local barons, was sometimes only ruling a few square kilometers of territory. The **Spring and Autumn Period** (770-476 B.C.) and the **Warring States Period** (475-221 B.C.), which came at the end of the Zhou era, were when philosophers such as Confucius were teaching. Shi Huang Di (literally the "First Emperor") of Qin (r. 221-210 B.C.) then conquered all his rivals and founded the **Qin Dynasty** (221-207 B.C.). During his short reign the various local walls along the northern border of China were unified into the Great Wall and Chinese writing, currencies, and measurements were standardized.

The **Han Dynasty** (206 B.C.-A.D. 220) is held in high regard by most Chinese. The official annals record the deeds of the "good" Han Dynasty Emperor Wu (r. 140-87 B.C.) in detail, for example, and credit his reign with the opening of the Silk Road through Northwest China to Turkestan and Persia, and with effecting central control over the country. Also, paper and the compass were invented. After the Han fell in the face of a massive rebellion, three centuries of disunity followed.

The period that began with the reunification of China by the short-lived **Sui Dynasty** (581-618) and that was dominated by the **Tang Dynasty** (618-907) has been called China's most prosperous and creative time. The Grand Canal was built, control was effected over the Silk Road route as far as Central Asia, Buddhist art and architecture reached their zenith, and the examination system was universalized to bring the best and the brightest into the service of the

3

emperor. In addition, Chinese literature was at a high point under the Tang.

The **Song Dynasty** was founded in 960 after another period of short-lived dynasties. Not able to consolidate its rule, it was pushed southward by the steppe tribes until it collapsed in 1279. Culturally, though, the Song era was a time of unprecedented innovation: silk and porcelain factories were founded, moveable-type printing and gunpowder were invented, the magnetic-needle compass was designed and applied to shipping, and canal locks on China's elaborate waterway system were in use. The Mongols, after brutally conquering all China, set up their court at Dadu in the north (on the site of present-day Beijing) and became the **Yuan Dynasty** (1271-1368).

The rebellion against the Yuan rulers started less than a hundred years after they had come to power. The following **Ming Dynasty** was founded in 1368. The Ming emperors built their imposing palace, the Forbidden City, at Beijing. The thirteen Ming Tombs in suburban Beijing, containing huge hoards of wealth, are another example of the talent and riches that the Ming rulers drew to the capital city. Still, this period, with its nostalgia for past grandeur, was not as innovative as the Tang and Song.

The **Qing Dynasty** (1644-1911) was established by the Manchus, who conquered the whole of China from their homeland in the Northeast. They had an initial period of imperial greatness, and at the same time assimilated Chinese culture. Beginning in the early 1800s, though, the Qing court weakened in the face of successive internal rebellions and the external threat from Western powers eager for trading rights.

What you can find out about the dynasties of China, however, won't be complete without some knowledge of the other interesting aspects of Chinese civilization. You might want to begin with some general knowledge of China's political history and then read in detail on a different theme.

Perhaps you're interested in China's rich **ART HISTORY**. Just as formidable as China's dynastic history, it has developed, besides, a unique array of symbols and traditions. You might want to concentrate on the religious art and carvings of China, or on the two most distinctive Chinese genres—landscape painting and porcelain. The latter both flourished during the creative Tang and Song dynasties: the establishment at that time of imperial porcelain kilns near the best deposits of clay, and the official sponsorship of painters, encouraged an artistry that some claim has never been matched.

The development of **TRADE AND TECHNOLOGY** is another theme you can use to approach China. Keep in mind that over the past centuries Westerners have made a flip-flop in how they view Chinese development. At first, influenced by Marco Polo's *Travels* and the detailed reports of Jesuit missionaries, scholars in the West regularly referred to China as a sort of rational and highly developed paradise. Then, as the Industrial Revolution pushed the West into a frenzy of development, China came to be seen by some—particularly Western diplomats and businessmen—as a backward and decaying society.

Because both viewpoints were relative to the West, which was first behind China and then ahead of it, they exaggerated the actual conditions of China. Nonetheless, it is clear from the history books that China's economy reached a peak and then slowed down. Innovation, apparent in such important inventions as printing to such ostensibly common changes as adopting the chair for daily use, was sweeping the country from the 9th through 12th centuries. Afterward, development leveled off. Chinese society then fell into an intricate, self-contained cycle—a system of agriculture and trade that sustained a population of millions for several centuries.

The driving force behind China's technological achievements was China's great tradition of **LEARNING AND SCHOLARSHIP**. The thousands of well-designed bridges and buildings, the elaborate system of medicines and therapeutic treatments, and the highly productive agriculture techniques all are the result of careful study and scientific analysis. The classical scholars documented these achievements in the official history of each dynasty and in monographs on everything from shipbuilding to chemistry. If you also look into the elaborate and ritualized world of the Mandarins, with its grueling examinations, bitter rivalries, and continuous shuffling of officials from place to place, you can gain a full picture of the 2,000-year-long grip that the scholars had on China. At the same time you will gather insight into China as a whole.

China is also interesting to consider in terms of its **SOCIALIST CULTURE**. Socialism is rather new compared to the thousands of years of Chinese civilization, but it has brought a new set of circumstances to China. In the past forty years of reconstruction after the decades of war and rebellion that had devastated the country, China's economy has had a remarkable expansion. The fields situated on the east central plains is one place where you can see the impact of this. They used to be a crazy quilt of crops, each small plot tilled by a farmer or tenant. These were punctuated by family graveyards decorated with colorful flower wreaths and paper memorial banners. Today they stretch for miles without a break. These and other changes—the lack of widespread street crime, for example, and the almost full employment—will all be apparent when you visit China.

Alongside this modern development, however, everywhere you'll still find evidence of the rich history of China: canals and terraces built over centuries by laborers determined to tame their environment; paintings and ceramics; palaces and ruins that tell of powerful dynasties; and temples, pagodas and huge rock carvings of Chinese religions. You'll also find such subtle pleasures as, say, watching a sunset over Hangzhou's West Lake.

The thing to remember about China is that, though it may be large and diverse beyond imagination, and steeped in centuries of civilization very different from the West's, it need not be a mysterious world apart. China is more open now than at any time before. With a little curiosity and some Chinese language, you'll have plenty of opportunities to enjoy this vast and eclectic land. With a little effort, you'll be able to piece together your experiences and discover for yourself what makes this part of the world Chinese.

Dean Arkema

Pronunciation Guide

1. The Chinese Phonetic Alphabet (*Pinyin*)

Common Alphabet

A a	ah or a in father
B b	similar to "bay" with a shorter vowel
C c	same as the "ts" in rats
D d	similar to "day" with a shorter vowel
E e	pronounced between "u" in up and "oo" in book
F f	same as F in English
G g	similar to "gay" with a shorter vowel
H h	similar to "hah"
I i	same as E in English
J j	like "jee-ay" in English
K k	like English "kay" with a shorter vowel
L l	same as L in English
M m	same as M in English
N n	similar to "nay" with a short vowel
O o	close to English "oh"
P p	like English "pay" with a short vowel
Q q	like "chee-oh" in English keeping both the "ee" and "oh" short
R r	similar to the "r" in English "read"
S s	same as S in English
T t	similar to the "ta" in English "table" with a shorter vowel
U u	like the "oo" in English "ooze"
V v	like the "va" in English "vane" with a shorter vowel
W w	pronounced as "wah" in English
X x	similar to English "she"
Y y	similar to "yah" in English
Z z	like the "ds" in English "beds", or like "dzay" with a shorter vowel

---

T I P S

Chinese phonetic system (*Hànyǔ Pīnyīn*)

Pǔtōnghuà (standard Chinese), based on a northern China dialect, is used in broadcasts and taught in schools throughout China. To popularize pǔtōnghuà, a Chinese Phonetic System (Hànyǔ Pīnyīn) or the romanization of Chinese language was invented. It uses the 26 English letters as its consonants and vowels to pronounce different characters and words with four basic tones. To pronounce Chinese words correctly, it is wise to learn pīnyīn first. And this is also a short-cut for people who have not learned Chinese before.

Unique Alphabet

Zh zh   to form this sound, raise the tip of the tongue to touch the front of the hard palate (just behind the alveolar ridge), then release the tongue just enough for the air to flow to pass through with some friction

Ch ch   with the tip of the tongue first curled back to touch the hard palate, then released just enough to allow the air flow to pass through

Sh sh   to form this sound, let the tip of the tongue curl back to approach but not touch the front of the hard palate, leaving a narrow fissure between the two, and let the air flow pass through this fissure with some friction

Ü ü   to form this sound, first pronounce *i* then transform to *u*, just like French "u" or German "ü"

2. The Four Basic Tones in *Pinyin*

⁻ First tone   keeps steadily to the highest pitch.

ˊ Second tone   starts at the middle pitch and rises steadily to the highest pitch.

ˇ Third tone   first drops, relatively slowly, to the lowest pitch, then rises quickly to the highest pitch.

ˋ Fourth tone   falls steadily from the highest to the lowest pitch.

Pronunciation

T I P S

To pronounce Chinese characters correctly, you must have a good command of the "four tones" of pǔtōnghuà. This is important because any single pīnyīn word means something different depending on what tone you use. The word ma, for instance, can mean "mommy" (mā), "hemp" (má), "horse" (mǎ), or "curse"(mà). So if you want to say "mommy" but use the third tone, then you've said "horse." Mistakes like this might confuse your listeners a bit, but at worst it will provide some comic relief. Anyway, even if you use some wrong tones in a sentence, you can usually still be understood.

The Basics

Nín hǎo.
How are you?

As an ancient Chinese proverb says, "Everything is difficult in the beginning"—and learning a foreign language is certainly no exception. But if you're planning to travel to China, there is nothing more valuable that you can take along than some Chinese language. Your spoken Chinese will give you a chance to meet ordinary Chinese (who will immediately love you for speaking their language), as well as being useful in getting a good deal in China's bustling markets or in getting out of a tough bind or two.

Meeting and Greeting

Hello (How are you?)	Nín hǎo!
Good morning!	Zǎoshàng hǎo!
Have you had your (lunch/dinner)?	Chīle méiyǒu?
What a fine day it is!	Jīntiān tiānqì zhēnhǎo!
Good afternoon!	Xiàwǔ hǎo!
Good evening!	Wǎnshàng hǎo!
Good night!	Wǎn ān!
Good-bye!	Zài jiàn!
How do you do?	Nín hǎo!
I am (American).	Wǒ shì (Měigguó rén).
My name is (George Brown).	Wǒ jiào (Qiáozhì Bùlǎng).
I am glad to meet you.	Hěn gāoxìng rènshi nǐ.
It's a long time since we last met.	Hǎojiǔ méi jiàn le.

Requests

Could you help me?	Néng bāng wǒ yíxià ma?
Can I ask you a question?	Néng wèn nǐ yí ge wèntí ma?
Could you do me a favor?	Néng bāng wǒ ge máng ma?
Do you mind if I (smoke)?	Kěyǐ (chōuyān) ma?
Could you give me a hand?	Qǐng bāng wǒ ná yīxià.
Please tell me...	Qǐng gàosù wǒ...

T I P S

Chinese names

The order of Chinese names is just the opposite of that of Western names. The Chinese put the family name (surname) first and the given name second. For example, Zhāng Xiǎojiāng—Zhāng is the family name and Xiǎojiāng is the given name.

Chinese family names are usually one character—as in Zhāng, Mǎ and Lǐ—and are easy to pronounce. There are also some family names which have two characters—as in Oūyáng and Zhūgě. Perhaps you've heard that Han Chinese have a total of only one hundred family names.

Key Words

您好！

早上好！

吃了没有？

今天天气真好！

下午好！

晚上好！

晚安！

再见！

您好！

我是（美国人）。

我叫（乔治·布朗）。

很高兴认识你。

好久没见了。

能帮我一下吗？

能问你一个问题吗？

能帮我一个忙吗？

可以（抽烟）吗？

请帮我拿一下。

请告诉我……

Day and Date

three days ago	dàqiántiān	大前天
the day before yesterday	qiántiān	前天
yesterday	zuótiān	昨天
today	jīntiān	今天
tomorrow	míngtiān	明天
the day after tomorrow	hòutiān	后天
three days from now	dàhòutiān	大后天
morning	zǎochén	早晨
noon	zhōngwǔ	中午
afternoon	xiàwǔ	下午
evening	wǎnshàng	晚上
night	yèlǐ	夜里
China	Zhōngguó	中国
United States	Měiguó	美国
Britain	Yīngguó	英国
France	Fǎguó	法国
Germany	Déguó	德国
Canada	Jiānádà	加拿大
Australia	Àodàlìyà	澳大利亚
Spain	Xībānyá	西班牙

TIPS

Although there are a few names that are very common, there are actually hundreds of names in use today. In modern times, women continue to use their own family names after marriage.

Chinese given names can have one character or two characters. Nowadays, there is a tendency for people to want one character for their given names.

Chinese have a unique custom for exchanging names. It's usually not polite to ask a person's name upon meeting for the first time. Most Chinese feel comfortable small talking for a while and then slipping in a Nǐ guì xìng? (Can I have your family name?) after things warm up.

Where is the (toilet)?	Nǎlǐ yǒu (cèsuǒ)?
Could you please pass me that (salad)?	Qǐng dìgěi wǒ nàpán (shālā).
Could you tell me how to get to (the Imperial Palace)?	Qǐng gàosù wǒ, (Gùgōng) zěnme zǒu?
Excuse me. (Make way.)	Qǐng ràng yí ràng.
Excuse me. (Sorry.)	Duì bù qǐ.
Excuse me. (May I ask...)	Qǐng wèn...

Expressing Thanks

Thanks. (Thank you.)	Xièxiè.
That's all right.	Méi guānxi.
Thank you very much.	Shífēn gǎnxiè.
Thank you for your (invitation/ gift/help).	Xièxiè nǐ de (yāoqǐng/lǐwù/ bāngzhù).
Thank you for your (hospitality/ kindness).	Duōxiè nǐ de (kuǎndài/hǎoyì).
I've had enough, thank you.	Wǒ gòu le, xièxiè.
Thank you for all what you've done for me.	Xièxiè nǐ wèi wǒ suǒ zuò de yí qiè.
Please convey (my/our) thanks to him.	Qǐng nǐ dài (wǒ/wǒmen) xièxiè tā.

Polite Remarks

Congratulations! (Marriage, birth of a child, promotion, etc.)	Zhùhè nǐ!
Come in, please!	Qǐng jìn.

T I P S

We, you and they

Making wǒ (I), nǐ (you), and tā (he/she/it) into their plural forms is simpler in Chinese than in English. You just need to add mén. Examples:

wǒ (I)	wǒmén (we)
nǐ (you)	nǐmén (you)
tā (he, she, it)	tāmén (they)

哪里有(厕所)？

请递给我那盘(色拉)。

请告诉我,(故宫)怎么走？

请让一让。

对不起。

请问……。

谢谢。

没关系。

十分感谢。

谢谢你的(邀请/礼物/帮助)。

多谢你的(款待/好意)。

我够了,谢谢。

谢谢你为我所做的一切。

请你代(我/我们)谢谢他。

祝贺你！

请进。

Key Words

Italy	Yìdàlì	意大利
Switzerland	Ruìshì	瑞士
New Zealand	Xīnxīlán	新西兰
Austria	Àodìlì	奥地利
Holland	Hélán	荷兰
Belgium	Bǐlìshí	比利时
Denmark	Dānmài	丹麦
Sweden	Ruìdiǎn	瑞典
Norway	Nuówēi	挪威
Portugal	Pútáoyá	葡萄牙

(To refer to people from a certain country, simply add the word ren to the name of the country, as in *Zhongguo* for "China" and *Zhongguoren* for "Chinese", and as in *Měiguó* for "America" and *Měiguórén* for "American".)

help	bāngmáng	帮忙
smoke	chōuyān	抽烟
man's toilet	nán cèsuǒ	男厕所
lady's toilet	nǔ cèsuǒ	女厕所
book	shū	书
ham	huǒtuǐ	火腿
clothes	yīfu	衣服
umbrella	sǎn	伞
cup	bēizi	杯子
Summer Palace	Yíhéyuán	颐和园

TIPS

Pronouns

Singular: wǒ (I) nǐ (you) tā (he) tā (she) tā (it)
Plural: wǒmén (we) nǐmén (you) tāmén (they)

Verbs

shì (be, am, are, is, was, were)
qù (go, goes, went, gone)

Sit down, please!	Qǐng zuò.
Can I help you?	Xūyào wǒ bāngmáng ma?
You're welcome.	Búyào kèqì.
Wish you (a happy birthday/recover soon/luck).	Zhù nǐ (shēngrì kuàilè/zǎorì huīfù jiànkāng/zǒuyùn).
I hope you'll have chance to visit (the United States).	Xīwàng nǐ yǒu jīhuì qù (Měiguó).
Wish you a good time in China.	Xīwàng nǐ zài Zhōngguó guòde yúkuài.

Questions

May I have your family name?	Gùi xìng?
What's your surname?	Nǐ xìng shénme?
May I have your first name?	Nǐ jiào shénme míngzi?
This is Mr. Zhang Xiaojiang.	Zhèshì Zhāng Xiǎojiāng xiān-sheng.
Where is the (hotel/railway station/shop/post office)?	(Fàndiàn/huǒchēzhàn/shāngdiàn/yóujú) zài nǎlǐ?
Do you have (shirts/blouses/silk/jadeware)?	Yǒu méi yǒu (chènshān/nǚ chènshān/sīchóu/yùqì)?
What (color/size)?	Shénme (yánsè/chǐcùn)?
How much is it?	Duōshǎo qián?
Have you got enough? (food, money)	Gòu bú gòu?
What time is it now?	Xiànzài jǐdiǎn?
What direction should we take?	Wǒmen gāi wǎng nǎge fāngxiàng zǒu?
Taxi!	Chūzū chē.

T
I
P
S

"To be"

Chinese grammar is simpler than English. The verb "to be," for instance, doesn't change forms. I, you, he, she, it, we and they all take the same verb form. Examples:

Wǒ shì (I am)	Wǒmén shì (we are)
Nǐ shì (you are)	Nǐmén shì (you are)
Tā shì (he/she/it is)	Tāmén shì (they are)

请坐。
需要我帮忙吗？
不要客气。
祝你(生日快乐/早日
恢复健康/走运)。
希望你有机会去(美
国)。
希望你在中国过得愉
快。

贵姓？
你姓什么？
你叫什么名字？
这是张小江先生。

(饭店/火车站/商店
/邮局)在哪里？
有没有(衬衫/女衬衫
/丝绸/玉器)？
什么(颜色/尺寸)？
多少钱？
够不够？

现在几点？
我们该往哪个方向走？
出租车！

Key Words

English	Pinyin	Chinese
Great Wall	Chángchéng	长城
Zhongshan Park	Zhōngshān Gōngyuán	中山公园
Temple of Heaven	Tiāntán	天坛
east	dōng	东
west	xī	西
south	nán	南
north	běi	北
left	zuǒ	左
right	yòu	右
bright	qíngtiān	晴天
sultry	mēn	闷
humid	shī	湿
rain	xiàyǔ	下雨
snow	xiàxuě	下雪
sweat	chūhàn	出汗
bustling business	Shēngyì xīnglóng	生意兴隆
May you a great fortune	Gōngixǐ fācái	恭喜发财
good health	shēntǐ jiànkāng	身体健康
good luck	hǎo yùnqì	好运气
Everything turns out well	Shìshì shùnlì	事事顺利

Did it, is it, or will it?

T I P S

Chinese verbs do not have different forms for present, past and future. You just need to add le after the verb to indicate past, and add jiāng before the verb to indicate future. Example:

Wǒ qù. (I go.)
Wǒ qù le. (I went.)
Wǒ jiāng qù. (I will go.)

I want to get a taxi.	Wǒ yào yí liàng chūzū chē.
Could you take me to the (Friendship Store/the Great Wall Hotel/airport)?	Qù bú qù (Yǒuyì Shāngdiàn/ Chángchéng Fàndiàn/jīchǎng)?
Do you stop at (Wangfujing Street/the Beijing Hotel)?	(Wángfǔjīng/Běijīng Fàndiàn) tíng bù tíng?
Are you happy about the (food/ service/performance)?	(Fàncài/fúwù/yǎnchū) hǎo bù hǎo?
Are you open on Sunday? (Restaurant, shop, government dept., etc.)	Xīngqīrì xiū bù xiūxi?
When does the (bank/restaurant) (open/close)?	(Yínháng/cānguǎn) jǐdiǎn (kāi/ guān) mén?

Exclamations

Hurry up!	Gǎn kuài!
There's no other way!	Zhēn méi bànfǎ!
I can't help it!	Wǒ méi bànfǎ.
Very good!	Tài hǎo le!
Excellent!	Hǎo jí le!
Extremely good!	Bàng jí le!
Wonderful!	Tài jīngcǎi le!
Terrific!	Méi zhì le!/Gài le!
My god! (My goodness!)	Tiān na!
That's too bad!	Zhēn zāo gāo!

Questions

T
I
P
S

Questions in English are formed by raising the tone at the end and changing the word order. Again, Chinese has a shortcut—simply add ma at the end of the sentence. (Ma has no stress or tone.) Examples:

Nǐ yào ma? (Do you want it?)
Tā qù ma? (Is he going?)
Nǐ hǎo ma? (How are you?)
Nǐ tóngyì ma? (Do you agree?)
Tā yuànyì ma? (Is he willing to?)
Tā bù xiǎng qù kàn ma? (She doesn't want to see it, does she?)

我要一辆出租车。

去不去（友谊商店/长城饭店/机场）？

（王府井/北京饭店）停不停？

（饭菜/服务/演出）好不好？

星期日休不休息？

（银行/餐馆）几点（开/关）门？

赶快！

真没办法！

我没办法。

太好了。

好极了。

棒极了。

太精彩了。

没治了/盖了！

天哪！

真糟糕！

Key Words

| Everything turns out just as wished | Wànshì rúyì | 万事如意 |
| May you have a son | Zǎo shēng guì zǐ | 早生贵子 |

Numbers

one	yī	一
two	èr	二
three	sān	三
four	sì	四
five	wǔ	五
six	liù	六
seven	qī	七
eight	bā	八
nine	jiǔ	九
ten	shí	十
eleven	shíyī	十一
twelve	shíèr	十二
thirteen	shísān	十三
fourteen	shísì	十四
fifteen	shíwǔ	十五
sixteen	shíliù	十六

T I P S

Courteous phrases

Qǐng (please), zhù (wish) and xīwàng (hope) are common in polite speech. There are also some other courteous phrases. Examples:

Lǚtú yúkuài. (Have a pleasant journey.)
Shēnghuó yúkuài. (Have a happy life.)
Wànshì rúyì. (Wish you every success.)
Yílù píng'ān. (Have a safe journey.)
Shēntǐ jiànkāng. (Wish you good health.)
Chángmìng bǎisui. (Wish you a long life.)
Shēngrì kuàilè. (Happy birthday.)

How disappointing!	Zhēn sǎoxìng!
What a (fine/bad) day!	Tiānqì zhēn (hǎo/zāo)!
Look out! (Be careful!)	Xiǎo xīn!
Ridiculous!	Jiǎnzhí kěxiào!
That's regretful!	Zhēn yíhàn.
What a pity!	Tài kěxī le.
What luck!	Zhēn xìngyùn.
I'm here!	Wǒ lái le!
I'm totally disappointed.	Dà shī suǒ wàng.
What's wrong with you? (I don't feel well.)	Nǐ zěnme le?
I don't feel well.	Wǒ bù shūfu.

On the Phone

Hello!	Wèi.
Who do you want to speak to?	Nǐ zhǎo shuí?
Can I speak to (Mr. George Brown)?	Wǒ zhǎo (Qiáozhì Bùlǎng xiānsheng).
It's me.	Wǒ jiù shì.
Just a minute, please. (Hold on.)	Qǐng děng yì děng.
This is (George Brown) speaking.	Wǒ shì (Qiáozhì Bùlǎng).
He is not in.	Tā bú zài.
Do you want to leave a message for him?	Yào bú yào liúhuà?
Please tell him I've called.	Qǐng gàosù tā, wǒ láiguò diànhuà.
i'll tell him.	Wǒ huì gàosù tā de.

T
I
P
S

What to say when you're sure

Dāngrán la! (Certainly!)
Kěndìng! (Definitely!)
Juéduì! (Absolutely!)
Méi wèntí! (No problem!)

真扫兴！

天气真（好/糟）。

小心！

简直可笑！

真遗憾。

太可惜了。

真幸运。

我来了！

大失所望。

你怎么了？

我不舒□

喂！

你找□

□□（乔治·布朗先生）。

□就是。

请等一等。

我是（乔治·布朗）。

他不在。

要不要留话？

请告诉他，我来过电话。

我会告诉他的。

Key Words

seventeen	shíqī	十七
eighteen	shíbā	十八
nineteen	shíjiǔ	十九
twenty	èrshí	二十
thirty	sānshí	三十
forty	sìshí	四十
fifty	wǔshí	五十
sixty	liùshí	六十
seventy	qīshí	七十
eighty	bāshí	八十
ninety	jiǔshí	九十
one hundred	yìbǎi	一百
a thousand	yìqiān	一千
ten thousand	yíwàn	一万
a million	yì bǎiwàn	一百万

The number "2" has two different spoken forms. It is almost always said liǎng —— as in liǎng kuài qián (two *yuan*). However, when used in a number, it is said èr. For example, the telephone number 834-2323 is said bā sān sì èr sān èr sān.

The Calendar

Monday	Xīngqī yī	星期一
Tuesday	Xīngqī èr	星期二
Wednesday	Xīngqī sān	星期三
Thursday	Xīngqī sì	星期四

TIPS

Negatives

It is much easier to make a sentence negative in Chinese than in English. You just need to add a bù (not) in front of the verb. Examples:

Wǒ qù. (I go.) Wǒ bú qù. (I don't go.)

Wǒ chī. (I eat.) Wǒ bù chī. (I don't eat.)

Wǒ yào. (I want.) Wǒ bú yào. (I don't want.)

I'll call back later.	Guò yīhuìr, wǒ zài qù diànhuà.
Operator.	Jiēxiànyuán!
I want to make a long-distance call.	Wǒ xiǎng dǎ chángtú.
(The United States), please.	Wǒ yào (Měiguó).
Collect call, please.	Duìfāng fùkuǎn.
How long will I have to wait?	Yào děng duō jiǔ?
You've got the wrong number.	Nǐ dǎcuò le.
The phone number is correct, but I am not the person you want.	Hàomǎ méicuò, dàn wǒ búshì nǐ yàozhǎo de rén.

Apologies

Excuse me.	Duì bù qǐ!
I apologize.	Wǒ hěn bàoqiàn.
I beg your pardon.	Qǐng zài shuō yí biàn.
I wasn't intending to...	Wǒ búshì yǒuyì de.
I'm sorry.	Qǐng yuánliàng.
I'm not able to help.	Méi bànfǎ.
That's all right.	Méi guānxi.

Help

In the off-chance that you run into an emergency, these simple sentences could be of some use:

Help!	Jiù mìng a!
Call the (police/doctor/ambulance).	Kuài jiào (jǐngchá/yīshēng/jiùhù chē).

T
I
P
S

What one?

The equivalents of this, that, these, which, and where in Chinese are: zhè, nà, zhè xiē, nà xiē, nǎ gè, and nǎ lǐ, respectively. Examples:

Zhè shì wǒmen de lǚguǎn. (This is our hotel.)
Nà shì zhǎnlǎnguǎn. (That is an exhibition hall.)
Zhè xiē bēizi hén hǎo kàn. (These cups look nice.)
Nǐ yào nǎ běn shū? (Which book do you want?)
Wǒmen de shǐguǎn zài nǎ lǐ? (Where is our embassy?)

过一会儿,我再去电话。
接线员!
我想打长途。

我要(美国)。
对方付款。
要等多久?
你打错了。
号码没错,但我不是你
要找的人。

对不起!
我很抱歉。
请再说一遍。
我不是有意的。
请原谅。
没办法。
没关系。

救命啊!
快叫(警察/医生/救护
车)。

Key Words

Friday	Xīngqī wǔ	星期五
Saturday	Xīngqī liù	星期六
Sunday	Xīngqī rì	星期日
January	Yī yuè	一月
February	Èr yuè	二月
March	Sān yuè	三月
April	Sì yuè	四月
May	Wǔ yuè	五月
June	Liù yuè	六月
July	Qī yuè	七月
August	Bā yuè	八月
September	Jiǔ yuè	九月
October	Shí yuè	十月
November	Shíyī yuè	十一月
December	Shíèr yuè	十二月

Time

one o'clock	yìdiǎnzhōng	一点钟
one ten	yìdiǎn shífēn	一点十分
two fifteen	liǎngdiǎn shíwǔfēn	二点十五分
a quarter past two	liǎngdiǎn yíkè	二点一刻
two twenty	liǎngdiǎn èrshí	二点二十

TIPS

Zhè, nà, and nǎ can be used together with measure words like gè, as well as specific measure words. Examples:
Zhè gè dìfāng wǒ lái guò. (I've been to this place before.)
Zhè zhāng zhàopiàn hén hǎo kàn. (This picture looks nice.)
Nà pán cídài hén hǎo tīng. (That cassette is pleasant to listen to.)
Nǐ yào nǎ zhāng bàozhǐ? (Which newspaper do you want?)

I'm having a (heart attack/ stomach trouble).	Wǒ de (xīnzàng bìng/wèi bìng) fàn le.
Send me to the hospital.	Kuài sòng wǒ qù yīyuàn.
I'm dying.	Wǒ bùxíng le.
Bring me back to my hotel.	Kuài sòng wǒ huí lǚguǎn.
There's a fire.	Zháo huǒ le!
There's been a traffic accident.	Chū jiāotōng shìgù le.
I was hit by a (car/bicycle).	Wǒ bèi (qìchē/zìxíng chē) zhuàng le.

When asking help, *qǐng* (please), *néng bù néng* (could you), and *kěyǐ bù kěyǐ* (can you) are often used.

Good-byes

Good-bye!	Zài jiàn.
Have a pleasant journey! (By train, plane, etc.)	Yí lù shùn fēng.
See you soon./See you later.	Huí tóu jiàn/yí huìr jiàn.
See you tomorrow.	Míngtiān jiàn.
I'm afraid I must go now.	Wǒ gāi zǒu le.
Take good care of yourself.	Duōduō bǎozhòng.
Hope to meet you again.	Xīwàng wǒmen zài jiànmiàn.
Come again if you have a chance.	Yǒu jīhuì zài lái.
Write to us if you have time.	Yǒu kòng lái xìn.
Please say hello for me to your (wife/husband/sister).	Wèn nǐ (tàitai/zhàngfu/jiějie) hǎo.
We'll see you off here.	Bù yuǎn sòng le.

T I P S

Is it better or best?

Adjectives in Chinese do not have to change their forms when they are used to indicate different degrees. What you only need to do is to add bǐjiào (relatively) or zuì (most) before the adjectives. Examples:

hǎo (good)	gānjing (clean)
bǐjiào hǎo (better)	bǐjiào gānjing (cleaner)
zuì hǎo (best)	zuì gānjing (cleanest)

Sometimes you may add yìdiǎn (a bit) or gèng (more) before the adjectives to indicate comparative degrees.

我的(心脏病/胃病)犯
了。

快送我去医院。

我不行了。

快送我回旅馆。

着火了!

出交通事故了。

我被(汽车/自行车)撞
了。

再见!

一路顺风!

回头见/一会儿见。

明天见。

我该走了。

多多保重。

希望我们再见面。

有机会再来。

有空来信。

问你(太太/丈夫/姐
姐)好。

不远送了。

Key Words

three thirty	sāndiǎn sānshí	三点三十
half past three	sāndiǎn bàn	三点半
four forty-five	sìdiǎn sìshíwǔ	四点四十五
a quarter to six	wǔdiǎn sānkè	五点三刻
four fifty	sìdiǎn wǔshí	四点五十
ten to six	wǔdiǎn wǔshí	五点五十

What You May Hear

Nín hǎo!	Hello!
Xièxie.	Thank you.
Xíng.	OK.
Bù xíng.	Won't do.
Hǎo.	Good.
Bù hǎo.	Not good.
Kě yǐ.	Can be done.
Bù kěyǐ.	Can't be done.
Yǒu.	Have/there is
Méiyǒu.	Have not/ there isn't.
Děng yi děng.	Wait a second.
Qǐng jìn.	Please come in.

T Examples:

I Zhège píngguǒ bǐ nàge tián yìdiǎn. (This apple is a bit sweeter than that one.)

Zhège yánsè bǐ nàge gèng xiānyàn. (This color is fresher than that one.)

P You may also add jí le (extremely) after the adjectives to indicate the superlative degree. Examples:

S Piàoliàng jí le! (Really beautiful!)

Tǎoyàn jí le! (Really disgusting!)

Xiānměi jí le! (Extremely delicious!)

Signs

shànglóu / xiàlóu
Upstairs /
Downstairs

rùkǒu / chūkǒu
Entrance / Exit

nán cèsuǒ
Men's Toilets

nǚ cèsuǒ
Women's Toilets

gōngyòng diànhuà
Public Telephone

Travel

CUSTOMS

Huānyíng lái Zhōngguó!
Welcome to China!

Traveling in China is great fun either by air or by train. Trains, however, are the main means of inter-city transportation in China, and along with the sea and river boats, they provide a great way to make getting where you're going an interesting part of your trip. (Long-distance buses are for trekkers who like bumpy rides to out-of-the-way places.) If your time is short, on the other hand, there are planes shuttling among the big cities. Travelers from abroad have to pay FEC for air and train tickets.

At Customs

Can I have your passport and Customs Declaration Form?

Qǐng chūshì hùzhào hé hǎiguān shēnbào dān.

Are you a (tourist)?

Nǐ shì lái (lǚyóu) de?

This is my first time to come to China.

Wǒ shì dì yī cì lái Zhōngguó.

This is my passport.

Zhèshì wǒ de hùzhào.

We (four) are in a group.

Wǒmen yígòng (sì) ge rén.

I am sorry. I didn't know that you don't allow to take (Renminbi) out of China.

Duì bù qǐ, wǒ bù zhīdào (rénmínbì) bùnéng dài chūqù.

This (painting) is a gift from one of my Chinese friends.

Zhè zhāng (huà) shì yí ge Zhōng guó péngyǒu sònggěi wǒ de.

I was told by the shop that I can take this (vase) out.

Shāngdiàn gàosù wǒ, zhè ge huāpíng néng dàichūqù.

It has a wax seal on it.

Yǒu huǒqī yìn.

This is the receipt.

Zhèshì fāpiào.

Any other problems?

Hái yǒu wèntí ma?

I have nothing to declare.

Wǒ méiyǒu yào bàoguān de dōngxi.

I've lost my (passport).

Wǒ de (hùzhào) bú jiàn le.

Could you do me a favor?

Néng bāng wǒ ge máng ma?

Can I phone my embassy?

Néng gěi dàshǐguǎn dǎ ge diàn-huà ma?

Money in China

Excuse me. Can I use (U.S. dollars) in China?

Qǐng wèn, (měiyuán) zhèlǐ néng yòng ma?

T I P S

Customs and money exchange

As China became more open in the 1980s, the Chinese Customs simplified its procedures. So long as you don't have contraband (e.g., munitions, drugs, and pornographic publications and tapes) with you, all the procedures will be short and simple.

Antiques, precious paintings and calligraphy works, and

Key Words

请出示护照和海关申报单。

你是来（旅游）的?

我是第一次来中国。

这是我的护照。

我们一共（四）个人。

对不起，我不知道（人民币）不能带出去。

这张（画）是一个中国朋友送给我的。

商店告诉我，这个花瓶能带出去。

有火漆印。

这是发票。

还有问题吗?

我没有要报关的东西。

我的（护照）不见了。

能帮我个忙吗?

能给大使馆打个电话吗?

请问，（美元）这里能用吗?

passport	hùzhào	护照
customs	hǎiguān	海关
customs declaration form	hǎiguān shēnbào dān	海关申报单
duty	guānshuì	关税
duty free	miǎnshuì	免税
foreign currency	wàihuì	外汇
jewelry	zhūbǎo	珠宝
calligraphy and painting	shūfǎ hé huìhuà	书法和绘画
antique	gǔdǒng	古董
drugs	dúpǐn	毒品
contraband	zǒusī	走私
health certificate	jiànkāng zhèngmíng	健康证明
open	kāi	开
close	guān	关
suitcase	xiāngzi	箱子
luggage	xíngli	行李
check	zhīpiào	支票
Bank of China	Zhōngguó Yínháng	中国银行
Friendship Store	Yǒuyì Shāngdiàn	友谊商店
exchange	duìhuàn	兑换
exchange counter	duìhuàn chù	兑换处
U. S. dollar	měiyuán	美元

TIPS

ancient coins cannot be taken out of China unless you are able to show the receipt from the shops where you bought the article and show the untouched wax seal or other certificates from certain departments.

Renminbi also cannot be taken out of China. Again, if you keep your FEC exchange receipt, you can exchange your remaining FEC back to foreign currencies before leaving China.

Where can I exchange (U.S. dollars) for FEC?

Nǎlǐ néng bǎ (měiyuán) huànchéng duìhuànquàn?

What time does the Bank of China open?

Zhōngguó Yínháng shénme shíhòu kāimén?

Can I have my money changed in the hotel?

Fàndiàn lǐ néngbùnéng huàn qián?

Excuse me. I want exchange (U.S. dollars) for Renminbi.

Láojià, wǒ xiǎng bǎ (měiyuán) huànchéng rénmínbì.

I want to exchange (800) dollars.

Wǒ yàohuàn (bābǎi) měiyuán.

What is today's exchange rate?

Jīntiān de duìhuànlǜ shì duōshǎo?

Please give me large notes.

Qǐng gěi wǒ dàpiàozi.

Please give it to me in tens.

Qǐng gěi wǒ shíyuán yī zhāng de.

Excuse me. Can I use my credit card in China?

Qǐng wèn, Zhōngguó néngyòng xìnyòngkǎ ma?

Where can I cash my traveler's checks?

Zài nǎlǐ néng duìhuàn lǚxíng zhīpiào?

Can I take Renminbi out of China?

Rénmínbì kěyǐ dài chūjìng ma?

I want to change my Renminbi back to (U.S. dollars).

Wǒ xiǎng bǎ rénmínbì huànhuí (měiyuán).

Here is my Foreign Exchange Certificate receipt.

Zhèshì wǒ de wàihuì duìhuàn zhèngmíng.

Chinese currency

Renminbi is Chinese currency. Its unit is the yuán, which is also called kuài by many people. There are notes for one yuan, two yuan, five yuan, ten yuan, fifty yuan and one hundred yuan. Under the yuán, there is the jiǎo (ten cents), also called the máo, with notes for one jiao, two jiao and five jiao. Under the jiao is the fēn (cent) with coins (notes as well) for one fen, two fen and five fen.

FEC has the same value as Renminbi. Foreigners coming to China have to exchange their foreign currencies for FEC for use in China. There are notes for one yuan, five yuan, ten yuan and fifty yuan. When you exchange your money, the bank will give you a FEC exchange receipt. Save these, as you can use them to exchange your remaining FEC back to foreign currencies before you leave China.

哪里能把(美元)换成
兑换券?

中国银行什么时候开
门?

饭店里能不能换钱?

劳驾,我想把(美元)换
成人民币。

我要换(八百)美元。

今天的兑换率是多少?

请给我大票子。

请给我十元一张的。

请问,中国能用信用卡
吗?

在哪里能兑换旅行支
票?

人民币可以带出境吗?

我想把人民币换回(美
元)。

这是我的外汇兑换证
明。

Key Words

British Sterling	yīngbàng	英磅
Japanese Yen	rìyuán	日元
Hong Kong dollar	gǎngbì	港币
Deutsche Mark	Xīdé mǎkè	西德马克
FEC receipt	wàihuìquàn	外汇券
Renminbi	rénmínbì	人民币
exchange rate	duìhuàn lù	兑换率
FEC (Foreign Exchange Certificate) receipt	wàihuìquàn duìhuàn zhèngmíng	外汇券 兑换证明
yuan	yuán	元
jiao	jiǎo	角
fen	fēn	分
credit card	xìnyòng kǎ	信用卡
traveler's check	lǔxíng zhīpiào	旅行支票
use	shǐyòng	使用

Exchange

You cannot use foreign currencies while traveling in China. You must have them converted into Foreign Exchange Certificates (FEC) or Renminbi at the Bank of China. There are banks at airports, hotels, and friendship stores. In most cases, you will be asked to pay FEC for your hotel room, restaurant bill, taxi fare, and air and train tickets. However, Renminbi can be used in ordinary shops. Credit cards can be used in many big hotels and designated shops.

Money exchange can only be done at the bank. Any private exchange is illegal. You may meet people asking to exchange foreign currencies, but it would be best to refuse, since violating Chinese regulations could get you into unnecessary trouble. And it's only fair to warn you that the black-marketeers are sometimes con artists looking to cheat you.

Booking an Air Ticket

Can I go by (plane) to (Shang-hai)?

Dào (Shànghǎi) qù néng zuò (fēijī) ma?

Is there a regular flight to (Shanghai)?

Shìfǒu měitiān dōu yǒu qù (Shànghǎi) de bānjī?

Where can I buy an air ticket?

Nǎlǐ néng mǎidào fēijīpiào?

Could you tell me where (the CAAC office) is?

(Mínháng bànshìchù) zài nǎlǐ?

How much is the ticket?

Jīpiào duōshǎo qián?

I want (three) tickets, (first class/economy class).

Wǒ mǎi (sānzhāng) (tóuděng cāng/jīngjìcāng) de.

Please give me a window seat.

Wǒ yào kào chuānghu de zuòwèi.

Is there a discount for children?

Xiǎohái piányi diǎn ma?

I want to reroute my ticket.

Wǒ xiǎng gǎi yíxià hángbān.

When will I arrive at the airport?

Shénme shíhòu yīngdào jīchǎng?

Is there a passengers' bus to and from the airport?

Jīchǎng yǒu jiēsòng de kèchē ma?

How much should the fare to be to the (airport)?

Qù (jīchǎng) duōshǎo qián?

How long does it take to the (air-port)?

Dào (jīchǎng) yào duōshǎo shíjiān?

Planes

How long is the flight to (Shang-hai)?

Dào (Shànghǎi) yào fēi duōcháng shíjiān?

When will we arrive at (Shang-hai)?

Shénme shíhòu néng dào (Shànghǎi)?

T
I
P
S

International airlines

Many international airlines have service to the major cities of China, such as Beijing, Shanghai, Guangzhou, Tianjin, Hangzhou, Kunming, Harbin, Shantou, Xiamen and Urumqi. Of course Beijing is the hub of all international airlines. When you book a ticket, you should know what airline you would like to take, both its English and Chinese names and the code. The following list will help.

Key Words

到(上海)去能坐(飞机)吗？

是否每天都有班机？

哪里能买到飞机票？

(民航办事处)在哪里？

机票多少钱？

我买三张(头等舱/经济舱)的。

我要靠窗户的座位。

小孩便宜点吗？

我想改一下航班。

什么时候应到机场？

机场有接送的客车吗？

去(机场)多少钱？

到(机场)要多少时间？

到(上海)要飞多长时间？

什么时候能到(上海)？

boarding	shàng fēijī	上飞机
departing	xià fēijī	下飞机
take off	qǐfēi	起飞
landing	jiàngluò	降落
flight	hángbān	航班
plane	fēijī	飞机
airport	jīchǎng	机场
pilot	fēixíngyuán	飞行员
CAAC office	Mínháng bànshìchù	民航办事处
first class	tóuděng cāng	头等舱
economy class	jīngjìcāng	经济舱
gate	rùkǒu	入口
exit	chūkǒu	出口
plane ticket	jīpiào	机票
ticket office	shòupiào chù	售票处
seat	zuòwèi	座位
safety belt	ānquándài	安全带
this side	zhè biān	这边
that side	nà biān	那边
departure hall	hòujī tīng	候机厅
weather	tiānqì	天气
temperature	qìwēn	气温

Is it (cold) in (Shanghai)?	(Shànghǎi) (lěng bù lěng)?
What place shall we land at next?	Xià yí zhàn shì nǎlǐ?
Where are we now?	Wǒmen xiànzài dào nǎr le?
What's that city?	Nàshì shénme chéngshì?
Where should I have my baggage checked?	Shénme dìfāng tuōyùn xíngli?
When will Flight No. (232) take off?	(Èrsān'èr) hào hángbān shénme shíhòu qǐfēi?
Could you tell me where Gate (No. 5) is?	(Wǔ hào) rùkǒu zài nǎlǐ?
Please get me a cup of (ice water).	Qǐng gěi wǒ yì bēi (bīngshuǐ).
This safety belt is broken.	Ānquándài huài le.
I would like a copy of *China Daily*.	Wǒ yào fèn Zhōngguó Rìbào.
When will (breakfast) begin?	Shénme shíhòu chī (zǎofàn)?
Where is (the Customs)?	(Hǎiguān) zài nǎlǐ?
Can I have my goods duty-free?	Wǒ kěyǐ yǒu miǎnshuì wùpǐn ma?
I can't find my (suitcase).	Wǒ de (xiāngzi) zhǎo bù dào le.
·This is my (baggage claim tag).	Zhèshì (xínglǐpái).
Are there any carts?	Yǒu xiǎo tuīchē ma?
Where is the exit?	Chūkǒu zài nǎlǐ?

Trains

Which way is it to the (train station)?	Qù (huǒchēzhàn) zěnme zǒu?

Flights

T
I
P
S

Flights between big cities in China are mainly on Boeing 747s, Boeing 737s and other large planes. There are two classes—first class and economy class. Flights between medium-sized cities are on smaller planes such as the Yun-7 and Yun-8, and have only one class. In China, safety is regarded as most important. If the weather is not good, flights might be delayed. Holdups at the airport are not uncommon, so be prepared with a good book—or, better yet, wander around and practice your Chinese.

（上海）（冷不冷）？

下一站是哪里？

我们现在到哪儿了？

那是什么城市？

什么地方托运行李？

（232）号航班什么时候
起飞？

（5）号入口在哪里？

请给我一杯（冰水）。

安全带坏了。

我要份《中国日报》。

什么时候吃（早饭）？

（海关）在哪里？

我可以有免税物品吗？

我的（箱子）找不到了。

这是（行李牌）。

有小推车吗？

出口在哪里？

去（火车站）怎么走？

Key Words

information office	wènxùnchù	问讯处
baggage	xíngli	行李
baggage claim area	xíngli fáng	行李房
baggage claim tag	xíngli pái	行李牌
check (baggage)	tuōyùn	托运
how much	duōshǎo qián	多少钱
railway station	huǒchē zhàn	火车站
train 119	yāoyāojiǔ cì lièchē	119 次 列车
train ticket	huǒchē piào	火车票
soft sleeper	ruǎnwò	软卧
hard sleeper	yìngwò	硬卧
soft seat	ruǎnzuò	软座
hard seat	yìngzuò	硬座
waiting room	hòuchē shì	候车室
luggage rack	xíngli jià	行李架
coach	chēxiāng	车厢
platform	zhàntái	站台
seat	zuòwèi	座位
special express	tèkuài	特快
through train	zhíkuài	直快
express	kuàichē	快车
slow train	mànchē	慢车

Trains

T I P S

Trains are the core of China's transportation network. Passenger trains have four classes: soft berth, hard berth, soft seat and hard seat. Soft berth and soft seat are what is called first class in the West. You'll have to buy tickets a day or two beforehand to guarantee a seat. Traveling by train is actually ideal for tourists, because it gives you a chance to see the beautiful Chinese countryside and meet people. There are four types of passenger trains in China: special express, through train, express and slow train.

Which window sells tickets to (Nanjing)?	Qù (Nánjīng) de piào zài nǎge chuāngkǒu mài?
I want to buy a ticket to (Suzhou), train (119).	Wǒ mǎi yì zhāng qù (Sūzhōu) de piào, (yāoyāojiǔ) cì de.
I want a (soft berth/soft seat/hard berth/hard seat).	Yào (ruǎnwò/ruǎnzuò/yìngwò/yìngzuò).
How much?	Duōshǎo qián?
Can I use Renminbi to buy the ticket?	Kěyǐ yòng rénmínbì mǎi ma?
When will the next train be?	Xiàbānchē shénme shíjiān?
Is there an afternoon train?	Yǒu xiàwǔ de huǒchē ma?
Is there a train to (Xi'an)?	Yǒu qù (Xǐ'ān) de huǒchē ma?
When will it leave?	Shénme shíhòu kāichē?
How long will it wait at this station?	Zhège zhàn tíng duōjiǔ?
Can I have my ticket changed to (tomorrow's) train?	Néng huànchéng (míngtiān) de huǒchē ma?
Does the train serve food on board?	Huǒchēshàng yǒu fàn chī ma?

Boats

T I P S

There are two main boat routes in China. One skips along the coast from Dalian in the north down to Guangzhou. The other runs the length of the Changjiang River (Yangtze) from Chongqing to Shanghai, stopping at the river ports between. The boats, which have a total of five classes (from rat-level down in the hold to a very comfortable first class), are an interesting alternative to the trains. In addition, there are the canal boats that shuttle between Hangzhou and Suzhou on the Grand Canal. Tickets for boats can be bought at special ticket offices (these are not in the railroad stations) or you can have them reserved for you at a China International Tourist Service (CITS) office.

去(南京)的票在哪个窗口卖?

我买一张去(苏州)的票,(119)次的。

要(软卧/软座/硬卧/硬座)。

多少钱?

可以用人民币买吗?

下班车什么时间?

有下午的火车吗?

有去(西安)的火车吗?

什么时候开车?

这个站停多久?

能换成(明天)的火车吗?

火车上有饭吃吗?

What You May Hear

Gèwèi lǔkè qǐng zhùyì...	Passingers attention, please.
Qǐng chūshì...	Please show your...
hùzhào	passport
shēnbàodān	declaration form
xíngli	luggage
Běijīng dào le.	Arrived in Beijing.
Wù diǎn le.	Be late.
Tiānqì bùhǎo.	Weather is bad.
Nǐ qù nǎlǐ?	Where are you going?
Yào chūzūchē ma?	Need a taxi?
Huānyíng nǐ!	You are welcome.
Qǐng gēn wǒ lái.	Follow me, please.

119次

The opposite of ... is

T   qǐchuáng (get up)   shuìjiào (go to bed)

     zǎo (early)   wǎn (late)

I   dà (big)   xiǎo (small)

     gāo (tall)   ǎi (short)

     pàng (fat)   shòu (thin)

     shēn (deep)   qiǎn (shallow)

P   duō (more)   shǎo (less)

     yǒu (have)   wú (haven't)

     lái (come)   qù (go)

S   lěng (cold)   rè (hot)

     hēi (black)   bái (white)

     guì (expensive)   jiàn (cheap)

     hǎo (good)   huài (bad)

Signs

chūgǎng / rùgǎng
Departure / Arrival

hǎiguān
Customs

xíngli fáng
Luggage Claim Area

mínháng shòupiàochù
CAAC Ticket Office

hòuchēshì
Waiting Room

Health

> Wǒ yáténg.
> I've got a toothache.

"Preparedness averts peril," a Chinese saying, is the theme of this part—though we hope you'll never have to use it. Most Chinese doctors don't speak English, so you might use these simple sentences to help solve quickly any health problems that come up.

Seeing a Doctor

Where is the hospital?	Nǎlǐ yǒu yīyuàn?
I'm not feeling well.	Wǒ yǒudiǎn bù shūfu.
Is there a clinic in the hotel?	Lǚguǎn yǒu yīwùshì ma?
Does the small shop in the hotel sell (medicine)?	Xiǎomàibù yǒu (yào) mài ma?
I want to buy some (painkillers).	Wǒ xiǎng mǎi (zhǐtòngpiàn).
I have a headache.	Wǒ tóutòng.
When does the (hospital) open?	(Yīyuàn) shénme shíhòu kāimén?
Can you accompany me to the (hospital)?	Nǐ néng péiwǒ qù (yīyuàn) ma?
Can the doctor pay a home visit?	Yīshēng chūzhěn ma?
I've had my finger cut.	Wǒ de shǒu gēpò le.
Where is the (pharmacy)?	(Yàofáng) zài nǎlǐ?
Do I have to show a prescription when buying medicine?	Mǎiyào yào chǔfāng ma?

In the Hospital

I've got a cold, Doctor.	Dàifu, wǒ gǎnmào le.
I have a sore (throat/cough/fever).	Wǒ (hóulong tòng/késou/ fāshāo).

Good medical care

T
I
P
S

Despite the best of preparations and good health, people still sometimes become sick when traveling because of the change of weather and tiredness. In the event of illness, China's hospitals and clinics can provide medical service. The larger hospitals in China all have doctors with high levels of professionalism who can provide good service. You can fully trust them. Although in the past there were no private doctors and clinics, there now are a few. It's still best to go to larger hospitals, though.

After dozens of years of effort, infectious diseases in China have been reduced to a minimum, and some have even been eliminated. But in some places that travelers frequently visit certain infectious diseases are again being found, including VD and AIDS (though only a few cases of the latter have been found).

Key Words

哪里有医院？

我有点不舒服。

旅馆有医务室吗？

小卖部有（药）卖吗？

我想买（止痛片）。

我头痛。

（医院）什么时候开门？

你能陪我去（医院）吗？

医生出诊吗？

我的手割破了。

（药房）在哪里？

买药要处方吗？

大夫，我感冒了。

我（喉咙痛/咳嗽/发烧）。

hospital	yīyuàn	医院
clinic	yīwùsuǒ	医务所
emergency treatment	jízhěn	急诊
emergency ward	jízhěnshì	急诊室
not feeling well	bù shūfu	不舒服
medicine	yào	药
pharmacy	yàofáng	药房
APC (aspirin)	āsīpǐlín	阿斯匹林
painkiller	zhǐtòng piàn	止痛片
doctor	yīshēng	医生
nurse	hùshì	护士
register	guàhào	挂号
cold	gǎnmào	感冒
abdominal pain	dùzitòng	肚子痛
stomachache	wèitòng	胃痛
headache	tóutòng	头痛
footache	jiǎo tòng	脚痛
toothache	yá tòng	牙痛
dizzy	tóuyūn	头晕
loose bowels	fùxiè	腹泻

Chinese medicine

T
I
P
S

   Traditional Chinese medicine has a history of more than 2,500 years and is still popular in China though Western medicine is practiced in most hospitals. Traditional Chinese medicine is effective in fighting various chronic diseases —even cancer, according to a recent report. These days, all over China treatment with traditional Chinese medicine and Western medicine goes hand-in-hand. Should you become sick, you might consider being treated by a doctor of traditional Chinese medicine. The Chinese herbal medicine the doctor prescribes, which often comes in big balls, may not be pleasant to the eye, but it is potent. It's worth a try if your Western medicine doesn't seem to be having the right effect.

I feel like (vomiting/dizzy).	Wǒ yǒudiǎn (ěxīn/tóuyūn).
No pain there.	Zhèlǐ bùténg.
What's wrong with me?	Wǒ shénme bìng?
Probably you've got a cold.	Nǐ kěnéng shì zhāoliáng le.
Please give me some medicine.	Qǐng gěi wǒ diǎn yào.
My foot's sprained.	Wǒ jiǎo niǔ le.
I feel pain here.	Zhèlǐ téng.
How long before I'm recovered?	Duōjiǔ néng hǎo?
Does this matter?	Yàojǐn ma?
Do I have to have an operation?	Yào kāidāo ma?
Is it serious?	Yánzhòng ma?
I have (heart disease/high blood pressure/toothache/loose bowels).	Wǒ yǒu (xīnzàng bìng/gāoxuèyā/yáténg bìng/fùxiè).
I'm pregnant.	Wǒ huáiyùn le.
Can I have some Chinese medicine?	Néng gěidiǎn zhōngyào ma?
Will I be able to drink wine?	Néng hējiǔ ma?
Will I be able to go out tomorrow?	Míngtiān néng chūmén ma?
Should I come again?	Háiyào lái kàn ma?
I'm feeling better now.	Wǒ jué de hǎo duō le.
Thank you, Doctor.	Xièxiè nǐ, dàifu.

T I P S

Acupuncture

Acupuncture, which has been around for more than 4,000 years, is regularly used in China to treat all sorts of diseases. You've probably seen the scary long needles, but don't let them keep you away. Some of the Westerners who have lived long-term in China and have had some time to get used to the idea swear by acupuncture for sinuses, migraines, and other ailments—not to mention the acupuncture clinics becoming more and more common in the West. Acupuncture anaesthesia is now used for both major and minor surgery, proving effective and safe without aftereffects.

我有点(恶心/头晕)。

这里不疼。

我什么病？

你可能是着凉了。

请给我点药。

我脚扭了。

这里疼。

多久能好？

要紧吗？

要开刀吗？

严重吗？

我有(心脏病/高血压/牙疼病/腹泻)。

我怀孕了。

能给点中药吗？

能喝酒吗？

明天能出门吗？

还要来看吗？

我觉得好多了。

谢谢你，大夫。

Key Words

laboratory test	huàyàn	化验
blood test	yànxuè	验血
X-ray checkup	tòushì	透视
penicillin	qīngméisù	青霉素
allergy	guòmǐn	过敏
reaction	fǎnyìng	反应
side effect	fù zuòyòng	副作用
high blood pressure	gāo xuèyā	高血压
hepatitis	gānyán	肝炎
take medicine	chīyào	吃药
Chinese medicine	Zhōngyào	中药
Western medicine	Xīyào	西药
have an injection	dǎzhēn	打针
gauze	shābù	纱布
adhesive plaster	xiàngpígāo	橡皮膏
absorbent cotton	miánhuā	棉花
mercurochrome	hóngyàoshuǐ	红药水
tincture of iodine	diǎnjiǔ	碘酒
gentian violet	zǐyàoshuǐ	紫药水

Qigong

T I P S

If you're out in the early morning you'll probably run into groups of people practicing martial arts (gōng fu)—they'll be mostly in parks but also just anywhere on the sidewalks. Some of these people are actually doing qìgōng, a breathing exercise with a history of thousands of years. People believe that qigong can help build up one's health, cure some diseases and even prolong one's life. There are many schools of qigong, each with its own movements. Some are easy to learn, others are difficult. Some are mild, others are violent. To learn qigong, it's best to find a good teacher. On the other hand, books on self-taught qigong are also available in English in many hotels or bookshops.

Taking Medicine, Having an Injection

How should I take this medicine?	Zhè yào zěnme chīfǎ?
How many times a day?	Yìtiān jǐcì?
How many pills each time?	Yícì jǐpiàn?
Should I take the medicine before or after my meals?	Fànqián chī háishì fànhòu chī?
Can I take these two medicines together?	Zhè liǎngzhǒng yào néng yìqǐ chī ma?
Do I need an injection everyday?	Měitiān dǎ yìzhēn ma?
Are there any side effects?	Yǒu méi yǒu fǎnyìng?
Is it possible to avoid having the injection?	Bù dǎ zhēn, xíng ma?
Is this an intramuscular injection?	Shì jīròu zhùshè ma?
Is this a disposable needle?	Shì yícìxìng zhēntóu ma?
I am allergic to penicillin.	Wǒ duì qīngméisù guòmǐn.

T I P S   Medicine

Medicines like aspirin, vitamins, and common cold remedies are available from drug stores. Most drug stores in China do not require a doctor's prescription. Usually a drug store has both a Chinese medicine section and a Western medicine section. If you want to, you can try out some Chinese medicine. Contraceptives are sold in the Western medicine section of all drug stores. At some places contraceptives are provided free of charge—a service given by the government to help reduce China's overlarge population.

What You May Hear

这药怎么吃法？

一天几次？

一次几片？

饭前吃还是饭后吃？

这两种药能一起吃吗？

每天打一针吗？

有没有反应？

不打针，行吗？

是肌肉注射吗？

是一次性针头吗？

我对青霉素过敏。

shìbiǎo	take temperature
dǎzhēn	have an injection
Tòng bú tòng?	Does it hurt?
Tǎngxià.	Lie down.
Fàngsōng.	Take it easy.
yàofāng	prescription
yàofáng	pharmacy
chīyào	take medicine
Nǎlǐ bù shūfu?	Where is the discomfort?
xiūxi	have a rest
Nǐ hěnkuài huì hǎo de.	You will get well very soon.
Méi shénme dà wèntí.	Nothing serious.

Ordinal numbers

This is also an easy part of Chinese. You just need to add dì in front of the numbers to make them into ordinal numbers. Example:

dìyī (first)   dìliù (sixth)
dìèr (second)   dìqī (seventh)
dìsān (third)   dìbā (eighth)
dìsì (fourth)   dìjiǔ (ninth)
dìwǔ (fifth)   dìshí (tenth)

Signs

yīyuàn
Hospital

ménzhěnbù
Outpatient Department

guàhàochù
Registration Office

jízhěnshì
Emergency Room

yàofáng
Pharmacy

Transfortation

> **Yìzhāng Tiānānmén.**
> A ticket to Tiananmen.

To travel in cities you can go by taxi, public bus, or bicycle; while in Beijing, there is also a fast and convenient subway. Sometimes, you'll probably want to get out for walks by yourself and meet some ordinary Chinese. By starting with a few simple Chinese phrases and sentences and then trying them out on your own, you might surprise yourself by heading home from your trip being able to speak some Chinese. The real advantage will be feeling closer to all the things you'll experience and setting the stage for some wonderful memories of your trip.

Buses and Trolley Buses

Excuse me. Which bus should I take to get to the (Jianguo Hotel)?	Qǐngwèn, dào (Jiànguó Fàndiàn) zuò jǐlù chē?
How much to the (zoo)?	Dào (dòngwùyuán) duōshǎo qián?
I want (three) tickets, please.	Mǎi (sān zhāng) piào.
Please tell me when to get off.	Dàozhàn qǐng jiào wǒ yìshēng.
How many stops before the Art Gallery?	Dào Měishùguǎn háiyǒu jǐ zhàn?
Excuse me. Where is the bus stop for bus (52)?	Qǐng wèn, (wǔshíèr lù) chēzhàn zài nǎlǐ?
Excuse me. I'm getting off.	Duì bù qǐ, wǒ yào xiàchē.
Excuse me, please.	Qǐng ràng yí ràng.
Where should I transfer to bus (4)?	Nǎlǐ néng huàn (sì lù) chē?
Does this bus go to the (Summer Palace)?	Zhè tàng chē qù (Yíhéyuán) ma?
Excuse me. When is the last run?	Qǐng wèn, mòbān chē shénme shíjiān?

Subways

Where is the subway entrance?	Dìtiě zhànkǒu zài nǎlǐ?
Which direction should I go?	Gāi wǎng nǎge fāngxiàng?
Is it the correct direction to go toward (Qianmen)?	Zhèshì dào (Qiánmén) de fāngxiàng ma?

T I P S

Buses

Since China's cities are densely populated, the buses are often very crowded—especially during rush hour. Many people will be waiting at the stops, so if you're too polite you'll never make it onto the bus. Don't worry, a little pushing won't offend anyone. Pay the conductor (sometimes there's two—one at the front and one at the back doors) for your ticket once you're on the bus. Again, because the passengers get packed in tight, you'll want to work your way to the door one stop ahead of time.

Key Words

请问,到(建国饭店)坐
几路车?

到(动物园)多少钱?

买(三张)票。

到站请叫我一声。

到美术馆还有几站?

请问,(52 路)车站在哪
里?

对不起,我要下车.

请让一让。

哪里能换(4 路)车?

这趟车去(颐和园)吗?

请问,末班车什么时间?

地铁站口在哪里?

该往哪个方向?

这是到(前门)的方向吗?

bus stop	qìchē zhàn	汽车站
trolley bus stop	diànchē zhàn	电车站
first run	tóubān chē	头班车
last run	mòbān chē	末班车
bus No. 3	sānlù qìchē	三路汽车
get on	shàng chē	上车
get off	xià chē	下车
transfer	dǎo chē	倒车
traffic lights	hónglù dēng	红绿灯
red light	hóngdēng	红灯
green light	lùdēng	绿灯
bus stop name	zhànmíng	站名
express bus	kuàichē	快车
buy a ticket	mǎipiào	买票
month pass	yuèpiào	月票
subway	dìtiě	地铁
entrance	rùkǒu	入口
exit	chūkǒu	出口
coach	chēxiāng	车厢
direction	fāngxiàng	方向
time	shíjiān	时间
how many stops	jǐ zhàn	几站
taxi	chūzū chē	出租车

T I P S

Bus fare

Bus fare in China is very cheap. It ranges from 10 fen to 40 fen (equivalent to 2 to 8 American cents). There are two sorts of routes. One is a fixed charge—20 fen will get you anywhere along the line. The second is a rate according to the number of stops you'll go. The conductor will ask you Nǐ qù nǎlǐ? (Where are you going?) and you should be prepared to either say where or point to it on a map. If you're alone, tell the conductor Wǒ yào mǎi yì zhāng piào (I want to buy one ticket), or liǎng zhāng piào for two, and so forth.

How many stops are there before (Qianmen) Station?	Dào (Qiánmén) háiyǒu jǐ zhàn?
Does this subway go to (Yonghegong Monastery)?	(Yōnghégōng) qù bú qù?
How long do we have to wait for the next subway?	Xià yí tàng dìtiě yào děng duōjiǔ?
Where should I transfer to the round-the-city subway?	Nǎlǐ néng huàn huánxiàn dìtiě?
How much is the ticket?	Duōshǎo qián yì zhāng piào?
May I sit here?	Kěyǐ zuò zài zhèr ma?
Is this seat taken?	Zhèr yǒu rén ma?
Where should I wait for the subway to (Hepingmen)?	Qù (Hépíngmén) de dìtiě zài nǎr děng?
What is the next stop?	Xià yí zhàn shì nǎlǐ?
Make way, please. We want to get off.	Qǐng ràng yí ràng, wǒmen yào xiàchē.

Taxis

Where can I get a taxi?	Nǎlǐ néng jiàodào chūzū chē?
What's the fare per kilometer?	Yì gōnglǐ duōshǎo qián?
I want to go to the (Shangrila Hotel).	Wǒ qù (Xiānggélǐlā Fàndiàn).
To the (Exhibition Center), please.	Qù (Zhǎnlǎn Zhōngxīn).
Can you wait for me?	Néng děng wǒ yíxià ma?
I'll be back in (fifteen) minutes.	Wǒ (shíwǔ) fēnzhōng huílai.

T
I
P
S

Bus routes and operating hours

Bus routes are called lù in Chinese. In Beijing, the inner-city bus numbers are one or two digits, as in bus 1 and bus 27; the suburban bus numbers are three digits starting from three hundred, as in bus 332 and bus 360. Trolley bus numbers are three digits starting from one hundred, as in trolley bus 114 and trolley bus 103.

Public buses normally run from 5:00 am to 11:30 pm. Suburban buses begin later and stop earlier. There are some routes in the city that operate throughout the night.

Key Words

到（前门）还有几站？

（雍和宫）去不去？

下一趟地铁要等多久？

哪里能换环线地铁？

多少钱一张票？

可以坐在这儿么？

这儿有人吗？

去（和平门）的地铁在哪儿等？

下一站是哪里？

请让一让，我们要下车。

哪里能叫到出租车？

一公里多少钱？

我去（香格里拉饭店）。

去（展览中心）。

能等我一下吗？

我（十五）分钟回来。

driver	sījī	司机
odometer	jìchéngqì	计程器
kilometer	gōnglǐ	公里
fare	chēfèi	车费
starting fare	qǐjià	起价
wait	děngyíxià	等一下
stop	tíngyíxià	停一下
fast	kuàiyìdiǎnr	快一点儿
receipt	shōujù	收据
car	xiǎo wò chē	小卧车
van	miànbāo chē	面包车
charge	shōufèi	收费
time	shíjiān	时间
mileage	lǐchéngshù	里程数
bicycle	zìxíng chē	自行车
rent a bicycle	zū zìxíng chē	租自行车
park a bicycle	cún zìxíng chē	存自行车
parking fee	cúnchēfèi	存车费
tire pump	qìtǒng	汽筒
leak	lòuqì	漏气
front tire	qiántāi	前胎
rear tire	hòutāi	后胎
repair	xiūlǐ	修理
repair shop	xiūlǐpù	修理铺

T
I
P
S

Minibuses

In addition to public buses and trolley buses, there are minibuses running on certain routes, mainly the tourist routes. They charge more than public buses—about 3 yuan each person—but are cheaper than a taxi. They have regular stops but will stop for you anywhere if you wave them down.

Go back to the hotel, please.	Xiànzài huí fàndiàn.
Please stop here for a moment.	Qǐng zài zhèlǐ tíng yíxià.
Please drive faster.	Qǐng kāi kuài yìdiǎnr.
We want (two) taxis.	Yào (liǎng liàng) chūzū chē.
Please turn on the meter.	Qǐng dǎkāi jìchéngqì.
What is the starting fare?	Qǐjià duōshǎo?
Can I have a receipt, please.	Qǐng gěi wǒ yí ge shōujù.

Renting a Car

I want to rent a car.	Wǒ yào zū yí liàng chē.
I need a van.	Wǒ yào yí liàng xiǎo miànbāo chē.
What is the rate per day?	Měitiān zūjīn duōshǎo?
Do you charge for time or for mileage?	Àn shíjiān suàn, háishì àn lǐchéng suàn?
How do you charge for extra mileage?	Chāochū de lǐchéng zěnme suàn?
Can I rent a car for half a day?	Kěyǐ zū bàntiān ma?

Bikes

Where can I rent a bicycle?	Nǎlǐ yǒu zū zìxíng chē de?
Can I rent a bicycle here?	Zhèlǐ zū zìxíng chē ma?
What is the rental for an hour?	Yì xiǎoshí duōshǎo qián?

Taxis

T
I
P
S

   Only big cities in China have taxis. They are run by state-owned automobile companies, hotels and travel agencies. Recently, some illegal private taxis can also be found. Be careful. They might overcharge you. These illegal taxis usually do not have the yellow taxi lights on the top. When riding in a taxi, you should check whether or not the driver uses the odometer. If not, you should ask him to turn it on. If you have any complaints about the taxi, note the plate number and report it to the taxi control department.
   Taxi fare currently is normally 1.00 yuan to 3.00 yuan per kilometer according to different cars. The starting fare is 12.00 yuan.

现在回饭店。

请在这里停一下。

请开快一点。

要（两辆）出租车。

请打开计程器。

起价多少？

请给我一个收据。

我要租（一）辆车。

我要（一）辆小面包车。

每天租金多少？

按时间算，还是按里程算？

超出的里程怎么算？

可以租半天吗？

哪里有租自行车的？

这里租自行车吗？

一小时多少钱？

Key Words

take a walk	sànbù	散步
east	dōng	东
south	nán	南
west	xī	西
north	běi	北
left	zuǒ	左
right	yòu	右
front	qián	前
back	hòu	后
avenue	lù	路
street	jiē	街
lane	xiàng	巷
alley	hútòng	胡同
park	gōngyuán	公园
department store	bǎihuò gōngsī	百货公司
intersection	shízì lùkǒu	十字路口
five minutes	wǔfēnzhōng	五分钟
ten minutes	shí fēnzhōng	十分钟
a quarter of an hour	yíkèzhōng	一刻钟
walk forward	yìzhízǒu	一直走

Subway

T
I
P
S

There are only two subway routes in Beijing—one runs from Shijingshan to the Beijing Train Station and the other is a round-the-city route. The two interlink at Fuxingmen Station and part at Beijing Train Station. The subway fare is 50 fen for one way. Intervals between two subway trains vary between rush hour and the day time but are normally 3 to 5 minutes. The door of the subway opens and closes automatically–there is no need to push any button. Be careful not to fall from the platform as there is an electrified rail on the tracks. Each station has its own style of architecture and lights, which are worth looking at if you have time.

Do you have bicycles to lease now?	Xiànzài yǒu chē ma?
I want a (lady's/man's) bicycle.	Yào yí liàng (nǚchē/nánchē).
I want this one.	Yào zhè yi liàng.
Do I have to pay in advance?	Yào xiān fùqián ma?
How much do I owe you?	Wǒ gāi gěi nǐ duōshǎo?
This one is no good, please get me another one.	Zhè liàng bù hǎo, qǐng huàn yí liàng.
Can I use this tire pump?	Néng yòng yíxià qìtǒng ma?
When do you close?	Shénme shíhòu guānmén?
I'll be back at (five).	Wǒ (wǔdiǎn) huílái.
Please return my passport.	Qǐng huán wǒ hùzhào.
The tire of my bicycle leaks.	Wǒ de chētāi lòuqì.
The (front/rear) tire.	(Qián/hòu) tāi.
The brakes are broken.	Zhá huài le.
When do you think it can be repaired?	Shénme shíhòu néng xiūhǎo?
OK. Come back at (three) in the (afternoon).	Hǎo, (xiàwǔ) (sāndiǎn) láiqǔ.

On Foot

I'm going for a walk.	Wǒ xiǎng qù sànsàn bù.
Is there a park nearby?	Fùjìn yǒu gōngyuán ma?
Is (Tiananmen Square) far from here?	(Tiān'ānmén) lí zhèlǐ yuǎn ma?

Bicycles

T
I
P
S

The bicycle is definitely the most convenient and popular form of transportation in China, while private cars are rare. At rush hour, bicycles move like streams in the streets, which has made China famous as "Kingdom of Bicycles." (In Beijing alone there are altogether more than three million bicycles.) Part of the appeal of the bicycle is avoiding the crowds and delays that are common when taking China's overloaded public buses. In addition, you'll enjoy the chance you have on a bike to get a street-level impression of China.

现在有车吗？

要一辆（女车/男车）。
要这一辆。
要先付钱吗？
我该给你多少？
这辆不好，请换一辆。

能用一下气筒吗？
什么时候关门？
我（五点）回来。
请还我护照。
我的车胎漏气。
（前/后）胎。
闸坏了。
什么时候能修好？

好。（下午）（三点）来取。

我想去散散步。
附近有公园吗？
（天安门）离这里远吗？

Key Words

forward	wǎngqián	往前
backward	wǎnghòu	往后
eastward	wǎngdōng	往东
westward	wǎngxī	往西
turn	guǎiwān	拐弯
lost	mílù	迷路
man's room	nán cèsuǒ	男厕所
lady's room	nǚ cèsuǒ	女厕所
charge	shōufèi	收费

Rent a bike

T I P S

You can rent a bike from many hotels and bicycle repair shops. There are designated bicycle parking areas almost everywhere, usually watched over by bicycle attendants. The parking fee is cheap—five fen during daytime and 20 fen at night. Of course, you will see people parking their bikes anywhere that's convenient: on the sidewalks, at the entrance of the subway, and in front of shops. However, the bike owner runs the risk of having the bike removed as penalty.

Could you tell me how to get there?	Nǐ néng gàosù wǒ zěnme zǒu ma?
Walk (westward) from the (Beijing Hotel).	Cóng (Běijīng Fàndiàn) (wǎng xī).
It takes about (a quarter hour) to get there.	Dàyuē (yī kèzhōng) kě dào.
Does this alley lead to main street?	Zhètiáo xiǎo hútòng néng guòqù ma?
Is the (Art Gallery) far from here?	(Měishùguǎn) lí zhèr yuǎn ma?
Start out from here, turn (north) at the intersection, and it's not too long before you'll see (Dong'an Mall).	Chūmén (wǎngběi) bùyuǎn, jiùshì (Dōng'ān Shìchǎng).
What is the name of the street in front?	Qiánmiàn nàtiáo jiē jiào shénme míngzi?
What is the meaning of *hutong*?	Hútòng shì shénme yìsi?
Huotong is a Beijing dialect for small alley.	Běijīng rén guǎn xiǎoxiàng jiào hútòng.
I am lost.	Wǒ mílù le.
Excuse me. Where is the (Beijing Hotel)?	Duì bù qǐ, (Běijīng Fàndiàn) zài nǎr?
Down the street to the (east).	Yìzhí wǎng (dōng).
Is there a toilet nearby?	Fùjìn yǒu cèsuǒ ma?

On foot

T
I
P
S

Chinese like to go for strolls in the cool of day after their dinner. You should feel free to join them. The streets of most cities are tree-shaded, although lawns are scarce in many places and in some northern cities (like Beijing) streets are fairly dusty, especially during spring time. It's wise to bring along a pair of low-heeled shoes or traveler's boots if you plan to do a lot of walking.

If you get turned around on your stroll, you may have to ask for directions. People will be more than willing to help, but be advised that there are many local dialects in China. In addition, people in different places will use different expressions for directions. The southern people will say front, back, left, and right, while the northern people will say east, west, north, and south.

你能告诉我怎么走吗？

从（北京饭店）（往西）。

大约（一刻钟）可到。

这条小胡同能过去吗？

（美术馆）离这儿远吗？

出门（往北）不远，就是
（东安市场）。

前面那条街叫什么名
字？

胡同是什么意思？

北京人管小巷叫胡同。

我迷路了。

对不起，（北京饭店）在
哪儿？

一直往（东）。

附近有厕所吗？

What You May Hear

Qǐng mǎi piào.	Buy your tickets, please.
Duōshǎo qián?	How much?
Nín qù nǎlǐ?	Where are you going?
xiàchē	get off
Qǐng ràngyiràng.	Please let me pass.
Xiàchē ma?	Are you getting off?
dǎochē	transfer buses
Xiàzhàn shì...	The next stop is...
Dǎkāi piào.	Show your tickets.
Xiān xià hòu shàng.	Let people off first, then you may get on.
Duìbùqǐ.	Sorry.
Láojià.	Excuse me.

Toilets

TIPS

The other thing you might want to know for your strolls is about public restrooms. There are toilets in all hotels, big shops, airports and railway stations, but other places may not necessarily have them. In Beijing, you will find that there are public toilets located conveniently around the city. You just need to ask a passerby, Cèsnǒ zài nǎlǐ? (Where is the toilet?), and they will be able to tell you. However, be prepared to find that these toilets are not as clean as those in the West. These roadside toilets do not provide toilet paper or soap (you should take some small packets of tissue paper along wherever you go), and some even don't have tap water. However, there are now some pay-toilets which are relatively clean. The fee is normally 10 fen to 20 fen.

Signs

chūzū qìchē zhàn
Taxi Station

kāiwǎng...
Leaving for...

tíng
No Parking

xiūlǐ zìxíngchē
Bicycle Repair

fēiyǐnyòng shuǐ
Unpotable Water

Hotel

Néng bāng wǒ yíxià ma?
Could you help me?

In recent years, many four- and five-star hotels have been built in China with complete facilities. And the service people have studied English. There are also some medium-sized and small hotels built in the 50s or 60s. The rooms in these aren't quite as posh as the most expensive hotels, but they are equipped with a bath and TV. There are also some still smaller inns and hostels, though the conditions of these are usually not too good. The rooms have no bath and no hot water. But they do have fairly low rates. If you're thinking of choosing these to save your money for other things, be clear that you're giving up the modern convenience found at the upper end.

Check In

Excuse me. Do you have rooms available?	Qǐngwèn yǒu kōng fángjiān ma?
I need a (single/twin) room.	Wǒ yào yí ge (dānrén/ shuāngrén) fángjiān.
How much is a (single/twin) room per day?	(Dānrén/shuāngrén) fángjiān yì tiān duōshǎo qián?
I have already booked a room. My name is (Jackson).	Wǒ dìng le yí ge fángjiān. Wǒ jiào (Jiékèxùn).
Is there a bath and hot water in the room?	Yǒu yùshì hé rèshuǐ ma?
I need (two) rooms on the (fourth) floor.	Wǒ yào (liǎng) jiān (sì)céng de fángjiān.
I don't want the room facing the street.	Wǒ búyào línjiē de fángjiān.
I want to stay for (two) days.	Wǒ zhù (liǎng) tiān.

Check Out

Please connect me with the main desk.	Qǐng jiē zǒngfúwùtái.
My room number is (274).	Wǒ zhù (èrqīsì hào) fángjiān.
Please make up my bill.	Qǐng jiézhàng.
I'll leave at (one) o'clock (this afternoon).	Wǒ (xiàwǔ) (yìdiǎn) líkāi.
Will I be able to pay by credit card?	Kěyǐ yòng xìnyòngkǎ fùqián ma?
Can I leave my luggage here?	Xíngli néng zàn cún zài zhèlǐ ma?
I'm going to (Tianjin) and will be back (tomorrow).	Wǒ dào (Tiānjīn) qù, (míngtiān) huílái.
Please keep my room for me.	Qǐng bǎolíu wǒ de fángjiān.

T
I
P
S

Tipping

Tipping is illegal in China. You do not have to pay tips in the hotel or for the taxi. The wages paid to the hotel staff and taxi drivers already include the service charges. In the past, some service people would even consider a tip insulting, but now they know that tips are well intentioned.

Key Words

请问有空房间吗?

我要一个(单人/双人)
房间。

(单人/双人)房间一天
多少钱?

我订了一个房间。我叫
(杰克逊)。

有浴室和热水吗?

我要(两)间(四)层的房
间。

我不要临街的房间。

我住(两)天。

请接总服务台。

我住(274 号)房间。

请结帐。

我(下午)(一点)离开。

可以用信用卡付钱吗?

行李能暂存在这里吗?

我到(天津)去,(明天)
回来。

请保留我的房间。

hotel	lǚguǎn	旅馆
reception	fúwùtái	服务台
service people	fúwùyuán	服务员
book a room	dìng fángjiān	订房间
room available	kōng fángjiān	空房间
room rate	fángfèi	房费
single room	dānrénfáng	单人房
double room	shuāngrén-fáng	双人房
Palace Hotel	Wángfǔ Fàndiàn	王府饭店
Jianguo Hotel	Jiànguó Fàndiàn	建国饭店
business hours	yíngyè shíjiān	营业时间
main service desk	zǒng fúwùtái	总服务台
leave	líkāi	离开
come back	huílai	回来
bathroom	yùshì	浴室
hot water	rèshuǐ	热水
cold water	lěngshuǐ	冷水
water pipe	shuǐguǎn	水管
makeup a bill	jiézhàng	结帐
credit card	xìnyòng kǎ	信用卡

T I P S **Don't drink the tap water**

Tap water in China is unpotable. The Chinese do not drink tap water. They are used to drinking boiled water, or cold or hot water. There will usually be boiled water in thermoses in your hotel room.

Service

When can my luggage be sent here?	Wǒ de xíngli shénme shíhòu néng sòng dào?
When will we have hot water?	Jǐdiǎnzhōng yǒu rèshuǐ?
When does breakfast begin?	Shénme shíhòu chī zǎofàn?
Can I have my breakfast sent to my room?	Zǎofàn kěyǐ sòngdào fángjiān lǐ lái ma?
Please give me one more blanket.	Qǐng zài gěi wǒ yì tiáo tǎnzi.
I need some towels.	Wǒ háiyào liǎng tiáo máojīn.
There is no soap in my room.	Yùshìlǐ méiyǒu féizào.
Please wake me at (six) o'clock tomorrow morning.	Míngzǎo (liùdiǎn) qǐng jiàoxǐng wǒ.
Any messages for me?	Yǒu wǒ de xìn ma?
I want to talk to the restaurant manager.	Wǒ yào zhǎo cāntīng jīnglǐ.
I need (a) thermos of boiled water.	Wǒ yào (yì píng) kāishuǐ.
Where is the wall socket?	Chāzuò zài nǎlǐ?

Problems

My toilet is leaking.	Mǎtǒng lòushuǐ.
My basin is blocked up.	Xǐliǎnchí dǔzhù le.
The heating is not working.	Nuǎnqì bú rè.
The air conditioner doesn't work.	Kōngtiáo huài le.
The lamp's broken.	Táidēng bú liàng le.
I can't open the window.	Chuānghu dǎ bù kāi.

T
I
P
S

Safety

Large hotels in China are very safe. You do not have to worry about having your belongings lost or stolen. But it's always a good idea to keep track of your valuables—consider having them kept in the hotel safe. But don't be too worried. There's a joke that a hotel service person ran after a tourist to return him his discarded magazines and used razors.

Key Words

我的行李什么时候能
送到？

几点钟有热水？

什么时候吃早饭？

早饭可以送到房间里
来吗？

请再给我一条毯子。

我还要两条毛巾。

浴室里没有肥皂。

明早（六点）请叫醒我。

有我的信吗？

我要找餐厅经理。

我要（一瓶）开水。

插座在哪里？

马桶漏水。

洗脸池堵住了。

暖气不热。

空调坏了。

台灯不亮了。

窗户打不开。

room number	fánghào	房号
upstairs	shànglóu	上楼
downstairs	xiàlóu	下楼
(first) floor	(yì) cénglóu	（一）层楼
voltage	diànyā	电压
wall socket	chāzuò	插座
TV	diànshì	电视
refrigerator	diànbīngxiāng	电冰箱
breakfast	zǎofàn	早饭
lunch	wǔfàn	午饭
supper	wǎnfàn	晚饭
boiled water	kāishuǐ	开水
ice water	bīngshuǐ	冰水
tea cup	chábēi	茶杯
thermos bottle	nuǎnpíng	暖瓶
towel	máojīn	毛巾
clean	gānjìng	干净
dirty	zāng	脏
air conditioner	kōngtiáojī	空调机
break down	huàile	坏了
take a bath	xǐzǎo	洗澡
soap	féizào	肥皂
key	yàoshi	钥匙

T I P S Toiletries

Soap, toothbrushes and toilet paper are provided by Chinese hotels, but most of these items are Chinese-made. If you have a special preference, you'd be best to bring your own. Foreign soaps are available in stores. Foreign toilet paper, however, is rare—while the Chinese toilet paper is sometimes less soft.

Laundry

Where should I put my laundry?	Yào xǐ de yīfu fàngzài nǎli?
Can I have this drycleaned?	Néng gānxǐ ma?
When can I get my laundry back?	Shénme shíhòu néng xǐhǎo?
Can it be done sooner?	Néng kuài yì diǎnr ma?
This silk blouse should be hand washed.	Zhèjiàn sīchènshān yào shǒu xǐ.
I need it (this afternoon).	(Xiàwǔ) yào.

Mail

How much does it cost to send it airmail to (the United States)?	Jì (Měiguó) hángkōng xìn duō shǎoqián?
Please give me (three) (2) *yuan* stamps.	Mǎi (sān zhāng) (liǎng) yuán de yóupiào.
I'd like to send it airmail.	Wǒ jì hángkōng xìn.
How long will it take this letter to arrive?	Duōjiǔ néng dào?
How much does it cost to mail a postcard?	Jì míngxinpiàn duōshǎo qián?
How many times a day is the mail collected?	Yìtiān kāi jǐ cì xìnxiāng?
Did I write it correctly?	Zhèyàng xiě duì bú duì?
How much does it cost to post it?	Yóufèi duóshǎo?
I want to remit (50) *yuan* to (Shanghai).	Wǒ yào huì (wǔshí) yuán dào (Shànghǎi).
Could you help fill in this form for me?	Nǐ néng bāng wǒ tián yíxià ma?
Do you have wrapping paper and rope?	Yǒu bāozhuāng zhǐ hé shéngzi ma?

T
I
P
S
Laundry

Laundry service in most hotels is fairly good. Your laundry will be washed and returned to you in a day, half a day or even a few hours at your request. If your clothes are cut or a hole has been burned, the laundry can mend it by hand to make it good as new.

Key Words

要洗的衣服放在哪里？

能干洗吗？

什么时候能洗好？

能快一点吗？

这件丝衬衫要手洗。

（下午）要。

寄（美国）航空信多少钱？

买（三张）（两）元的邮票。

我寄航空信。

多久能到？

寄明信片多少钱？

一天开几次信箱？

这样写对不对？

邮费多少？

我要汇（50）元到（上海）。

你能帮我填一下吗？

有包装纸和绳子吗？

toilet	mǎtǒng	马桶
blanket	máotǎn	毛毯
laundry	xǐyīfu	洗衣服
dryclean	gānxǐ	干洗
hand wash	shǒuxǐ	手洗
remit money	huìkuǎn	汇款
letter paper	xìnzhǐ	信纸
glue	jiāoshuǐ	胶水
stamp	yóupiào	邮票
envelop	xìnfēng	信封
commemorative stamp	jìniàn yóupiào	纪念邮票
airmail	hángkōng	航空
surface mail	píngxìn	平信
postcard	míngxìn piàn	明信片
parcel	bāoguǒ	包裹
express mail	kuàidì	快递
address	dìzhǐ	地址
name	xīngmíng	姓名
register	guàhào	挂号
telephone exchange	zǒngjī	总机
operator	jiēxiànyuán	接线员
telephone	diànhuà	电话
busy line	zhànxiàn	占线

Postage

T
I
P
S

Postal service in China is state run, so postage is cheap. Postage for domestic surface letters is 20 fen and for domestic airmail is 30 fen. Postage for overseas airmail letters is 2 yuan. Now there are express mail services available in big post offices, big hotels and office buildings.

I'd like to buy some (commemorative/special) stamps.	Wǒ yào mǎi (jìniàn/tèzhǒng) yóupiào.
Do you have (panda) stamps?	Yǒu (xióngmāo) yóupiào ma?
How much does each set cost?	Měi tào duōshǎo qián?

Phone Calls

Do I have to dial "0" first to get an outside connection?	Dǎ wàixiàn yào xiānbō líng ma?
Extension (938), please.	Qǐng jiē (jiǔsānbā) fēnjī.
Could you please tell him to give me a call?	Qǐng zhuǎngào tā, gěi wǒ huíge diànhuà, xíng ma?
My telephone number is (378-6542).	Wǒ de diànhuà shì (sānqībā liùwǔsìèr).
I'll be at the hotel (this afternoon).	Wǒ (xiàwǔ) zài lǚguǎn.
How much per minute?	Yì fēnzhōng duōshǎo qián?
Try it again, please.	Qǐng zài shìshì.
The number is correct. Please try again.	Hàomǎ méicuò, qǐng zài jiē yícì.
Please cancel the call I booked just now.	Qǐng qǔxiāo wǒ yào de diànhuà.

Using the phone

Ⓣ   If you're making a phone call from a hotel, first dial "0" (in some hotels dial "9") then the phone number. If the number you call is an exchange, the operator will ask you the extension number. The operator will then say either Zhàn xiàn (The line's busy) or Méi rén jiē (Nobody answers the phone). In most cases, whoever answers the phone will ask Nǐ zhǎo shuí? (Whom are you looking for?) instead of telling you who he or she is. This is not impolite, it's just the way Chinese do it. If you make an international phone call through the operator, you may hear Qǐng děng yì děng (Hold on, please!) or Nín de diànhuà lái le (Your phone call is through).

Ⓘ

Ⓟ

Ⓢ   What you'll hear most often when making phone calls is: Wéi (Hello), Nǐ zhǎo shuí? (Whom are you looking for?), Qǐng děng yì děng (Hold on, please!), Bú zài (He/she is not in), and Zhàn xiàn (The line is busy).

我要买(纪念/特种)邮票。

有(熊猫)邮票吗?

每套多少钱?

打外线要先拨"0"吗?

请接(938)分机。

请转告他,给我回个电话,行吗?

我的电话是(378-6542)

我(下午)在旅馆。

一分钟多少钱?

请再试试。

号码没错,请再接一次。

请取消我要的电话。

Key Words

wait	děngdài	等待
public telephone	gōngyòng diànhuà	公用电话
telephone bill	diànhuà fèi	电话费
domestic long-distance	guónèi chángtú	国内长途
International long-distance	guójì chángtú	国际长途
long-distance exchange	chángtútái	长途台
not connected	bù tōng	不通
no answer	méi rén jiē	没人接
The phone doesn't work	diànhuà huài le	电话坏了
How to use the phone	zěnme dǎ fǎ	怎么打法
telephone number	diànhuà hàomǎ	电话号码
telefax	chuánzhēn	传真
cable address	diànbào guàhào	电报挂号
telex	diànchuán	电传

Electric appliances

T I P S

The voltage of the electricity in China is 220V/50Hz —different from that of the United States. In few hotels, there are two types of wall sockets: 220V and 110V. However, it would be best to use electric appliances suitable to China's voltage, or else bring along with you a converter (220V to 110V).

China Central TV (CCTV) has an English news program every night at 10:00 on Channel Eight.

You can readily receive BBC and VOA English shortwave broadcasts in China. These come in especially clear at night and in the morning.

Telegrams, Telexes, and Telefaxes

I'd like to send a telegram to (Qingdao).	Wǒ yào fā ge diànbào dào (Qīngdǎo).
This is the cable address.	Zhèshì diànbào guàhào.
I don't know how to write Chinese.	Wǒ búhuì xiě Zhōngwén.
Could you help write it for me, please?	Nǐ néng bāngwǒ xiě yíxià ma?
Do you have a telex machine?	Yǒu diànchuánjī ma?
May I send it myself?	Wǒ kěyǐ zìjǐ fā ma?
Do you have a fax machine?	Yǒu chuánzhēnjī ma?
I'd like to send it to (England) by fax.	Wǒ yào chuánzhēn dào (Yīng-guó) qù.
This is the fax number.	Zhèshì chuánzhēn hàomǎ.

Barbershops

I need a haircut.	Wǒ yào lǐfà.
I'd like it rather (long/short).	Lǐde (cháng/duǎn) yìdiǎnr.
Please just trim it.	Xiūqù yìdiǎnr jiù kěyǐ.
How much does it cost to have a permanent wave done?	Tàngfà duōshǎo qián?
Just wash and blow dry it.	Xǐtóu bìng chuīgān.
Can you do modern styles?	Huì zuò xīnshì fàxíng ma?
The blower is too hot.	Chuīfēngjī kāi de tàitàng le.
I like this style.	Wǒ xǐhuān zhèzhǒng shìyàng.
I'd like my hair dyed into a fair color.	Wǒ yào rǎn jīnhuángsè de.

T
I
P
S

Long-distance phone calls

As noted previously, not many Chinese families have their own phone. And you can't dial long-distance from public telephones. To make a long-distance call, you'll need to go either to a telecommunications center or a nearby post office. Bring along something to pass the time, though, because placing the call can sometimes take half an hour. Nowadays, you can also make long-distance calls from rooms in big hotels.

Key Words

我要发个电报到(青岛)。

| haircut | lǐfà | 理发 |
| hair washing | xǐfà | 洗发 |

这是电报挂号。

我不会写中文。

| hair curling | tàngfà | 烫发 |
| hair dyeing | rǎnfà | 染发 |

你能帮我写一下吗?

| conditioner | hùfàsù | 护发素 |
| hair cream | fàrǔ | 发乳 |

有电传机吗?

我可以自己发吗?

有传真机吗?

我要传真到(英国)去。

| hair style | fàxíng | 发型 |

What You May Hear

这是传真号码。

Yǒu kòng fángjiān ma?	Do you have vacant rooms?
Shénme shíhòu dào de?	When did you arrive?
Nǐ jiào shénme míngzi?	What's your name?
Chīdiǎn shénme?	What would you like to eat?

我要理发。

理得(长/短)一点。

修去一点就可以。

烫发多少钱?

Gòu le ma?	Have you had enough?
Qǐng děng yi děng.	Please wait a second.
Diànhuà zhànxiàn.	The line is busy.

洗头并吹干。

会做新式发型吗?

吹风开得太烫了。

我喜欢这种式样。

我要染金黄色的。

Xiān bōlíng.	Dial "0" first.
Qǐng biéguà diànhuà.	Hold on, please.
Méirén jiē.	No answer.
Lǐ shénme yàng shì de?	What hair style do you prefer?

T
I
P
S

Telex and telefax

Telex and telefax facilities are now available in China, and are used mostly by institutions having international business. Post offices and big hotels now also provide telex and telefax services.

Signs

fàndiàn
Hotel

shāngpǐnbù
Shopping Center

shāngwù zhōngxīn
Business Office

zhōngcāntīng
**Chinese
Restaurant**

měifà tīng
Barbershop

Eating

Wèidào hǎo jí le!
Delicious!

Most visitors are eager for the chance to try the authentic Chinese delicacies found only in China—some of the Chinese restaurants in the West having adapted their dishes somewhat. (You won't find chop suey or fortune cookies in China.) A true connoisseur will also want to sample the many regional flavors. The problem, though, is finding the right restaurant and then ordering the food. The following section is geared to helping you open the door to genuine Chinese cooking.

Breakfast in a Hotel

I'll have (Chinese) breakfast.	Wǒ yào chī (Zhōngguó) zǎocān.
I would like to make a reservation for tomorrow.	Wǒ yùdìng míngtiān de.
Do you have (fried crullers)?	Yǒu (yóutiáo) ma?
A bowl of (soybean milk), please.	Yì wǎn (dòujiāng).
(With/without) sugar.	(Yào/búyào) táng.
A tray of (steamed dumplings), please.	Yí tì (xiǎolóng bāozi).
If you don't have (steamed dumplings), (noodles) will be fine, too.	Méiyǒu (bāozi), (miàntiáo) yě kěyǐ.
Do you have a (ham) (sandwich)?	Yǒu (huǒtuǐ) (sānmíngzhì) ma?
A (fried egg), please.	Yí ge (jiānjīdàn).
Another glass of (orange juice), please.	Zài lái yì bēi (júzishuǐ).
That's all.	Jiù zhèxiē.
How much is it altogether?	Yígòng duōshǎo qián?
Here is (twenty) *yuan*.	Zhèshì (èrshí) yuán.

Eating in a Restaurant

Waiter!	Fúwùyuán!
Can we have the menu, please?	Qǐng gěi wǒmen càidān.
Can you please recommend some dishes?	Néng tuījiàn jǐ ge cài ma?
I would like to have (prawns).	Wǒ xǐhuān chī (xiā).
Good, a (stir-fried shrimp), please.	Hěnhǎo, lái yí ge (qīngchǎo xiārén).

T
I
P
S

Fried crullers and beancurd milk

Like milk, eggs, and bread in the West, fried crullers and beancurd milk, often eaten together with pancakes, constitute the most common breakfast in China. If you take a walk in a Chinese town in early morning, you will run into many food stands, some of them mounted on wheels or large tricycles, where crullers are served hot right out of the frying pan.

Key Words

我要吃(中国)早餐。	breakfast	zǎocān	早餐
我预定明天的。	lunch	wǔcān	午餐
	dinner	wǎncān	晚餐
有(油条)吗?	waiter,	fúwùyuán	服务员
一碗(豆浆)。	waitress		
(要/不要)糖。	Miss	xiǎojiě	小姐
一屉(小笼包子)。	reservation	yùdìng	预定
	menu	càidān	菜单
没有(包子),(面条)也	seat	zuòwèi	座位
可以。	like	xǐhuān	喜欢
有(火腿)(三明治)吗?	don't like	bù xǐhuān	不喜欢
一个(煎鸡蛋)。	want	yào	要
再来一杯(橘子水)。	don't want	bú yào	不要
	enough	gòule	够了
就这些。	table	zhuōzi	桌子
一共多少钱?	napkin	cānjīn	餐巾
这是(二十)元。	beancurd milk	dòujiāng	豆浆
	fried cruller	yóutiáo	油条
	milk	niúnǎi	牛奶
服务员!	rice congee	dàmǐ zhōu	大米粥
请给我们菜单。	millet congee	xiǎomǐ zhōu	小米粥
能推荐几个菜吗?	pickled mixed	pàocài	泡菜
我喜欢吃(虾)。	vegetables		
很好,来一个(清炒虾	bread	miànbāo	面包
仁)。	egg	jīdàn	鸡蛋
	ham	huǒtuǐ	火腿
	butter	huángyóu	黄油

T
I   ### Two musts
P
S
　　Roast Peking Duck and Mongolian Hot-pot are two of China's most famous dishes. The 120-year-old Quanjude Peking Duck Restaurant, carrying on the tradition in Beijing, serves an all-duck dinner at which duck meat, liver, webs and blood are skillfully cooked into dishes with fantastic names.

Any (chicken) dishes?	Yǒu shénme (jī) ma?
A (crispy fried chicken), please.	(Xiāngsūjī) yí ge.
A big plate of fresh vegetables, please.	Yí dà pán xīnxiān shūcài.
I (don't) like (fish) very much.	Wǒ (bù) xǐhuān chī (yú).
Do you have any soup?	Yǒu shénme tāng?
(Two bowls) of (hot-and-sour soup), please.	(Liǎng wǎn)(suānlàtāng).
(A bowl) of rice, please.	(Yì wǎn) mǐfàn.
Is this dish very hot?	Zhège cài hěn là ma?
Do you have (steamed rolls)?	Yǒu (huājuǎn) ma?
Is this enough?	Gòu ma?
And (four) bottles of (beer), too.	Zài yào (sì píng) (píjiǔ).
Can we move to the table (by the window)?	Néng huàndào (kàochuāng) de zhuōzi qù ma?
Please bring us some (paper napkins).	Qǐng gěi yìxiē (cānjīnzhǐ).
I don't know how to use chopsticks.	Wǒ búhuì yòng kuàizi.
Can we have some forks, please?	Néng gěi jǐbǎ chāzi ma?
It's delicious!	Wèidào hǎojí le.
We're really enjoying the meal.	Wǒmen chī de hěnmǎnyì.
Bring us the bill, please.	Kāi zhàngdān.

Four major regular cuisines

T I P S

Chinese cooking consists of many regional styles, but the most famous four regional cuisines are from Guangdong, Sichuan, Shandong and Jiangsu. The Guangdong (or Cantonese) style, which is most common in overseas Chinese restaurants, is noted for its mild-tasting, lightly-cooked dishes and for the great variety of seafood. Sichuan dishes are hot and spicy. This, perhaps, developed in an effort to overcome problems created by the damp weather. The Jiangsu style is known for the use of soya sauce and for being slightly sweet, while Shandong food (to which Beijing cooking belongs) uses just as much soya sauce, but tends to be salty.

有什么(鸡)吗?

(香酥鸡)一个。

一大盘新鲜蔬菜。

我(不)喜欢吃(鱼)。

有什么汤?

(两碗)(酸辣汤)。

(一碗)米饭。

这个菜很辣吗?

有(花卷)吗?

够吗?

再要(四瓶)(啤酒)。

能换到(靠窗)的桌子
去吗?

请给一些(餐巾纸)。

我不会用筷子。

能给几把叉子吗?

味道好极了。

我们吃得很满意。

开帐单。

Key Words

jam	guǒjiàng	果酱
sandwich	sānmíngzhì	三明治
tea (black tea, green tea, jasmine tea)	chá (hóng- chá, lǜchá, huāchá)	茶(红茶、绿茶、花茶)
beer	píjiǔ	啤酒
Coca-Cola	Kěkǒu Kělè	可口可乐
chopsticks	kuàizi	筷子
fork	chā	叉
knife	dāo	刀
spoon	chí	匙
ingredients	zuóliao	作料
coffee	kāfēi	咖啡
soda water	qìshuǐ	汽水
orange juice	júzishuǐ	桔子水
mineral water	kuàngquán- shuǐ	矿泉水
ice water	bīngshuǐ	冰水
ice cream	bīngqílín	冰淇淋
hot water	kāishuǐ	开水
snacks	xiǎochī	小吃
pastries	diǎnxīn	点心
Beijing dishes	Běijīng cài	北京菜

Chopsticks

T
I
P
S

The fundamental utensil for Chinese food is chopsticks. Of course spoons are also common these days. Normally, chopsticks are made from bamboo or wood. Expensive ones are made from mahogany and ivory. If you find using chopsticks is difficult, don't hesitate to ask for a fork. Knives, however, are usually unnecessary, for Chinese food is always prepared by cutting the ingredients into small cubes, slices, and shreds. You won't find anything like beef steak that makes a knife an absolute necessity.

Do you accept traveler's checks?	Nǐmen shōu lǚxíng zhīpiào ma?
Will Renminbi do?	Rénmínbi xíng bù xíng?
Let's drink to our friendship!	Wèi wǒmen de yǒuyi gānbēi!
To your health! Cheers!	Zhù nǐ shēntǐ jiànkāng! Gānbēi!

Making a Reservation

Do you take reservations?	Kěyǐ yùdìng ma?
I would like to make a reservation for (Saturday) (evening).	Wǒ yào dìng (Xīngqīliù)(wǎn-shàng) de.
There will be (seven) people.	(Qī) ge rén.
We will arrive at (8 o'clock).	Wǒmen (bādiǎn) dào.
How much is it per person?	Měirén duōshǎo qián?
Does (fifty *yuan*) also include (drinks)?	(Wǔshí yuán) bāokuò (yǐnliào) ma?
Do you have (whiskey)?	Yǒu (wēishìjì) ma?
Don't make the dishes too hot, please.	Cài búyào tàilà.
I (don't) want (roast duck).	Wǒ (búyào/yào) (kǎoyā).

Looking for a Restaurant

I am starving.	Wǒ è huài le.
Is there a (restaurant) nearby?	Fùjìn yǒu (cānguǎn) ma?
A (Chinese/Western) food restaurant.	(Zhōng/Xī) cānguǎn.

Wait, there's more

T
I
P
S

The number of courses at formal dinners—up to a dozen or even twenty to thirty—always amazes visitors. The dinner begins with four to eight cold dishes, followed by seven or eight hot dishes, and then chow mein, soup, pastries, dessert, and fruits. One thing to remember is not to take too much of the first few courses. You won't want to pass on the good ones which follow. As a courtesy, your host may choose the best parts of the dishes and put them on your plate. You'll find it impossible to stop this, but if you're really full, you can always leave what you don't want on your plate.

你们收旅行支票吗？

人民币行不行？

为我们的友谊干杯！

祝你身体健康！干杯！

可以预定吗？

我要订（星期六）（晚上）的。

（七）个人。

我们（八点）到。

每人多少钱？

（五十元）包括（饮料）吗？

有（威士忌）吗？

菜不要太辣。

我（不要／要）（烤鸭）。

我饿坏了。

附近有（餐馆）吗？

（中／西）餐馆。

Key Words

Guangdong (Cantonese) dishes	Guǎngdōng cài	广东菜
Sichuan dishes	Sìchuān cài	四川菜
Shandong dishes	Shāndōng cài	山东菜
fried rice	chǎofàn	炒饭
rice	mǐfàn	米饭
steamed rolls	huājuǎn	花卷
steamed buns	mántou	馒头
noodles with soup	tāngmiàn	汤面
fried noodles	chǎomiàn	炒面
boiled dumplings	jiǎozi	饺子
steamed dumplings	zhēngjiǎo	蒸饺
soup	tāng	汤
bottoms up	gānbēi	干杯
drink	hē	喝
eat	chī	吃
glass	bēizi	杯子
plate	pánzi	盘子
bowl	wǎn	碗
green vegetables	qīngcài	青菜
beef	niúròu	牛肉
mutton	yángròu	羊肉

It's called what?

T
I
P
S

At a Chinese banquet, you are likely to be struck by the imaginative names of the dishes. Often you won't be able to get the slightest idea of what you're eating by reading the menu. Instead, the names sometimes describe how the dish looks. Mǎyǐ shàngshù (Ants Climbing the Tree), for example, is actually a dish of stir-fried mince meat with bean noodles. Táohuā Fàn (Flood of Peach Blossoms) is made with rice cakes, tomato sauce and shrimps. If you want to know how wide and deep the Chinese imagination can run, simply read the menu.

Not too expensive.	Bú yào tàiguì de.
We want something (hot and spicy).	Wǒmen xiǎng chī (là) de.
How can I get there?	Zěnme zǒu?
Is it far from here?	Yuǎn bù yuǎn?
Do I have to go there by car?	Yào zuòchē ma?
Can it be reached in (ten minutes)?	(Shí fēnzhōng) néng dào ma?
What's the name of the restaurant?	Cānguǎn jiào shénme míngzi?
Is the place crowded?	Rén duō ma?
Will they serve if we go there now?	Xiànzài qù néng chīdào fàn ma?

During the Meal

Waiter, this is not what we ordered.	Fúwùyuán, zhè búshì wǒmen diǎn de cài.
I asked for (sweet-and-sour pork).	Wǒ yào de shì (gǔlǎo ròu).
Are there any (tooth picks)?	Yǒu (yáqiān) ma?
Can I take this menu away?	Wǒ néng názǒu zhège càidān ma?
This dish is a bit too cold.	Zhège cài liáng le.
Any more glasses?	Háiyǒu bēizi ma?
Please wipe it.	Qǐng cā yī cā.
Can I have some (soya sauce), please.	Zài gěi yìdiǎnr (jiàngyóu).

T
I
P
S

"Dry the cup"

At a traditional or formal banquet, you will find in front of you three different-sized wine glasses. The smallest is for Máotái (a fiery liquor made with grain), the medium one is for wine (most Chinese wines are sweet, though dry wine is becoming popular) and the largest for beer. Toasting is usually done with Maotai—and in the course of a banquet, there may be many toasts. The Chinese phrase for toasting is Gān Bēi, literally meaning "dry the cup." Often they mean what they say.

不要太贵的。

我们想吃（辣）的。

怎么走？

远不远？

要坐车吗？

（十分钟）能到吗？

餐馆叫什么名字？

人多吗？

现在去能吃到饭吗？

服务员，这不是我们点的菜。

我要的是（古老肉）。

有（牙签）吗？

我能拿走这个菜单吗？

这个菜凉了。

还有杯子吗？

请擦一擦。

再给一点（酱油）。

Key Words

fish	yú	鱼
shrimp	xiā	虾
seafood	hǎixiān	海鲜
chicken	jī	鸡
duck	yā	鸭
sour	suān	酸
sweet	tián	甜
bitter	kǔ	苦
hot	là	辣
salty	xián	咸
sweet-and-sour pork	gǔlǎo ròu	古老肉
crispy fried duck	xiāngsū yā	香酥鸭
spicy chicken cubes with peppers	làzijī dīng	辣子鸡丁
beef shreds with onions	yángcōng niúròusī	洋葱牛肉丝
sweet-and-sour fish	tángcù yú	糖醋鱼
mushu pork	mùxūròu	木须肉
beancurd casserole	shāguō dòufu	沙锅豆腐
sauteed bean sprouts	qīngchǎo dòuyá	清炒豆芽

TIPS

Pigs, snakes and frogs

The variety of Chinese food is dazzling. Some people say Chinese cuisine includes just about everything but what is poisonous. Well, not quite. Even some poisonous things, such as snake and scorpions, are the delicacies of some Chinese dinner tables. Bear paws, camel humps, bird nests and shark fins are all sought-after, expensive dishes.

On the other hand, the humble status of pork, the most common meat, does not put off Chinese chefs. They can conjure it into dozens of mouth-watering dishes.

Cold Drinks

It is really hot.	Tiān tàirè le.
I'm tired and thirsty, too.	Wǒ yòulèi yòukě.
I am dying for a (cold drink).	Wǒ xiǎng hē (lěngyǐn).
Where can I buy a (cold drink), please?	Nǎr yǒu (lěngyǐn) mài?
(Two bottles) of (mineral water), please.	(Liǎng píng)(kuàngquánshuǐ).
With ice, please.	Yào jiā bīng de.
Do you have (iced coffee)?	Yǒu (bīng kāfēi) ma?
(Iced) (coke) will do.	(Bīng)(kělè) yě xíng.
Do you have (soda water)?	Yǒu (qìshuǐ) ma?
Umm... the (yogurt) is good.	Zhēn guò yǐn, (suānnǎi) búcuò.
Do you have (icecream)?	Yǒu (bīngqílín) ma?
I want (two) (strawberry) ice-creams.	Wǒ yào (liǎng fèn) (cǎoméi) bīngqílín.

A Quick Lunch

I hear Chinese snacks are really good.	Tīngshuō Zhōngguó xiǎochī hěn bàng.
Is there a good snack restaurant?	Nǎlǐ yǒu hǎode xiǎochī diàn?
Will there be one where we go sightseeing today?	Jīntiān cānguān de dìfāng huì yǒu ma?
Is it expensive?	Guì ma?
(Sichuan) style?	(Sìchuān) fēngwèi?

Rice, steamed buns and boiled dumplings

T I P S

There is another more basic regional difference that has developed in Chinese cuisine—southerners like rice, while northerners eat more food made with wheat. The northerners' New Year dinner always includes boiled dumplings (jiǎozi), with the whole family making the dinner together—a sort of ritual of yearly reunion.

Nowadays this is all changing. Food made with wheat gradually is becoming common in the south, while rice is already a staple food for many northerners. Southerners, for

Key Words

天太热了。

我又累又渴。

我想喝(冷饮)。

哪儿有(冷饮)卖?

(两瓶)(矿泉水)。

要加冰的。

有(冰咖啡)吗?

(冰)(可乐)也行。

有(汽水)吗?

真过瘾,酸奶不错。

有(冰淇淋)吗?

我要(两份)(草莓)冰

淇淋。

听说中国小吃很棒。

哪里有好的小吃店?

今天参观的地方会有吗?

贵吗?

(四川)风味?

Chinese cabbage with mushrooms	mógū càixīn	蘑菇菜心
hot-and-sour soup	suānlàtāng	酸辣汤
chicken eggs with tomatoes	jīdàn chǎo xīhóngshì	鸡蛋炒西红柿
spring rolls	chūnjuǎn	春卷
steamed juicy pork dumplings	shāomài	烧麦
small steamed dumplings	xiǎolóng-bāo	小笼包
sesame sweet-rice dumplings	zhīma tāngtuán	芝麻汤团
wontons	húntún	馄饨
shish kebab	yángròu chuàn	羊肉串
almond-flour tea	xìngrén chá	杏仁茶
fruits	shuǐguǒ	水果
banana	xiāngjiāo	香蕉
apple	píngguǒ	苹果
pear	lí	梨
orange	júzi	桔子
peach	táozi	桃子
watermelon	xīguā	西瓜

TIPS

instance, insist on eating noodles (a wheat product) when celebrating a birthday, for the long noodles are considered a symbol of a long life. But the popularity of noodles in the south is only a rather recent development. Some people say spaghetti is an Italian version of Chinese noodles which Marco Polo introduced into Italy. The connection between the two is not very clear these days, though, as Chinese do not eat cheese and could not imagine their noodles being served as spaghetti. Noodles in China commonly come in a fast-food soup sold from street vendors or cold, served with vinegar and parsley (Sichuan-style).

What are the snacks?

Dōu yǒu shénme xiǎochī?

(*Dandan* noodles, beancurd milk....) Oh, over a dozen kinds.

(Dāndān miàn, dòufu nǎo), yígòng shíjǐ zhǒng.

It's really great.

Tài bàng le.

Is it open now?

Xiànzài kāimén ma?

Let's go right away.

Wǒmen mǎshàng qù.

How long will it take (on foot)?

(Zǒulù) yào duōjiǔ?

What are the famous (snacks) of China?

Zhōngguó háiyǒu shénme zhùmíng (xiǎochī)?

How are these (steamed corn-flour buns) made?

(Xiǎo wōwotóu) shì zěnme zuò de?

The empress used to eat these?

Huángtàihòu chī de?

It must be good.

Nà yídìng hěn   hǎochī.

Small restaurants

TIPS

Besides restaurants in big hotels, there are many small restaurants featuring regional delicacies. In fact, these are the places that offer the most colorful display of the local specialties. Usually they are crowded, and you may find that you have to wait—not standing at the entrance, but behind those who are eating and may finish sooner than others. Be careful to consider the cleanliness of the restaurant before eating, though, as the standards in some places are quite low.

都有什么小吃？

（担担面，豆腐脑），一共十几种。

太棒了。

现在开门吗？

我们马上去。

（走路）要多久？

中国还有什么著名（小吃）？

（小窝窝头）是怎么做的？

皇太后吃的？

那一定很好吃。

What You May Hear

Jǐ wèi?	How many?
Qǐng zuò.	Sit down, please.
Zhōngcān?	Chinese food?
Xīcān?	Western food?
Kǎoyā?	Roast duck?
Shuàn yángròu?	Mongolian hot pot?
diǎncài	order dishes
càidān	menu
Yào shénme yǐn liào?	What would you like to drink?
Hējiǔ ma?	Want some wine?
Gānbēi!	Cheers!
Zhùnǐ jiànkāng.	To your health.
Yào mǐfàn ma?	Want any rice?
Chī làde ma?	Do you eat hot dishes?
Gòu bú gòu?	Is it enough?
Huānyíng zàilái.	Welcome to come again.

Signs

fànguǎn
Restaurant

nèiyǒu yǎzuò
**V.I.P. Room
Available**

kǎoyā
**Roast Peking
Duck**

Sìchuān fēngwèi
Sichuan Cuisine

shuǐjiǎo / miàntiáo
**Dumplings /
Noodles**

Shopping

You'll probably be on the lookout for good buys while
you're there, and China will not disappoint you. For one,
China offers many items quite different from those in
other countries, such as silk, jade, and finely-wrought
unique handicrafts. In addition, besides the state-run
department stores, many free markets and private shops
have sprung up in recent years. Vendors at these places
sell just about everything. However, you will have to be
careful to not get cheated. An important thing to remember is that you should bargain at the free markets, while
the prices in the government stores are fixed. Just how
successful you can be while shopping in China depends
on your shopping experience, judgment, bargaining skills
and of course how much Chinese you know.

Shopping in a Department Store

Please show me that (piece) of (cloth).	Qǐng gěi wǒ kànkan (nàkuài) (liàozi).
Do you have any other color?	Háiyǒu biéde yánsè ma?
I'd like something brighter.	Wǒ yào xiānyàn yīdiàn de.
How much is it for (two) meters?	(Liǎng) mǐ duōshǎo qián?
I'll have (three) meters.	Wǒ yào (sān) mǐ.
I'd like to have a look at that (red) (sweater), please.	Wǒ xiǎng kànkan nàjiàn (hóng) (máoyī).
Do you have a (large) size one?	Yǒu (dà) hào de ma?
I don't like this color.	Wǒ bù xǐhuān zhège yánsè.
Is there anything (cheaper)?	Yǒu (piányi) yìdiànr de ma?
There is a stain on this one.	Zhèlǐ yǒu diǎn zāng.
Can you show me another one?	Néng huàn yí jiàn ma?
Can I try it on?	Néng shìshi ma?
This fits well.	Zhèjiàn hěn héshì.
I'll buy this one.	Wǒ yào zhèjiàn.
What time do you close?	Nǐmen shénme shíhòu guānmén?
Do you close at noontime?	Zhōngwǔ xiūxi ma?
Sorry, I don't think I'll take this.	Duì bù qǐ, wǒ búyào le.

Ordinary stores

T
I
P
S

Most stores in China are run by the state. However, the last several years have seen a mushrooming of (usually small) privately run stores. Again, unlike the state-run stores, bargaining is routine in private stores. You can get cheaper things from the ordinary shops downtown than from a Friendship Store, and you can also pay Renminbi, the Chinese currency every Chinese uses, however sometimes the quality of goods there may not be as good as in a Friendship Store. Of course if you are a shrewd shopper, you will get both.

In stores or on the streets in small-sized cities, foreigners are often followed by onlookers. Don't worry. They aren't hostile, only curious. Just give them a smile and go ahead with your own business.

Key Words

请给我看看（那块）
（料子）。

还有别的颜色吗？

我要鲜艳一点的。

（两）米多少钱？

我要（三）米。

我想看看那件（红）（毛
衣）。

有（大）号的吗？

我不喜欢这个颜色。

有（便宜）一点的吗？

这里有点脏。

能换一件吗？

能试试吗？

这件很合适。

我要这件。

你们什么时候关门？

中午休息吗？

对不起，我不要了。

antiques	gǔdǒng	古董
native and local products	tǔtè chǎn	土特产
handicrafts	shǒugōngyì pǐn	手工艺品
carpet	dìtǎn	地毯
chinaware	cíqì	磁器
carpet	dìtǎn	地毯
batik	làrǎn	蜡染
jewelry	zhūbǎo	珠宝
jadeite	fěicuì	翡翠
jade carving	yùdiāo	玉雕
tapestry	guàtǎn	挂毯
woven bambooware	zhúbiān	竹编
cloth	bù	布
batik cloth	làrǎn bù	蜡染布
like	xǐhuān	喜欢
not like	bù xǐhuān	不喜欢
painter	huàjiā	画家
calligrapher	shūfǎjiā	书法家
water color prints block	mùbǎn shuǐyìn	木版水印

Foreign articles

T
I
P
S

Before the 1970s, foreign articles, such as certain brands of liquor, cigarettes, and coffee, were rarely seen in China. Now they are readily available in big hotels, Friendship Stores (established especially for foreigners) and even ordinary Chinese stores. Hennesy, Johnnie Walker whiskey, Nescafe and U.S. cigarettes are all available with prices about the same as, if not cheaper than, in Western countries. However, if you have a strong preference for a particular brand, it's best to bring it along. For instance, China only has Qimen Black Tea, but it is not like those from India or Sri Lanka that are most common in the West. And instant sweetened milk powder is available everywhere, but it is difficult to get unsweetened low-fat milk powder.

At an Arts and Crafts Store

Do you have (cloisonne) (vases)? — Yǒu (jǐngtàilán) (huāpíng) ma?

Where are these made? — Nǎlǐ chǎn de?

There is a flaw here. — Zhèlǐ yǒudiǎn máobing.

How about this one? — Zhège zěnme yàng?

I like it very much. — Wǒ hěn xǐhuān.

Can you please wrap it up? — Qǐng bāo yíxià hǎo ma?

Can you please give me a receipt? — Qǐng gěi wǒ fāpiào.

What dynasty does this (porcelain bowl) belong to? — Zhège (cíwǎn) shì nǎge cháodài de?

Why is it so expensive? — Wèishénme zhème guì?

Can it be taken out of the country? — Kěyǐ dài chūjìng ma?

It can be taken out of China with this red wax seal. — Yǒu huǒqīyin jiùnéng dài chūqù.

Is the painting an original or a copy? — Zhèshì yuánhuà háishi fùzhìpǐn?

It's a wood block print. — Shì mùbǎn shuǐyin.

It's beautifully done. — Yin de zhēn piàoliàng.

Are there any (original) paintings? — Yǒu (yuánzuò) ma?

Is the painter alive? — Huàjiā hái huózhe ma?

Where is the Liulichang Cultural Street? — Liúlíchǎng Wénhuà Jiē zài nǎlǐ?

What do they sell there? — Nǎlǐ yǒu shénme dōngxi?

Key Words

有(景泰兰)(花瓶)吗？

哪里产的？

这里有点毛病。

这个怎么样？

我很喜欢。

请包一下好吗？

请给我发票。

这个(磁碗)是哪个朝代的？

为什么这么贵？

可以带出境吗？

有火漆印就能带出去。

这是原画还是复制品？

是木板水印。

印得真漂亮。

有(原作)吗？

画家还活着吗？

琉璃厂文化街在哪里？

那里有什么东西？

receipt	fāpiào	发票
place of origin	chǎndì	产地
antique	gǔdǒng	古董
calligraphy	zìhuà	字画
painting	huìhuà	绘画
original	yuánzuò	原作
imitation	fǎngzhìpǐn	仿制品
reproduction	fùzhìpǐn	复制品
embroidery	cìxiù	刺绣
silk	sīchóu	丝绸
woolen fabric	máoliào	毛料
arts and crafts	gōngyì pǐn	工艺品
seal	túzhāng	图章
stone	shítou	石头
ink	yìn ní	印泥
carve	kè	刻
name	míngzi	名字
ring	jièzhi	戒指
necklace	xiànglián	项链
this	zhège	这个
that	nàge	那个
large size	dàhào	大号
medium size	zhōnghào	中号
small size	xiǎohào	小号

T I P S

Antiques

China has a law that antiques of over 120 years of age are allowed to be taken out of the country only with shopping receipts and red wax seals on the objects. Therefore, it is advisable not to buy such things from free markets. This will help to avoid any complications with the Chinese Customs.

Do they sell jade?	Mài yùqì ma?
Any calligraphy works or paintings?	Yǒu zìhuà ma?
I would like to buy a chop.	Wǒ yào mǎi yí ge túzhāng.
What type of stone is this?	Zhèshì shénme shítou?
Is this blood stone?	Shì jǐxuèshí ma?
It's really beautiful!	Zhēnshì piàoliàng jíle.
Too expensive.	Tài guì le!
Can you carve my English name on it?	Néng bǎ wǒ de Yīngwén míngzi kèshàng ma?
Could you please translate my name into Chinese?	Qǐng nǐ bǎ wǒ de míngzi yìchéng Zhōngwén hǎo ma?
I would also like an (ink case).	Wǒ háiyào yì hé (yìnní).
I'll get the (green jade) (ring).	(Fěicuì) (jièzhǐ) wǒ yě yào le.
I would also like a (green jade) (bracelet).	Hái yào yí ge (fěicuì) (shǒu zhuó).
I love the jade incense burner.	Wǒ xǐhuān zhège yùxiānglú.
I can't afford it.	Wǒ mǎi bù qǐ.

Buying Books and Newspapers

Where can I find (English) (books and newspapers)?	Nǎr yǒu (Yīngwén) (shūbào) mài?
Where is the (Foreign Languages Bookstore)?	(Wàiwén shūdiàn) zài nǎlǐ?
Are there any (U.S.) (magazines)?	Yǒu (Měiguó) (zázhì) ma?

Newspapers, books and maps

T
I
P
S

Throughout China, there is a national bookstore chain called Xinhua Bookstores (Xīnhuǎ Shūdiàn) that sell books of all subjects. Periodicals, however, are sold mostly in post offices. There are of course also specialized bookstores carrying books and journals of such subjects as astronomy, geology, architecture, reference books and popular science books. Tourists out wandering for fun or at scenic sites are more likely to run into private book stands, which have

卖玉器吗？

有字画吗？

我要买一个图章。

这是什么石头？

是鸡血石吗？

真是漂亮极了。

太贵了！

能把我的英文名字刻上吗？

请你把我的名字译成中文好吗？

我还要一盒（印泥）。

（翡翠）（戒指）我也要了。

还要一个（翡翠）（手镯）。

我喜欢这个玉香炉。

我买不起。

哪儿有（英文）（书报）卖？

（外文书店）在哪里？

有（美国）（杂志）吗？

Key Words

color	yánsè	颜色
red	hóng	红
yellow	huáng	黄
blue	lán	蓝
green	lù	绿
purple	zǐ	紫
want	yào	要
don't want	bú yào	不要
expensive	guì	贵
cheap	piányi	便宜
department store	bǎihuò shāngdiàn	百货商店
arts and crafts	gōngyì měishù	工艺美术
store	shāngdiàn	商店
antique store	gǔdǒng diàn	古董店
Rongbaozhai Art Store	Róngbǎozhāi Wénwù Shāngdiàn	荣宝斋 文物 商店
friendship store	yǒuyì shāngdiàn	友谊商店
Liulichang	Liúlíchǎng	琉璃厂
Cultural Street	Wénhuà Jiē	文化街

T I P S

enjoyed brisk business in the last few years. Books, magazines, maps, and postcards can all be found at these small stands.

Among the national newspapers, *People's Daily* (Renmin Ribao) enjoys the largest circulation. *Guangming Daily* (Guangming Ribao) devotes most of its space to cultural and intellectual affairs. Evening papers such as the *Beijing Evening Gazette* (Beijing Wanbao) and the *Xinmin Evening Gazette* (Xinmin Wanbao) of Shanghai are popular because of their timely and wide coverage of local affairs. In addition to post offices, newspapers are also sold by private business people.

Does China have its own newspapers in (English)?

Zhōngguó yǒu zìjǐ de (Yīngwén) bàozhǐ ma?

I never imagined China publishes so many books in English!

Zhēn méi xiǎngdào Zhōngguó chūbǎn zhème duō Yīngwén shū.

Are there any phrase books for tourists?

Yǒu lǚyóu huìhuà ma?

Oh, a map of *Getting Around Beijing by Bus* in English.

Yǒu Yīngwén de Běijīng Lǚyóu Jiāotōng Tú.

Very good. It's extremely useful.

Tàihǎo le, zhè hěn shíyòng.

I really want a book to learn how to speak Chinese.

Wǒ xiǎng mǎi yì běn xuéshuō Zhōngwén de shū.

I'll have a copy of the (*Provincial Atlas of China*).

Wǒ mǎi yì běn (Zhōngguó Fēnshěng Dìtúcè).

The (children's books) are beautiful.

Zhèxiē (értóngshū) hěn piàoliàng.

I'll buy (a copy) for my granddaughter.

Wǒ gěi sūnnǚ mǎi (yì běn).

She will love it.

Tā yídìng xǐhuān.

I would also like a book about (Chinese women).

Wǒ háiyào yì běn yǒuguān (Zhōngguó fùnǚ) de shū.

I have really bought a lot today.

Jīntiān shōuhuò zhēndà.

English books on Chinese topics

T

I

P

S

To help foreigners get to know China, the Foreign Languages Press publishes a wide range of books on topics such as Chinese history, geography, traditional medicine, travel, art, philosophy, and religion. These are sold in book stands in hotels and all Foreign Languages Bookstores in the country. If you are unable to find a particular book in English or other foreign languages, don't hesitate to call or go to the Foreign Languages Press. It is always worth the trouble. Almost all textbooks teaching foreigners Chinese are published either by the Foreign Languages Press or its subsidiary, Sinolingua. Another subsidiary, Dolphin Books, publishes children's books—which are often bought by visitors as gift items. Books in English that may be of special interest to visitors include *China—A General Survey, Provincial Atlas of China, Traditional Chinese Exercises, An Outline History of China,* and many more. Of course, the map of Beijing in English is very handy to all travelers.

中国有自己的(英文)报纸吗？

真没想到中国出版这么多英文书。

有旅游会话吗？

有英文的北京旅游交通图。

太好了，这很实用。

我想买一本学说中文的书。

我买一本(《中国分省地图册》)。

这些(儿童书)很漂亮。

我给孙女买(一本)。

她一定喜欢。

我还要一本有关(中国妇女)的书。

今天收获真大。

Key Words

English newspaper	yīngwén bàozhǐ	英文报纸
English magazine	yīngwén zázhì	英文杂志
tourist map	lǚyóu tú	旅游图
transportation route map	jiāotōng tú	交通图
book	shū	书
map	dìtú	地图
foreign languages bookstore	wàiwén shūdiàn	外文书店
tourist guide book	lǚyóu shū	旅游书
buy	mǎi	买
mail	jì	寄
gift	lǐwù	礼物
children's book	értóng shū	儿童书
language book	xué yǔyán de shū	学语言的书
cartoon book	kǎtōng shū	卡通书
art book	huàcè	画册

English language reading materials

T

Want to keep up with what's going on at home or what's happening elsewhere in the world? Imported foreign newspapers and magazines such as the *New York Times*, *Newsweek*, the *Wall Street Journal*, *Life* magazine, *Reader's Digest*, and the *Washington Post*, can all be found in big hotels.

I

Thrillers, romances, detective stories and many other paperback books by Western publishers are also sold in these places. China itself publishes an English daily and a number

P

of English magazines. *China Daily*, which was launched in 1981, covers the international situation, world sports, politics, and economic affairs, as well as Chinese lifestyles,

S

cultural customs, events, etc. And of course for relaxation there is always the cross-word section. English language magazines include: *Beijing Review*, *China Today*, *China Pictorial*, *China Sports*, *Chinese Literature* and *Women of China*.

Buying Clothes and Shoes

I would like to buy (a) (silk) (blouse).	Wǒ xiǎng mǎi (yí jiàn) (sīchóu) (chènshān).
This one is very nice.	Zhèjiàn hěnhǎo.
What's the size?	Yào duōdà de?
I wear size (40).	Wǒ chuān (sìshí) hào.
What fabric is this?	Zhèshì shénme liàozi de?
Any (long sleeved/short sleeved) ones?	Yǒu (chángxiù/duǎnxiù) de ma?
Is (batik) (dyed) by (hand)?	(Làrǎn) shì (shǒugōng) (rǎn) de ma?
Where is (batik) produced?	(Làrǎn bù) shì nǎlǐ shēngchǎn de?
In which part of China is it produced?	Zài Zhōngguó de nǎ yí bùfèn?
Where are (kung fu) shoes sold?	Nǎlǐ yǒu (bùxié) mài?
I want size (25).	Wǒ yào (èrshíwǔ) hào.
What I want to buy most are a dozen (Mao caps).	Wǒ zuì xiǎng mǎi de shì (jūn-mào).
And (Mao suits) too.	Háiyǒu (Zhōngshān zhuāng).
These (silk ties) are of good quality, but the colors are too loud.	Zhèxiē (sīlǐngdài) zhìliàng hěn-hǎo, jiùshì yánsè tài xiānyàn.
Do you have any more conservatively colored silk ties?	Yǒu méi yǒu sù yìdiǎn de?
The (sports suits) are cheap. I'll get one for my son.	(Yùndòng fú) hěn piányi, wǒ yào gěi érzi mǎi yí tào.
It is well made.	Zuògōng hěn jīngxì.
Are these (shoes) washable?	Zhè (xié) néng xǐ ma?

T I P S
Recommended articles

carpets (*from Beijing, Tianjin, Xinjiang and Tibet*)
pottery and **ceramics** (*from Foshan near Guangzhou, Liling in Hunan, Jingdezhen in Jiangxi, and Yixing in Jiangsu*)
ivory articles (*from Guangzhou and Beijing*)
bambooware (*from Chengdu*)
lacquerware (*from Beijing and Fuzhou*)
cloisonne (*from Beijing*)
mahogany furniture (*from Beijing and Suzhou*)

Key Words

我想买(一件)(丝绸)
(衬衫)。

这件很好。

要多大的?

我穿(40)号。

这是什么料子的?

有(长袖/短袖)的吗?

(蜡染)是(手工)(染)的
吗?

蜡染布是哪里生产的?

在中国的哪一部分?

哪里有(布鞋)卖?

我要(25)号。

我最想买的是(军帽)。

还有(中山装)。

这些(丝领带)质量很好,
就是颜色太鲜艳。

有没有素一点的?

(运动服)很便宜,我要给
儿子买一套。

做工很精细。

这(鞋)能洗吗?

cashmere	kāisīmǐ	开司米
sweater	máoyī	毛衣
Mao cap	"Máoshì"	"毛式"
	màozi	帽子
Mao suit	Zhōngshān-zhuāng	中山装
worker's cap	yāshémào	鸭舌帽
sports suit	yùndòng fú	运动服
silk pajamas	sīchóu shuìyī	丝绸睡衣
silk blouse	sīchóu chènshān	丝绸衬衫
kung fu shoes	bùxié	布鞋
silk tie	sīchóu lǐngdài	丝绸领带
film	jiāojuǎn	胶卷
print film	chōngxǐ	冲洗
enlarge	kuòyìn	扩印
color prints film	cǎi juǎn	彩卷
black and white film	hēibái juǎn	黑白卷
Kodak	Kēdá	柯达
Fuji	Fùshì	富士
100 ASA	yìbǎidù	一百度
slides	huàndēngpiān	幻灯片

T
I
P
S

jewelry (*from Beijing, Shanghai and Suzhou*)
silk (*from Hangzhou, Suzhou, Wuxi and Shanghai*)
embroidery (*from Suzhou, Changsha, Chengdu and Guangzhou*)
furs and **leather** (*from Beijing and Hohhot*)
scrolls (Chinese paintings) (*from Beijing, Nanjing and Shanghai*)
reproductions of Chinese paintings (*from Rongbaozhai Art Store, Beijing*)
knives (*from Xinjiang, Tibet and Inner Mongolia*)

| Must it be drycleaned? | Yídìng yào gānxǐ ma? |
| I'll buy a pair for my (wife/ husband). | Wǒ yào gěi wǒ (tàitai/ xiānsheng) mǎi yì shuāng. |

Shopping in a Free Market

Is there a (free market) selling (clothes)?	Nǎlǐ yǒu mài (yīfu) de (zìyóu shìchǎng)?
How much is this (embroidered) (blouse)?	Zhèjiàn (cìxiù) (chènshān) duō shǎo qián?
It's too expensive. Can you bring the price down a little bit?	Tài guì le, néng piányi yìdiǎnr ma?
(80) yuan, OK?	(Bāshí) kuài, zěnme yàng?
(80) yuan is quite enough.	(Bāshí) kuài kěyǐ le.
(Two) more yuan. I'll give you (82) yuan.	Zài jiā (liǎng) kuài, wǒ gěi nǐ (bāshíèr) kuài.
I won't buy it for even one more yuan.	Duō yí kuài, wǒ yě bù mǎi.
You want (U.S. dollars)?	Nǐ yào (Měiyuán) ma?
I don't have them.	Wǒ méiyǒu.
Foreign Exchange Certificates?	Duì huàn quàn?
Sixty?	Liùshí?
It's a deal.	Chéng jiāo le.

Printing Film

| I need to have this film printed. | Wǒ yào chōngxǐ jiāojuǎn. |

Chops (seals)

T
I
P
S

Perhaps one of the conspicuous differences between Chinese and Westerners is that Chinese do not attach much importance to signatures, preferring to use chops. While in China, you may want to buy one. The carver can help you to choose a Chinese name to carve on the chop or you can ask a Chinese friend to give you a Chinese name. The seal makes an interesting souvenir, or can be a gift. Make sure that you don't forget to buy a small box of red paste to use with your seals. The price for the seals—which are made of stone, wood, or metal—can vary a great deal.

一定要干洗吗？

我要给我(太太/先生)
买一双。

哪里有卖(衣服)的(自
由市场)？

这件(刺绣)(衬衫)多少
钱？

太贵了，能便宜一点吗？

(80)块，怎么样？

(80)块可以了。

再加(两)块，我给你(82)
块。

多一块，我也不买。

你要(美元)吗？

我没有。

兑换券？

六十？

成交了。

我要冲洗胶卷。

Key Words

five yuan	wǔ kuài	五块
ten yuan	shí kuài	十块
twenty yuan	èrshí kuài	二十块
thirty yuan	sānshí kuài	三十块
fifty yuan	wǔshí kuài	五十块
a hundred yuan	yìbǎi kuài	一百块

Other gift items available in all cities

TIPS

paper cuts
handicrafts
souvenir stamps
sandalwood fans
Chinese writing brushes
ink slabs
clothes
chopsticks (bamboo, wood and bone)
chops (seals)

Can you take me to a film shop? — Nǐ néng dài wǒ qù chōngxǐdiàn ma?

When will it be ready? — Shénme shíhòu qǔ?

Will it be ready in (an hour)? — (Yì xiǎoshí) néng qǔ ma?

It won't be ready until (tomorrow). — (Míngtiān) cái néng qǔ.

I want to print some more pictures. — Wǒ háiyào jiāyìn jǐ zhāng.

How many days does it take? — Yào duōshǎo tiān?

Can you please make it faster? — Néng kuài yìdiǎnr ma?

I am leaving (tomorrow). — Wǒ (míngtiān) jiù yào zǒu le.

Do you sell film? — Yǒu jiāojuǎn mài ma?

Kodak (135). — Kēdá (yāosānwǔ).

Color prints. — Cǎisè de.

Slides, please. — Yào fǎnzhuǎn piān.

(400) ASA. — (Sìbǎi) dù.

(200) ASA will be fine, too. — (Liǎngbǎi) dù yě xíng.

(36) exposures. — (Sānshíliù) zhāng de.

(Two) rolls. — Mǎi (liǎng) ge.

Where are slides processed? — Nǎlǐ néng chōng fǎnzhuǎn piān?

Where is the China Photo Service? — Zhōngguó Túpiànshè zài nǎlǐ?

Are there any slide frames? — Yǒu huàndēng piān kuāng ma?

This kind, please. — Qǐng ná zhèzhǒng.

I'll have (two) boxes. — Wǒ yào (liǎng) hé.

T I P S Buying and printing film

Foreign film, like Kodak and Fuji, is sold in Chinese stores in just about every tourist place. Most of the film sold, however, is 100, 200 and 400 ASA. If you want to use 1000 ASA film for your camera, it is safest to bring it along with you on your trip. In case of emergency, it always pays to have some replacement batteries and camera flash bulbs. Developing color prints is easy in China, though developing Ektachrome slides is almost impossible.

你能带我去冲洗店吗？

什么时候取？

（一小时）能取吗？

（明天）才能取。

我还要加印几张。

要多少天？

能快一点吗？

我（明天）就要走了。

有胶卷卖吗？

柯达（135）。

彩色的。

要反转片。

（400）度。

（200）度也行。

（36）张的。

买（两）个。

哪里能冲反转片？

中国图片社在哪里？

有幻灯片框吗？

请拿这种。

我要（两）盒。

What You May Hear

Zhèjiàn héshì ma?	Does this fit you?
Wǒmén zhèlǐ méiyǒu.	We don't have...
Nǐ yào shénme?	May I help you?
Shōukuǎn chù	Cashier's counter
Shénme chǐcùn?	What's the size?
Mài wán le.	All sold out.
Shénme yánsè?	What's the color?
Nǎ yíjiàn?	Which one?
Zhǎo nǐ qián.	Here is your change.
Chéng jiāo le.	It's a deal.

T
I
P
S

Batteries and their sizes

It is very easy to get batteries in China, but they are classified by number.

D battery (No. 1)	yī hào diànchí
C battery (No. 2)	èr hào diànchí
AA battery (No. 5)	wǔ hào diànchí
AAA battery (No. 7)	qī hào diànchí

AAA batteries are not popular in China and sometimes can be difficult to get.

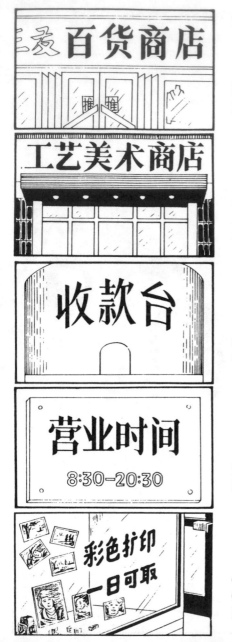

Signs

băihuò shāngdiàn
Department Store

gōngyì měishù
shāngdiàn
**Arts and Crafts
Store**

shōukuǎn tái
Cashier's Booth

yíngyè shíjiān
Business Hours

cǎisè kuòyìn
**Color Film
Processing**

Making Friends

The Chinese are a warm and hospitable people, so don't be shy to try to make some friends. One or two Chinese phrases, even if badly pronounced, will greatly reduce the distance between visitors and the Chinese. In fact, even sign language will bring smiles and helpfulness.

Meeting for the First Time

Hello.	Nín hǎo.
I am (American).	Wǒ shì (Měiguó rén).
I am from (Italy).	Wǒ cóng (Yìdàlì) lái.
Have you been to (Germany)?	Nǐ qùguò (Déguó) ma?
This is my first visit to (Shanghai).	Zhèshì wǒ dì yī cì lái (Shànghǎi).
I like (China) very much.	Wǒ hěn xǐhuān (Zhōngguó).
The (Great Wall) is really something.	(Chángchéng) shízài tài wěidà le.
Are there any other places for (sightseeing)?	Háiyǒu shénme hǎo (wán) de dìfāng?
I've been to the (Palace Museum).	Wǒ qùguò (Gùgōng).
I would like to learn to speak (Chinese).	Wǒ xiǎng xué shuō (Zhōngwén).
Can you teach me?	Nǐ néng jiāo wǒ ma?
I know a little (Chinese).	Wǒ huì yìdiǎnr (Zhōngwén).
I can't speak (Chinese) well.	Wǒ (Zhōngwén) shuō de bùhǎo.
My pronunciation is bad.	Wǒ fāyīn bùhǎo.
I can't understand.	Wǒ tīng bù dǒng.
Can you say that again?	Nǐ néng zài shuō yībiàn ma?
What's your family name?	Nǐ guì xìng?
How old are you?	Nǐ duōdà le?
Are you married?	Jié hūn le méi yǒu?

Hello, comrade

T
I
P
S

For years, husbands and wives in China have referred to each other as àirén (the person I love). But as contacts with the West have increased in recent years, they now more and more use Mr., Mrs., and Miss. To refer to their friends or colleagues, Chinese simply add the word tóngzhì (comrade) after the family name, as in Wáng tóngzhì (comrade Wang) or Lǐ tóngzhì (comrade Li). Strangers people run into when asking for directions or doing shopping are also addressed tóngzhì. In the big hotels and expensive restaurants, though, waitresses would rather be called xiǎojiě (miss) than tóngzhì.

Key Words

您好。

我是(美国人)。

我从(意大利)来。

你去过(德国)吗?

这是我第一次来(上海)。

我很喜欢(中国)。

(长城)实在太伟大了。

还有什么好(玩)的地方?

我去过(故宫)。

我想学说(中文)。

你能教我吗?

我会一点儿中文。

我(中文)说得不好。

我发音不好。

我听不懂。

你能再说 遍吗?

你贵姓?

你多大了?

结婚了没有?

Long time no see!	Hǎojiǔ bújiàn le!	好久不见了!
How are you?	Nǐ hǎo!	你好!
How have you been?	Nǐ jìnlái hǎo ma?	你近来好吗?
weather	tiānqì	天气
warm	nuǎnhuo	暖和
cold	lěng	冷
hot	rè	热
fine day	hǎotiān	好天
rainy	yǔtiān	雨天
windy	guāfēng	刮风
come	lái	来
go	qù	去
It's fun.	Hǎo wán	好玩
Chinese	Zhōngwén	中文
English	Yīngwén	英文
pronunciation	fāyīn	发音
not understand	bùdǒng	不懂
work	gongzuò	工作
job	gōngzuò	工作
marry	jiéhūn	结婚
children	háizi	孩子

Old Wang and Little Li

T I P S

A more respectful and polite way of saying nǐ is nín. When talking to strangers and people older than you it's OK to use nín, while you can use nǐ when you talk with good friends, people younger than you, and your subordinates. A very common and warm way of addressing people in China is to put the word lǎo (old) in front of the family name of older people and xiǎo (little or young) in front of the family name of younger people, as in Lǎo Wáng (Old Wang) and Xiǎo Lǐ (Little Li).

Do you have any kids?	Yǒu háizi ma?
Where do you work?	Nǐ zài nǎlǐ gōngzuò?
I'm a (professor).	Wǒshì (jiàoshòu).
My (wife) is an (engineer).	Wǒ (qīzi) shì (gōngchéngshī).
What's your job?	Nǐ zuò shénme gōngzuò?

Introductory Remarks

Please let me introduce Mr. (Yang).	Qǐng yǔnxǔ wǒ jièshào (Yáng) xiānsheng.
How do you do! This is Mr. (Wang).	Nǐ hǎo. Zhèshì (Wáng) xiān-sheng.
Nice meeting you.	Hěn gāoxìng rènshi nǐ.
I am (Brown).	Wǒ jiào (Bùlǎng).
When did you arrive?	Shénme shíhòu dào de?
I arrived (yesterday/in the afternoon/in the morning).	(Zuótiān/shàngwǔ/xiàwǔ) dào de.
Where are you staying?	Nǐ zhùzài nǎlǐ?
At the (Great Wall Hotel).	Zhùzài (Chángchéng Fàndiàn).
This is my first visit to China.	Shì dì yī cì lái Zhōngguó.
Bye!	Zàijiàn.
See you later.	Dāihuǐr jiàn.

Invitation

I'd like to invite you to (lunch/dinner).	Wǒ xiǎng qǐng nǐ chī (zhōngfàn/wǎnfàn).

T**I****P****S**

Unique greeting

Chinese greetings are similar to those of other countries except that the Chinese very rarely say "good afternoon" when running across friends or acquaintances around lunch or dinner time. They often say instead Nǐ chī guò wǔfàn le ma? (Have you had your lunch?) or Nǐ chī fàn le ma? (Have you had your meal?). The answer can be Chī guò le, nǐ ne? (I have, and you?) Although these are now merely greetings, they're based on concern for the person's well-being. In a business situation, however, even at these times a hearty Nǐ hǎo! (How are you!) is most appropriate.

有孩子吗?
你在哪里工作?
我是(教授)。
我(妻子)是(工程师)。
你做什么工作?

请允许我介绍(杨)先生。

你好! 这是(王)先生。

很高兴认识你。
我叫(布朗)。
什么时候到的?
(昨天/上午/下午)到
的。
你住在哪里?
住在(长城饭店)。
是第一次来中国。
再见。
呆会儿见。

我想请你吃(中饭
/晚饭)。

Key Words

comrade	tóngzhì	同志
Mister	xiānshēng	先生
Miss	xiǎojiě	小姐
Mrs	tàitai	太太
Ms	nǚshì	女士
professor	jiàoshòu	教授
teacher	jiàoshī	教师
engineer	gōngchéngshī	工程师
medical doctor	yīshēng	医生
lawyer	lǜshī	律师
businessman	shāngrén	商人
reporter	jìzhě	记者
accountant	kuàijìshī	会计师
student	xuéshēng	学生
painter	huàjiā	画家
artist	yìshùjiā	艺术家
invite someone to a meal	qǐng kè	请客
banquet	yànhuì	宴会
be late	chí dào	迟到
place	dìfāng	地方
difficult to find	bù hǎo zhǎo	不好找
don't have free time	méi kòng	没空

Invitation to a meal

TIPS

Chinese people, it's said, celebrate all occasions at the table. On your trip through China, you'll have plenty of opportunities to join in on the feasts. Usually, invitations are made beforehand. But sometimes, especially when it happens to be near lunch or dinner time, your host will give you an impromptu offer to join him at the meal. In many cases, this is just a customary gesture and you may politely refuse. Other times, the host will earnestly repeat the invitation. In that case, get ready for a mouth-watering Chinese meal.

I'm sorry. I am not free (today/tomorrow/this evening).	Duì bù qǐ, wǒ (jīntiān/míngtiān/jīnwǎn) méiyǒu kòng.
Can we have (lunch) together?	Hé wǒ gòngjìn (wǔcān), hǎo ma?
Can we find another time?	Gǎi tiān, hǎo ma?
I am afraid I can't come.	Wǒ kǒngpà bùnéng lái.
Do you want (tea/coffee)?	Nǐ yào (chá/kāfēi) ma?
What do you want to drink? (Beer, orange juice, mineral water, wine, Maotai liquor)	Nǐ xiǎng hēdiǎn shénme? (píjiǔ, júzishuǐ, kuàngquánshuǐ, pútáojiǔ, Máotáijiǔ.)
Shall we see a (movie/performance)?	Yìqǐ qù kàn (diànyǐng/yǎnchū) hǎo ma?
I hope you can make it to the (movie/performance).	Nǐ yídìng yào lái.
If you insist, I'd be glad to come.	Gōngjìng bù rú cóngmìng.
You are all invited to a banquet.	Qǐng dàjiā cānjiā yí ge yànhuì.

Calling on Someone

May I come in?	Néng jìnlái ma?
Sorry, I'm late.	Duì bù qǐ, wǒ lái wǎn le.
Haven't seen you for ages. How are you?	Hǎojiǔ méijiàn le, nǐ hǎo ma?
It's really (hot/cold) today.	Jīntiān zhēn (rè/lěng).
I am really pleased to see you.	Wǒ zhēn gāoxìng jiàndào nǐ.
How's everything with you?	Yíqiè dōuhǎo ma?
You look just the same.	Nǐ háishi lǎoyàngzi.
Do you mind my smoking?	Néng chōuyān ma?
Are you busy?	Gōngzuò máng ma?
I want to invite (you) (for dinner) (tomorrow). Are you free?	Wǒ xiǎng qǐng (nǐ) (míngtiān) lái (chīfàn), nǐ yǒu kòng ma?

T I P S

That's Mrs. who?

Chinese women do not automatically take their husbands' name after marriage. Perhaps as a way of maintaining equal status, they retain their own family names. For example, after Wang Guifen marries Mr. Li she is still called Wang Guifen. Of course, nowadays she might also accept it if you call her Mrs Li, after her husband's name.

对不起,我(今天/明天/今晚)没有空。

和我共进(午餐)好吗?

改天好吗?

我恐怕不能来。

你要(茶/咖啡)吗?

你想喝点什么?

(啤酒,橘子水,矿泉水,葡萄酒,茅台酒。)

一起去看(电影/演出)好吗?

你一定要来。

恭敬不如从命。

请大家参加一个宴会。

能进来吗?

对不起,我来晚了。

好久没见了,你好吗?

今天真(热/冷)。

我真高兴见到你。

一切都好吗?

你还是老样子。

能抽烟吗?

工作忙吗?

我想请(你)(明天)来(吃饭),你有空吗?

Key Words

sure to come	yídìng lái	一定来
Don't forget	Bié wàngjì	别忘记
smoke	chōuyān	抽烟
hotel	lǚguǎn	旅馆
guest house	bīnguǎn	宾馆
have meal together	yìqǐ chīfàn	一起吃饭
have tea	hēchá	喝茶
gift (present)	lǐwù	礼物
nice trip	lǚtú yúkuài	旅途愉快
pleasant journey	yílù shùnfēng	一路顺风
miss you	xiǎngniàn nǐ	相念你
thank you	xièxiè nǐ	谢谢你
hospitality	hàokè	好客
bye-bye	zàijiàn	再见
Hello	wèi	喂!
telephone	diànhuà	电话
telephone number	diànhuà hàomǎ	电话号码
extension	fēnjī	分机
address	dìzhǐ	地址
not in	búzài	不在
call back	huí diànhuà	回电话
staying at	zhùzài	住在
just a moment	děng yì děng	等一等

T
I
P
S

Age and salary

Unlike Westerners, Chinese do not avoid the subjects of age (niánlíng) and salary (gōngzī). You can be bold and ask all sorts of questions about these subjects, getting real insight into Chinese life.

Sorry, I don't have time (tomorrow).	Duì bù qǐ, wǒ (míngtiān) méiyǒu shíjiān.
In that case, we'll have to set up another time.	Nàme, wǒmen lìngwài zài yuē shíjiān ba.
Thank you for your kindness. I appreciate it very much.	Xièxiè nǐ de hǎoyì, wǒ xīnlǐng le.
There is a (soccer match) on (Sunday). Do you want to go?	(Xīngqīrì) yǒu yì chǎng (zúqiúsài), nǐ yuànyì qù ma?
That would be great!	Tài hǎo le.
We'll meet (at seven) at the (gate).	Wǒmen (qīdiǎn) zài (ménkǒu) jiàn.
I'll wait for you.	Wǒ děng nǐ.
I am definitely coming.	Wǒ yídìng lái.
I've brought (you) a (small present).	Wǒ gěi (nǐ) dàilái yí ge (xiǎo lǐwù).
Would you like to come to my hotel for (dinner)?	Dào wǒ lǚguǎn lái chī (wǎnfàn) hǎo ma?
Thank you for your hospitality.	Xièxiè nǐ de zhāodài.
I'm going home the (day after tomorrow).	Wǒ (hòutiān) huíguó.
Please do let me know when you come to the (United States).	Nǐ dào (Měiguó) lái, yídìng tōngzhī wǒ.
I'll pick you up at the (airport).	Wǒ dào (jīchǎng) qù jiēnǐ.
I'll miss you.	Wǒ huì xiǎngniàn nǐ de.
Have a nice journey!	Zhù nǐ yílù shùnfēng.

Jasmine or green tea

T
I
P
S

Chinese hosts always make tea for their guests. The most common teas they drink are jasmine tea (mòlì huā chá) and green tea (lǜ chá). Jasmine tea, which is preferred by northerners, is made by baking tea leaves together with jasmine flower petals—the tea then having a special fragrant aroma. People in the south tend to drink green tea, an unfermented tea of dark green color. In the far south, like Guangdong, black tea is also pretty common. Coffee has made its way into the Chinese cup only recently. While in ordinary stores, you will find only instant coffee, coffee beans can be found in stores catering for the special needs of foreigners—such as the Friendship Stores—in major cities.

对不起，我（明天）没有时间。

那么，我们另外再约时间吧。

谢谢你的好意，我心领了。

（星期日）有一场（足球赛），你愿意去吗？

太好了。

我们（七点）在（门口）见。

我等你。

我一定来。

我给（你）带来一个（小礼物）。

到我旅馆来吃（晚饭）好吗？

谢谢你的招待。

我（后天）回国。

你到（美国）来，一定通知我。

我到（机场）去接你。

我会想念你的。

祝你一路顺风。

Key Words

please wait	qǐng děng yíxià	请等一下
write it down	xiě xiàlái	写下来
say it again	zài shuō yíbiàn	再说一遍
My telephone number is...	Wǒ de diànhuà shì...	我的电话是
Good	Hǎo	好
OK.	Xíng	行
wait for your call	děng nǐ diànhuà	等你电话
switchboard; opeartor	zǒngjī	总机
room number	fánghào	房号
Hold on.	Bié guà	别挂
Monday	Xīngqī yī	星期一
Tuesday	Xīngqī èr	星期二
Wednesday	Xīngqī sān	星期三
Thursday	Xīngqī sì	星期四
Friday	Xīngqī wǔ	星期五
Saturday	Xīngqī liù	星期六
Sunday	Xīngqī rì	星期日

Chinese idioms

There is a rich pool of idioms, often four-character set phrases, in the Chinese language. To use these will add an air of learning to the conversation. The following are some of the most often used phrases. Try one out on a Chinese —you'll probably give him or her a real shock.

Bǎi wén bù rú yí jiàn

Meaning: Seeing is believing. Seeing something for oneself is a hundred times better than hearing from others.

Example: Chángchéng de qìshì nányí xiǎngxiàng. Zhè zhēn shì bǎi wén bù rú yí jiàn. The Great Wall's magnificence is beyond imagination. Seeing it gives me a much better idea than hearing it described a hundred times.
(*See Appendix 12 for more.*)

Calling a Friend by Phone

Hello.	Wèi.
Can I speak to Mr. (Liu), please?	Wǒ zhǎo (Liú) xiānsheng.
Hi. Can you guess who this is speaking?	Nǐ cāi wǒ shì shuí?
It's a surprise, isn't it?	Méi xiǎng dào ba.
I've just come from (New York).	Wǒ gāng cóng (Niǔyuē) lái.
Just arrived.	Gānggāng dào.
How are things with you?	Nǐ zěnme yàng?
Fine. Thank you.	Hěn hǎo, xièxiè.
Is your (wife) fine, too?	Nǐ (tàitai) hǎo ma?
I want to come and see you. Is it OK?	Wǒ xiǎng qù kànkan nǐ, kěyǐ ma?
Please tell me your address.	Qǐng gàosù wǒ nǐ de dìzhǐ.
Which bus should I take?	Wǒ zuò shénme chē kěyǐ dào?
At which stop should I get off?	Wǒ zài nǎzhàn xià?
Good. I'll meet you at the bus stop.	Hǎo, wǒ zài chēzhàn děngnǐ.
She isn't in.	Tā bú zài.
I'll call back again later.	Wǒ yìhuǐr zài dǎlái.
Please tell him to call me when he gets back.	Tā huílai hòu, qǐng tā gěi wǒ huí diànhuà.
Please tell her that I called.	Qǐng gàosù tā, wǒ láiguò diàn- huà.

What to wear on formal occasions

TIPS

Chinese tend to be very casual about their clothes. Today, the dark-colored clothes of a decade ago have been overtaken by colorful new fashions. Still, clothes for informal and formal occasions differ very little. The only conspicuous difference is that normally people change into clean or newly pressed clothes for the latter. It is not uncommon for women to wear pants to important functions. This is an advantage for you when packing—you don't need to make elaborate preparations in case a formal function comes up, just take along whatever you feel comfortable in.

Key Words

喂。

我找（刘）先生。

你猜我是谁？

没想到吧。

我刚从（纽约）来。

刚刚到。

你怎么样？

很好，谢谢。

你（太太）好吗？

我想去看看你，可以吗？

请告诉我你的地址。

我坐什么车可以到？

我在哪站下？

好，我在车站等你。

她不在。

我一会儿再打来。

他回来后，请他给我回电话。

请告诉她，我来过电话。

what time	jǐ diǎn	几点
one o'clock	yì diǎn	一点
two o'clock	liǎng diǎn	两点
ten o'clock	shí diǎn	十点
twelve o'clock	shí'èr diǎn	十二点
lifestyle	shēnghuó xíguàn	生活习惯
night life	yè shēnghuó	夜生活
music	yīnyuè	音乐
painting	huìhuà	绘画
sports	tǐyù	体育
play chess	xiàqí	下棋
weiqi (go)	wéiqí	围棋
chess	xiàngqí	象棋
see movie	kàn diànyǐng	看电影
fishing	diàoyú	钓鱼
dance	tiàowǔ	跳舞
travel	lǚxíng	旅行

Holidays

T
I
P
S

Xīnnián New Year's Day
Chūn Jié Spring Festival (late January or early February)
Guójì Láodòng Fùnǚ Jié International Women's Day (March 8)
Guójì Láodòng Jié International Labor Day (May 1)
Qīngnián Jié Youth Day (May 4)
Guójì Értóng Jié International Children's Day (June 1)
Guóqìng Jié National Day (October 1)

I'm staying at the (Friendship Hotel).

Wǒ zhù zài (Yǒuyì Bīnguǎn).

Building (Three), Room No. (485).

(Sānhào) lóu, (sìbāwǔ) hào fángjiān.

My phone number is (851-8888).

Wǒ de diànhuà shì (bāwǔyāo bā-bābābā).

Extension (3456).

(Sānsìwǔliù) fēnjī.

Just a moment please.

Qǐng děng yì děng.

I'll write it down.

Wǒ jì yíxià.

Talking About Hobbies

What do you do in your (spare time)?

Nǐ (yèyú shíjiān) gàn shénme?

I love (music).

Wǒ xǐhuān (yīnyuè).

Sometimes, I also go (fishing).

Yǒushí wǒ yě (diàoyú).

Do you like (soccer)?

Nǐ xǐhuān (zúqiú) ma?

I am a (basketball) player.

Wǒshì (lánqiú) yùndòng yuán.

I don't know how to play (chess).

Wǒ búhuì xià (xiàngqí).

Do you have (disco parties)?

Nǐmen yǒu (dísīkē wǔhuì) ma?

What time do you go to bed in the evening?

Nǐ wǎnshàng jǐdiǎn xiūxi?

How do you spend your weekends?

Zhōumò nǐ gàn xiē shénme?

Festivals

T
I
P
S

There are many traditional festivals in China each year, and the Chinese celebrate their festivals in different ways. Most of the festivals are related to a story which usually sings the praises of a historical figure, describes a beautiful legend or wishes a good harvest and happiness.... All the traditional festivals are based on the Chinese lunar calendar which is about 20 to 30 days in difference with the international calendar. You will be in luck if you come to China on one of these festivals, when you will get a glimpse of the long-

我住在(友谊宾馆)。

(三)号楼,(485)号房间。

我的电话是(8518888)。

(3456)分机。

请等一等。

我记一下。

你(业余时间)干什么?

我喜欢(音乐)。

有时我也(钓鱼)。

你喜欢(足球)吗?

我是(篮球)运动员。

我不会下(象棋)。

你们有(迪斯科舞会)吗?

你晚上几点休息?

周末你干些什么?

What You May Hear

Hǎojiǔ bújiàn.	Long time no see.
Shénme shíhòu dàode?	When did you arrive?
Rènshí nǐ zhēn gàoxìng.	Glad to meet you.
Huānyíng.	Welcome.
Bù yuǎn sòng le.	I'll see you off here.
Suíshí lái wán.	Come whenever you want.
Qǐng dàiwǒ xiàng...wèn hǎo.	Please say hello to... for me.
Bú jiàn bú sàn.	Do not leave without meeting.
Chōu yān ma?	Do you smoke?
Qǐng hēchá.	Please have some tea.
Zěnme huí shì?	What's the matter?
Búyào kèqì.	Make yourself at home.
Bào qiàn.	I'm sorry.
Zāo le.	Oh, it's too bad.

Signs

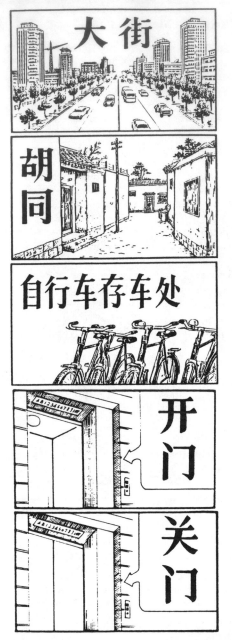

dàjiē
Main Street

hútòng
Alley

zìxíngchē
cúnchēchù
**Bicycle Parking
Zone**

kāimén
Open Door

guānmén
Close Door

Sightseeing

Zhào Zhāng xiàng ba.

Take a picture.

China's ancient civilization has left a wealth of places worth visiting. There are unique architectural wonders rising to imposing heights, such as the Great Wall and the Forbidden City; there are tombs and palaces of emperors and empresses underground; there are temples and monasteries of all ages and descriptions—in addition to factories and the scenic countryside. Having a good schedule, then, will be important, since you won't want to miss out on the best of the best. While out sightseeing, you'll probably enjoy learning something about China's history and culture, or you may want to take a lot of pictures—anyway, inquiries and conversation will be indispensable.

Preparing for a Trip

Where can I find a (tourist map of China)?	Nǎlǐ néng mǎidào (Zhōngguó lǚyóutú)?
Is it in English?	Shi Yīngwén de ma?
I also want (one) (road map).	Wǒ háiyào (yí fèn) jiāotōng lùxiàntú.
Where is (China International Travel Service) located?	(Zhōngguó Guójì Lǚxíngshè) zài nǎlǐ?
I need (an) (English speaking) (tourist guide).	Wǒ yào (yí ge) (Yīngyǔ) (dǎo yóu).
How much is it per hour? (What's the rate per hour?)	Měi xiǎoshí duōshǎo qián?
Are there any introductions to the tourist site?	Yǒu lǚyóudiǎn de jièshào ma?
What are the places to see in this city?	Zhège chéngshì yǒu shénme kěkàn de?
What's the (schedule) for (today)?	(Jīntiān) de (rìchéng) zěnme ānpái?
Are we going to come back for (lunch) at (noon time)?	(Zhōngwǔ) huílái (chīfàn) ma?
Is photographing allowed at (Tiananmen)?	(Tiān'ānmén) ràng pāizhào ma?
How long will it take on the road?	Lùshàng yào duōcháng shíjiān?
What time are we going to set off?	Shénme shíhòu chūfā?
What time will we be back in the (afternoon/evening)?	(Xiàwǔ/wǎnshàng) jǐdiǎn huílái?

How big is China?

T I P S

In land area, China ranks third in the world—next only to Russia and Canada—and is slightly larger than the United States. Its 9.6 million square kilometer territory extends about 5,200 kilometers from the west to the east. From north to south, it measures some 5,500 kilometers. China is divided into 31 provinces, autonomous regions (where mostly ethnic minorities live) and municipalities (the three largest cities in the country).
(For details, see Appendix 13.)

Key Words

哪里能买到（中国旅游图）？

是英文的吗？

我还要（一份）（交通路线图）。

（中国国际旅行社）在哪里？

我要（一个）（英语）（导游）。

每小时多少钱？

有旅游点的介绍吗？

这个城市有什么可看的？

（今天）的（日程）怎么安排？

（中午）回来（吃饭）吗？

（天安门）让拍照吗？

路上要多长时间？

什么时候出发？

（下午/晚上）几点回来？

tourist guide	dǎoyóu	导游
program (schedule)	rìchéng	日程
China International Travel Service (CITS)	Zhōngguó Guójì Lǚxíngshè	中国国际旅行社
China Travel Service (CTS)	Zhōnguó Lǚxíngshè	中国旅行社
China Youth Travel Service (CYTS)	Zhōngguó Qīngnián Lǚxíngshé	中国青年旅行社
sightseeing	guānguāng	观光
tourist sites	lǚyóudiǎn	旅游点
tourist bus	lǚyóu chē	旅游车
the Great Wall	Chángchéng	长城
the Palace Museum	Gùgōng	故宫
the Ming Tombs	Shísānlíng	十三陵
the Temple of Heaven	Tiāntán	天坛
the terra-cotta warriors	bīngmǎyǒng	兵马俑

Are we going to walk a lot to get to the site?	Chūqù cānguān yào zŏu hěnduō lù ma?
What's the weather going to be tomorrow?	Míngtiān tiānqì zěnme yàng?
Is it going to be a fine day?	Shì hǎotiān ma?
Is it going to rain?	Huì xiàyǔ ma?
Do we need to take umbrellas?	Yào dài yǔsăn ma?
Should we take our overcoats?	Yào dài dàyī ma?
Is the tourist bus air-conditioned?	Lǚyóu chē yŏu kōngtiáo ma?
Can you arrange it for us to go to (Guilin)?	Néng ānpái qù (Guilín) ma?

Visiting a Tourist Site

When was the (Great Wall) built?	(Chángchéng) shì năge niándài xiū de?
What was the function of these towers?	Fēnghuŏtái shì gàn shénme yòng de?
What is it on this?	Shàngmiàn xiě de shì shénme?
How many stone lions are there on the Marco Polo Bridge?	Lúgōuqiáo shàng yígòng yŏu duōshăo shí shīzi?
Wow, five hundred!?	Òu, wŭbăi ge!
Can we go and visit the (museum)?	Néng qù cānguān (bówùguăn) ma?
Mao Zedong used to live here?	Máo Zédōng yǐqián jiù zhù zài zhèli?
Chinese leaders have offices in there?	Zhōngguó lǐngdǎorén de bàngōngshì yě zài nàli?
Why are the Forbidden City's walls painted in vermillion?	Zǐjìnchéng de qiáng wèi shénme shì hóng de?
When were these (pottery soldiers and horses) unearthed?	(Bīngmǎyŏng) shì shénme shíhòu wājué chūlái de?

TIPS **The four seasons**

chūnjì (spring)	xiàjì (summer)
qiūjì (fall)	dōngjì (winter)

出去参观要走很多路吗？

明天天气怎么样？

是好天吗？

会下雨吗？

要带雨伞吗？

要带大衣吗？

旅游车有空调吗？

能安排去（桂林）吗？

（长城）是哪个年代修的？

烽火台是干什么用的？

上面写的是什么？

芦沟桥上一共有多少石狮子？

哦，500 个！

能去参观（博物馆）吗？

毛泽东以前就住在这里？

中国领导人的办公室也在那里？

紫禁城的墙为什么是红的？

（兵马俑）是什么时候挖掘出来的？

Key Words

weather	tiānqì	天气
clear	qíngtiān	晴天
gloomy	yīntiān	阴天
cloudy	duōyún	多云
drizzle	xiǎoyǔ	小雨
moderate rain	zhōngyǔ	中雨
heavy rain	dàyǔ	大雨
rainstorm	bàoyǔ	暴雨
temperature	qìwēn	气温
degree	dù	度
centigrade	shèshì	摄氏
Fahrenheit	huáshì	华氏
cool	liáng	凉
cold	lěng	冷
warm	nuǎnhuo	暖和
hot	rè	热
wind	fēng	风
windy	yǒufēng	有风
gale	dàfēng	大风
strong wind	qiángfēng	强风
tornado	lóngjuǎnfēng	龙卷风
typhoon	táifēng	台风
freezing	jiébīng	结冰
snow	xuě	雪
heavy snow	dàxuě	大雪
dry	gān	干
drought	gānhàn	干旱
damp	cháoshī	潮湿

T
I
P
S

Smoking

Except where there are signs forbidding smoking, smoking is not strictly restricted in public places. You may smoke at the home of your host, but it is best to ask permission first.

It's really something!	Tài wěidà le!
The gardens of Suzhou are really beautiful!	Sūzhōu de yuánlín zhēn piào liàng!
How long are we going to take?	Wǒmen yào zài zhèlǐ dāi duōjiǔ?
Excuse me, where is the rest room, please?	Duì bù qǐ, cèsuǒ zài nǎlǐ?

Visiting a Factory

How many workers are there in the factory?	Nǐmen yǒu duōshǎo gōngrén?
What do you produce?	Shēngchǎn shénme chǎnpǐn?
Is it a state factory or a private one?	Shì guóyíng de háishì sīyíng de?
How much does a worker make a month?	Gōngrén měiyuè gōngzī duō shǎo?
Is there any bonus?	Yǒu jiǎngjīn ma?
Is the salary of someone on leave of absence deducted?	Qǐngjià kòu bú kòu qián?
How long is the maternity leave?	Chǎnjià duōshǎo?
Are men and women workers paid the same?	Nánnǚ gōngzī yīyàng ma?
How long does it take to do this embroidery?	Xiù zhèfú huà yào duōshǎo shíjiān?
Have you studied painting before?	Nǐ xué guò huìhuà ma?
Did you design this (tea pot) yourself?	Zhè (cháhú) shì nǐ zìjǐ shèjì de ma?
Where are the products sold?	Chǎnpǐn xiāoshòu dào nǎlǐ?

TIPS

Dialects

   Sometimes when you're having trouble understanding someone in southeastern China—where there have always been a variety of dialects—the person will say the word slowly and "write" it with a finger on his or her open palm. This happens because, while dialects vary, the written language is understood by everyone. Unfortunately, this "help"

太伟大了!
苏州的园林真漂亮!

我们要在这里呆多久?
对不起,厕所在哪里?

你们有多少工人?

生产什么产品?
是国营的还是私营的?

工人每月工资多少?

有奖金吗?
请假扣不扣钱?

产假多少?
男女工资一样吗?

绣这幅画要多少时间?

你学讨绘画吗?

这(茶壶)是你自己设
计的吗?
产品销售到哪里?

Key Words

flood	hóngshuǐ	洪水
spring	chūntiān	春天
summer	xiàtiān	夏天
autumn	qiūtiān	秋天
winter	dōngtiān	冬天
sun	tàiyáng	太阳
moon	yuèliàng	月亮
earth	dìqiú	地球
go by oneself	dāndú qù	单独去
go together	yìqǐ qù	一起去
go in a group	jítǐ qù	集体去
plane	fēijī	飞机
train	huǒchē	火车
How many people?	Duōshǎo rén?	多少人
ask questions	tí wèntí	提问题
take a picture together	hé yǐng	合影
go out	chū qù	出去
come back	huílai	回来
factory	gōngchǎng	工厂
state-run	guóyíng	国营
private-run	sīyíng	私营
salary; wage	gōngzī	工资
worker	gōngrén	工人

TIPS

probably won't do you much good.
    There are pockets of Beijing dialect all through the south. In Kunming, for instance, the Ming rulers stationed a large contingent of soldiers to keep the peace after they had gained control of it. As the soldiers intermarried with the locals, the northern dialect became prevalent. In Hangzhou, once capital of the Southern Song, there are also signs of the Beijing dialect—the locals add an "r" to certain nouns.

How many hours do you work a day?	Yì tiān gōngzuò jǐ xiǎoshí?
Do you have a trade union?	Yǒu gōnghuì zǔzhī ma?
When was this place built?	Zhège dìfāng shénme shíhòu jiàn de?
Any other fringe benefits?	Hái yǒu bié de shōurù ma?

Visiting the Countryside

Is the new contract system good?	Shíxíng chéngbāo hǎo bù hǎo?
How many years is your contract?	Chéngbāo hétóng shì duōshǎo nián?
What do you do with the surplus labor force?	Duōyú de láodònglì zěnme chǔlǐ?
If everybody wants to work in the factory, what's happened to the land?	Dàjiā dōuxiǎng jìn gōngchǎng, tǔdì zěnme bàn?
Is it a marriage of free love or arranged by the parents?	Hūnyīn shì zìzhǔ de háishì fùmǔ bāobàn de?
How much does it cost to build a house like this?	Gài zhèyàng yí ge fángzi yào duōshǎo qián?
How many primary schools are there?	Zhèlǐ yǒu jǐsuǒ xiǎoxué?
Do you have enough food to eat?	Liángshi gòu chī ma?
Do you own this chicken farm yourself?	Yǎngjīchǎng shì nǐ zìjǐ de?
What's your annual income?	Nián shōurù duōshǎo?
Would you like to work in the city?	Nǐmen xǐhuān qù chénglǐ gōngzuò ma?

T I P S

Common flowers

Chinese people love flowers, and raising them is one of the most popular hobbies in China. Pots of flowers can be seen in offices and homes. Balconies of buildings everywhere are decorated with flowers. You may feel like asking Zhè shì shénme huā (What flower is this?) Or you can ask Zhè shì mòli huā ma? (Is this jasmine?) If so, the list in *Appendix 14* is essential.

一天工作几小时？

有工会组织吗？

这个地方什么时候建的？

还有别的收入吗？

实行承包好不好？

承包合同是多少年？

多余的劳动力怎么处理？

大家都想进工厂，土地怎么办？

婚姻是自主的还是父母包办的？

盖这样一个房子要多少钱？

这里有几所小学？

粮食够吃吗？

养鸡场是你自己的？

年收入多少？

你们喜欢去城里工作吗？

Key Words

bonus	jiǎngjīn	奖金
land	tǔdì	土地
workshop	chǎngfáng	厂房
dormitory	sùshè	宿舍
trade union	gōnghuì	工会
product	chǎnpǐn	产品
sale	xiāoshòu	销售
income	shōurù	收入
spending	zhīchu	支出
capital	zīchǎn	资产
contract	hétong	合同
farm	nóngchǎng	农场
grow; cultivate	zhòngzhí	种植
machine	jīqì	机器
grain	liángshi	粮食
ware house	cāngkù	仓库
working hours	gōngshí	工时
hire hands	gùgōng	雇工
automobile	qìchē	汽车
housing	zhùfáng	住房
ownership	suǒyǒu quán	所有权
manpower	láodònglì	劳动力
contract	chéngbāo	承包

Common trees

T
I
P
S

One of the first things visitors to China will notice is the tree-lined streets. There is a nation-wide awareness about the need to plant trees. In fact, China has an annual Arbor Day on March 12. The list of tree names in *Appendix 15* will help you to distinguish the different kinds of trees you see in China.

What's your education background?	Nǐ shì shénme wénhuà chéngdù?

Taking Photos

Can you please help me take a picture?	Qǐng nǐ tì wǒ pāi zhāng zhào, hǎo ma?
I want to take a photo (here).	Wǒ xiǎng zài (zhèlǐ) zhào zhāng xiàng.
Everything is set.	Dōu tiáo hǎo le.
Just press the button and that will be it.	Zhǐyào àn yíxià kuài mén jiù xíng le.
Can I take a picture of you?	Wǒ néng gěi nǐ zhào zhāng xiàng ma?
Please give me your address.	Qǐng liú xià nǐ de dìzhǐ.
I will definitely send it to you.	Wǒ yídìng jì gěi nǐ.
Let's take a picture together.	Ràng wǒmen yìqǐ zhào zhāng xiàng ba.
I'd like to take a picture with (Tiananmen) behind me.	Wǒ yào (Tiān'ānmén) zuò bèijǐng.
Smile!	Xiào yí xiào.
Is there a place to have these pictures printed?	Fùjìn yǒu chōngxǐ jiāojuǎn de dìfāng ma?

Talking with Chinese Tourists

Are you a tourist, too?	Nǐ yě shì lái lǚyóu de?
Where are you from?	Nǐ cóng nǎlǐ lái?

T I P S

Taking photos

China's beautiful scenery has always attracted camera buffs. If you want to have a Chinese stranger in a picture, feel free to make a request. Usually he or she will be happy to comply. However, please remember there are also a lot of Chinese who are shy and reserved. Don't press them, and at the same time don't feel disappointed if your invitation is turned down. You are not allowed to take pictures of military facilities—which are always clearly indicated with signs.

你是什么文化程度？

请你替我拍张照，好吗？

我想在（这里）照张像。

都调好了。
只要按一下快门就行了。

我能给你照张像吗？

请留下你的地址。
我一定寄给你。
让我们一起照张像吧。

我要（天安门）作背景。

笑一笑。
附近有冲洗胶卷的地方吗？

你也是来旅游的？
你从哪里来？

Key Words

take pictures	zhàoxiàng	照相
as a souvenir	liúniàn	留念
happy	gáoxìng	高兴
tired	lèi	累
toilet	cèsuǒ	厕所
What's the time?	jǐdiǎn	几点？
I am ...	Wǒ shì	我是美国人/英国人/法国人
American	Měiguórén	
(British)	(Yīngguórén)	
(French)	(Fǎguórén)	
call a taxi	jiào chē	叫车
be late	wǎn le	晚了
be quick	kuài diǎn	快点
Hurry up!	Bié mócèng!	别磨蹭
too late	lái bù jí	来不及
There's still time.	gǎnde shàng	赶得上
pay attention	zhùyì	注意
Be careful!	bié dàyì	别大意

T
I
P
S

Two slangs

The Beijing locals also have two slang words for "terrific" —méi zhì le (literally, ungoverned) and gài le (surpassing). If you try out one of these on a Beijinger, you will meet with delighted and amazed laughter.

Is (Hangzhou) a nice place to visit?

(Hángzhōu) hǎo wán ma?

How far away is (Nanjing) from here?

(Nánjīng) lí zhèlǐ duōyuǎn?

How many hours does it take (by train)?

(Zuò huǒchē) yào duōshǎo shíjiān?

Can we go there (by plane)?

Néng (zuò fēijī) ma?

I am (American). Where do *you* work?

Wǒ shì (Měiguórén), nǐ zài nǎlǐ gōngzuò?

How many days are you going to stay in (Beijing)?

Nǐ zài (Běijīng) dāi jǐtiān?

I am very pleased to have met you.

Hěn gāoxing yùdào nǐ.

I'll certainly go to (Chengdu) if I have the chance.

Rúguǒ yǒu jīhuì, wǒ yídìng qù (Chéngdū).

I wish you a nice time.

Zhù nǐ yú kuài.

（杭州）好玩吗？

（南京）离这里多远？

（坐火车）要多少时间？

能（坐飞机）吗？

我是（美国人），你在哪里工作？

你在（北京）呆几天？

很高兴遇到你。

如果有机会，我一定去（成都）。

祝你愉快！

What You May Hear

chūfā	set out
huílái	come back
dàole	Here we are.
bā/sì diǎn	eight/four o'clock
jíhé	gather; assemble
qǐng zhùyì	Please notice
zuǒbiān	left
yòubiān	right
qiánmiàn	front
Xiǎoxīn!	Be careful!
Xiūxi yíhuìr	Have a short rest.
Hái yǒu wèntí ma?	Any more questions?
lǎowài	foreigner
míngxìnpiàn	postcard
Jìnzhǐpāizhào	Photography prohibited

Measure words

T I P S

The use of measure words is the most difficult part of Chinese. English has measure words, too—as in "a *roll* of film." But in Chinese, some nouns aren't understandable unless used with the right measure word. The most common one is gè. Fortunately, ge can be used as a generic substitute in case you forget the right one. But it's still best to use the designated measure word. Please refer to the Appendix on page 244 for a list of common measure words. Examples:

yígè rén (one man)
yìběn shū (one book)
sānliàng qìchē (three cars)

Signs

huānyíng guānglín
Welcome

shòupiàochù
Ticket Office

ménpiào: 2 jiǎo
Admission: 20 fen

bù zhǔn suídìtǔtán
No Spitting

yóukè zhǐ bù
Visitors Keep Out

Entertainment

Travelers in China will find themselves in a world of wonders in the arts: there are various kinds of operas, dance and song performances, music, concerts, and so forth. Peking opera, perhaps the best known, is a typically Chinese form of traditional performance. Though you may have trouble understanding the dialogues and singing, the masks, costumes, music and acting will be a feast to the eye and the ear. There is also a colorful range of local operas. And the world famous Chinese acrobatic troupes give regular performances. On the other hand, if you feel nostalgic and want to see something Western, you can go to a concert by one of the several excellent orchestras of China or go to a Western-style opera.

Watching a Performance

What's on (tonight)?

(Jīntiān wǎnshàng) shénme jié-mù?

A (Peking opera)! That's great.

(Jīng jù), tài bàng le.

What's the title?

Jiào shénme míngzi?

At Crossroads (A well-known Peking opera).

Sān chà kōu.

Can you please tell me roughly what the story is about?

Néng jiǎndān jièshào yíxià gùshì qíngjié ma?

Can you please translate this sentence for me?

Néng fānyì yíxià zhèjù huà ma?

Is the (performer) famous?

Zhège (yǎnyuán) chūmíng ma?

What does a (red mask) represent?

(Hóng liǎn) dàibiǎo shénme yìsi?

At what age did they start training?

Tāmen cóng jǐ suì kāishǐ xùnliàn?

I would like to see a Chinese (folk) (dance).

Wǒ xiǎng kàn Zhōngguó (mínjiān) (wǔdǎo).

When will the (concert) (begin)?

(Yīnyuèhuì) shénme shíhòu (kāishǐ)?

Is there an introduction to the story in (English)?

Yǒu (Yīngwén) jièshào ma?

Sorry, I'm late.

Duì bù qǐ, wǒ lái chí le.

Can I get in?

Wǒ néng jìnqù ma?

Hurry up.

Gǎn kuài.

The performance will begin now.

Yǎnchū mǎshàng kāishǐ.

T I P S Peking opera

Peking opera, the most representative of all Chinese traditional drama forms, assumed its present form about two hundred years ago in Beijing (Peking). Like other traditional Chinese opera styles, Peking opera combines music, singing, dancing, and acrobatics, creating a quite unique form of art.

Peking opera is accompanied by orchestral music, and the main instruments are *jīnghú* (a 2-stringed fiddle) and gongs and drums of various sizes and shapes. The drum player doubles as the conductor of the band.

Characters in Peking operas wear exaggerated make-up,

Key Words

（今天晚上）什么节目？

（京剧），太棒了。

叫什么名字？

三岔口。

能简单介绍一下故事
内容吗？

能翻译一下这句话吗？

这个（演员）出名吗？

（红脸）代表什么意思？

他们从几岁开始训练？

我想看中国（民间）（舞
蹈）。

（音乐会）什么时候（开
始）？

有（英文）介绍吗？

对不起，我来迟了。

我能进去吗？

赶快。

演出马上开始。

performance	jiémù	节目
show	yǎnchū	演出
Peking opera	Jīngjù	京剧
acrobatics	zájì	杂技
local operas	dìfāngxì	地方戏
opera	gējù	歌剧
dance	wǔdǎo	舞蹈
concert	yīnyuèhuì	音乐会
symphony orchestra	jiāoxiǎngyuèduì	交响乐队
begin	kāishǐ	开始
end	jiéshù	结束
actor	nán yǎnyuán	男演员
actress	nǚ yǎnyuán	女演员
famous	zhùmíng	著名
introduction	jiǎnjiè	简介
buy a ticket	mǎipiào	买票
ticket price	piàojià	票价
front row	qiánpái	前排
back row	hòupái	后排
return a ticket	tuìpiào	退票
upstairs	lóushàng	楼上
downstairs	lóuxià	楼下

TIPS

representing particular types of roles. For instance, male characters who are frank and open-minded but rough, or those who are crafty and dangerous, are known as jìng or huāliǎn. Peking opera masks themselves are a highly developed type of art.

Movements in Peking opera are extremely abstract and often resemble those in a pantomime. Actions such as opening a door, riding horses and rowing boats are performed without the actual props. Besides Peking opera, other well-known local operas include yuèjù (of Guangdong), yuèjù (of Shanghai and its vicinity), huángméixi (of Anhui), Héběi bāngzi (of Hebei), and Hénán zhuìzi (of Henan).

Is there a (program) of the show?	Yǒu (jiémùdān) ma?

Getting Tickets

What (movie) is being shown (tomorrow)?	(Míngtiān) yǎn shénme (diànyǐng)?
I want (two) tickets for (today).	Wǒ yào (liǎng zhāng) (jīntiān) de piào.
Are there any tickets for (tomorrow)?	(Míngtiān) de piào háiyǒu ma?
(Front) rows, please.	Qǐng gěi wǒ (qián) pái de.
Preferably near the aisle.	Yào kào guòdào de.
How much is it?	Duōshǎo qián?
When will it begin?	Shénme shíhòu kāiyǎn?
How long will it last?	Yǎn duōcháng shíjiān?
Can I get the ticket (refunded)?	Wǒ xiǎng (tuìpiào).

Getting Seated

My seat is in the (8th) row.	Wǒ de zuòwèi zài (dì bā) pái.
Number (32).	(Sānshíèr) hào.
Is this seat taken?	Zhège wèizi yǒu rén ma?
This seat has been taken.	Yǒu rén.
Sorry, this is my seat.	Duì bù qǐ, zhèshì wǒ de zuò wèi.
You must be in the wrong seat.	Nǐ zuòcuò le ba!
Please let me pass.	Qǐng ràng yí ràng.
Where are your seats?	Nǐmen de wèizi zài nǎlǐ?
Upstairs?	Lóushàng?
When it is over, I'll wait in front of the gate.	Sànchǎng shí, wǒ zài ménkǒu děng nǐ.

T
I
P
S

Chinese musical instruments

Traditional Chinese music dates back several thousand years. You will have a chance to hear it while in China, as concerts are held regularly, or you may buy one to practice by yourself. The most common musical instruments are:

bǎnhú 2-stringed fiddle, high pitched
dízi 8-stop bamboo flute
èrhú 2-stringed fiddle, with a lower register

有(节目单)吗?

(明天)演什么(电影)?

我要(两张)(今天)的票。

(明天)的票还有吗?

请给我(前)排的。
要靠过道的。
多少钱?
什么时候开演?
演多长时间?
我想(退票)。

我的座位在第(八)排。
(32)号。
这个位子有人吗?
有人。
对不起,这是我的座位。
你坐错了吧!
请让一让。
你们的位子在哪里?
楼上?
散场时,我在门口等你。

Key Words

begin/curtain rises	kāiyǎn	开演
break	xiūxi	休息
ten minutes	shífēnzhōng	十分钟
which row	jǐpái	几排
seat	zuòwèi	座位
number	hàomǎ	号码
excuse me, please	qǐng ràng yíràng	请让一让
emergency	tàipíngmén	太平门
match	bǐsài	比赛
superb	jīngcǎi	精彩
fantastic	tài bàngle	太棒了
athlete	yùndòngyuán	运动员
coaches	jiàoliàn	教练
referee	cáipàn	裁判
baseball	bàngqiú	棒球
volleyball	páiqiú	排球
basketball	lánqiú	篮球
tennis	wǎngqiú	网球
table tennis	pīngpāngqiú	乒乓球
football (soccer)	zúqiú	足球
badminton	yǔmáoqiú	羽毛球
rugby	gǎnlǎnqiú	橄榄球
martial arts	wǔshù	武术

TIPS

jīnghú 2-stringed fiddle, with a higher register
pípa 4-stringed lute
sānxián 3-stringed guitar
shēng Chinese mouth organ
suǒnà Chinese cornet (woodwind)
xiāo vertical bamboo flute
yángqín dulcimer
yuèqín 4-stringed round mandolin
zhēng many-stringed zither

Discussing the Show

Today's (concert) was great.	Jīntiān de (yīnyuèhuì) zhēn jīngcǎi.
The (main characters) are all famous performers.	(Zhǔjué) dōushì zhùmíng yǎn-yuán.
It's too bad I couldn't understand.	Kěxī wǒ bùdǒng.
This is the first time I've seen a (Peking opera).	Wǒ shì dì yī cì kàn (Jīngjù).
I've never listened to Chinese folk music.	Wǒ cóng méi tīngguò Zhōngguó mínzú yīnyuè.
Are there any (tapes) I can buy?	Yǒu (lùyīndài) mài ma?
Which nationality is this (dance) from?	Zhèshì nǎge mínzú de wǔdǎo?

Watching a Sports Event

What sport do you like to play?	Nǐ xǐhuān shénme tǐyù huódòng?
I like to play (basketball).	Wǒ xǐhuān (lánqiú).
Are there any (tennis courts) here?	Zhèlǐ yǒu (wǎngqiú chǎng) ma?
Do you play (golf)?	Nǐ dǎ (gāoěrfū) qiú ma?
Who is playing with whom?	Shéi hé shéi bǐsài?
Which team is wearing the (white) (sports uniforms).	Chuān (báisè) (yùndòngfú) de shì nǎge duì?
The game has just begun.	Bǐsài gānggāng kāishǐ.
The match is really hot.	Dǎ de zhēn jǐnzhāng.
Have you seen a (rugby) game?	Nǐ kànguò (gǎnlǎn qiú) ma?

T
I
P
S
Table tennis and other sports

Chinese table tennis became world-known as the sport that set the ball rolling in the long process of normalization of Chinese-US relations in the 1970s. It was, and still is, the most popular sport in China. This is partly because it doesn't need much space and requires only very simple equipment. Chinese children, placing a few bricks as the net on a cement table, are fond of playing ping-pong for hours of fun.

At the same time, taijiquan (shadow boxing) and other

What You May Hear

今天的(音乐会)真精彩。

(主角)都是著名演员。

可惜我不懂。

我是第一次看(京戏)。

我从没听过中国民族音乐。

有(录音带)卖吗?

这是哪个民族的舞蹈?

你喜欢什么体育活动?

我喜欢(篮球)。

这里有(网球场)吗?

你打(高尔夫)球吗?

谁和谁比赛?

穿(白色)(运动服)的是哪个队?

比赛刚刚开始。

打得真紧张。

你看过(橄榄球)吗?

Jǐpái?	Which row?
Jǐhào?	Which seat?
Qǐng suíwǒlái.	Please follow me.
jiémù dān	program
mùjiān xiūxi	interval
Xǐhuān me?	Do you like it?
Hǎojí le!	It's wonderful!
guānzhòng	audience
Nǔshìmen,xiān-shēngmen	Ladies and gentle-men
bàomù yuán	announcer
Yǎnchū xiànzài kāishǐ.	The performance now begins.
Yǎnchū dàocǐ jié-sù.	The performance now ends.
Tài bàng le!	Great!
Hǎoqiú!	Good goal!
Jiā yóu!	Come on!
Sàn chǎng.	The show is over.

forms of martial arts are equally popular. Visitors to China can often see people practicing martial arts in public places.

If table tennis in China can be compared with baseball in the United States and soccer in Britain in degree of popularity, badminton in China is comparable to American-style football in the United States and rugby in Britain.

Other popular sports include swimming, volleyball, basketball, and of course football.

Tennis and golf, comparatively new to Chinese sports fans, and are mostly played in a small number of clubs.

Signs

diànyǐngyuàn
Cinema

kèmǎn
Sold out

dānhào / shuānghào
**Odd Numbers /
Even Numbers**

tàipíng mén
Emergency Exit

jìnzhǐ xīyān
No Smoking

English-Chinese Dictionary

This is a simplified dictionary for those who are learning Chinese or traveling in China. The Chinese expressions here are colloquial equivalents of the English entries. Where an entry has several meanings, a clarification of the intended meaning appears in parentheses. Abbreviations used are: noun (n), verb (v), and adjective (adj). Be aware that some Chinese expressions cannot be used syntactically like the corresponding English. However, they can be used effectively as replacements within the sentence patterns of the text.

a, an	yī, yígè	一，一个
a few	jǐgè	几个
a little	yìdiǎn	一点
a while	yíhuǐr	一会儿
about (approximately)	dàyuē	大约
about (concerning)	guanyu	关于
above	zài...zhī shàng	在……之上
accept	jiēshòu	接受
accident	shìgù, yìwài	事故，意外
accompaniment (music)	bànzòu	伴奏
accompany	péi	陪
accordion	shǒufēngqín	手风琴
accurate	zhèngquè, zhǔnquè	正确，准确
achievement	chéngjì, chéngguǒ	成绩，成果
acre	yīngmǔ	英亩
acrid	sè	涩
acrobat	zájì yǎnyuán	杂技演员
acrobatics	zájì	杂技
acrylic (fiber)	bǐnglún	丙纶
acting (performance)	biǎoyǎn	表演
action	xíngdòng, dòngzuò	行动，动作
activity	huódòng	活动
actor (actress)	yǎnyuán	演员
acupressure	diǎnxuè fǎ	点穴法
acupuncture	zhēnjiǔ	针灸
acupuncture anesthesia	zhēncì mázuì	针刺麻醉
acute	jíxìng	急性
adaptor (outlet board)	jiēxiànbǎn	接线板
adaptor (outlet cube)	sāntōng	三通
adaptor plug	zhuǎnjiē chātóu	转接插头
add	jiā	加
address (n)	dìzhǐ	地址
addressee	shōujiàn rén, duìfāng	收件人，对方

adhesive plaster	xiàngpí gāo	橡皮膏
adjust	tiáo	调
adjustment	tiáozhěng	调整
administrator	guǎnlǐ zhě	管理者
adore	rè'ài	热爱
adult	chéngrén, dàrén	成人，大人
advanced	xiānjìn	先进
advertisement manager	guǎnggào jīnglǐ	广告经理
aerobics	jiànměi cāo	健美操
aerogramme	hángkōng xìnjiàn	航空信件
affair (matter)	shìqing	事情
afraid	pà	怕
Africa	Fēizhōu	非洲
after meals	fànhòu	饭后
afternoon	xiàwǔ	下午
again	zài	再
agate	mǎnǎo	玛瑙
age (of a person)	niánlíng	年龄
agriculture	nóngyè	农业
AIDS	àizī bìng	爱滋病
air	kōngqì	空气
air conditioner	kōngtiáojī	空调机
air conditioning	kōngtiáo	空调
air force	kōngjūn	空军
air pump	qìbèng, qìtǒng	气泵，气筒
air sick	yùnjī	晕机
air valve	qìfá, qìmén	气阀，气门
airline	hángkōng gōngsī	航空公司
airmail	hángkōng	航空
airplane	fēijī	飞机
airport	fēijīchǎng	飞机场
airport departure tax	jīchǎng fèi	机场费
aisle	guòdào	过道
alarm clock	nàozhōng	闹钟
alcohol (fluid)	jiǔjīng	酒精
alcohol (liquor)	jiǔ	酒
alike	yíyàng, xiàng	一样，象
all	quánbù, dōu	全部，都
allergic	guòmǐn	过敏
allergy	guòmǐn zhèng	过敏症
alley	hútong	胡同
allspice	làméi	腊梅
almond	xìngrén	杏仁
almond gelatin	xìngrén dòufu	杏仁豆腐
almond-flour tea	xìngrénchá	杏仁茶
alone	dāndú	单独
already	yǐjīng	已经
also	yě	也

altitude	gāodù, hǎibá	海拔
altogether	yígòng	一共
always	zǒngshì, lǎoshì	总是，老是
ambulance	jiùhùchē	救护车
analyze	fēnxī	分析
ancient	gǔdài	古代
and	hé, gēn	和，跟
anemia	pínxuè zhèng	贫血症
anesthesia	mázuì	麻醉
anesthetist	mázuì shī	麻醉师
angina pectoris	xīn jiǎotòng	心绞痛
angry	shēngqì	生气
animal	dòngwù	动物
ankle	jiǎowàn	脚腕
anniversary	zhōunián	周年
another	lìng yí gè, biéde	另一个，别的
answer (phone)	jiē	接…
answer (reply)	huídá	回答
ant	mǎyǐ	蚂蚁
antenna (for TV, radio)	tiānxiàn	天线
anthropology	rénlèixué	人类学
antibiotic	kàngshēngsù	抗生素
antipyretic	tuìshāo	退烧
antique	gǔdǒng	古董
antiseptic cream	xiāodú gāo	消毒膏
anxious	zháojí	着急
any	rènhé	任何
apartment	danyuàn fáng, gōngyù	单元房，公寓
appetite	wèikǒu	胃口
applause	gǔzhǎng	鼓掌
apple	píngguǒ	苹果
apply for	shēnqǐng	申请
appreciate	xīnshǎng	欣赏
apprentice	xuétú	学徒
appropriate	héshì	合适
apricot	xìng	杏
April	sìyuè	四月
archaeology	kǎogǔ	考古
architecture	jiànzhù	建筑
area (measure)	miànjī	面积
area (realm)	lǐngyù, fànwéi	领域，范围
area (region)	dìqū	地区
argali sheep	tānyáng	滩羊
arm	gēbo, shǒubì	胳膊，手臂
armband	bìzhàng	臂章
armpit	yè	腋
army	bùduì, jūnduì	部队，军队
around (approximately)	zuǒyòu	左右

arrange	ānpái	安排
arrangement	ānpái	安排
arrive	dàodá	到达
art	yìshù	艺术
art director	yìshù zhǐdǎo	艺术指导
art exhibition	měishù zhǎnlǎn	美术展览
art gallery	huàláng	画廊
art museum	měishùguǎn	美术馆
art work	yìshùpǐn	艺术品
arthritis	guānjiéyán	关节炎
article (object)	wùpǐn	物品
arts and crafts	gōngyì měishù	工艺美术
arts and crafts store	gōngyì měishù shāngdiàn	工艺美术商店
ashtray	yānhuīgāng	烟灰缸
Asia	Yàzhōu	亚洲
ask	wèn	问
asparagus lettuce	wōsǔn	莴笋
aspen tree	báiyángshù	白杨树
aspirin	āsīpǐlín	阿斯匹林
assistant (n)	zhùshǒu, zhùlǐ	助手, 助理
assistant manager (hotel)	dàtáng jīnglǐ	大堂经理
assorted	jīngxuǎn	精选
assorted cold dishes	lěng pīnpán	冷拼盘
asthma	qìchuǎn	气喘
at	zài	在
athlete	yùndòngyuán	运动员
Atlantic Ocean	Dàxīyáng	大西洋
atomic	yuánzǐ	原子
attend class	shàngkè	上课
attend school	shàngxué	上学
attention	zhùyì	注意
audience	guānzhòng	观众
auditorium	lǐtáng	礼堂
August	bāyuè	八月
aunt (see Appendix H)	āyí	阿姨
Australia	Àodàlìyà	澳大利亚
Australian dollar	àoyuán	澳元
author	zuòzhě	作者
automatic	zìdòng	自动
autumn	qiūtiān	秋天
avenue	dàjiē	大街
awhile	yīhuìr	一会儿
azalea	dùjuānhuā	杜鹃花
back (direction)	hòu	后
back (n)	bèi	背
back door	hòumén	后门
back section (seating)	hòupái	后排

backpack	shuāngjiān kuàbāo	双肩挎包
backstage	hòutái	后台
backyard	hòuyuàn	后院
bad	huài	坏
badminton	yǔmáoqiú	羽毛球
bag	dài, dàizi	袋,袋子
baggage	xíngli	行李
baggage cart	xíngli chē	行李车
baggage claim area	xíngli tīng	行李厅
baggage claim office	xíngli bàngōngshì	行李办公室
baggage strap	xíngli dài	行李带
baggage tag	xíngli pái	行李牌
balcony (seating)	lóushàng zuòwei	楼上座位
balcony (terrace)	yángtái	阳台
Bali	Bālí	巴厘
ball	qiú	球
ball game	qiúsài	球赛
ballet	bāléiwǔ	芭蕾舞
ballpoint pen	yuánzhūbǐ	圆珠笔
ballroom	wǔtīng	舞厅
bamboo	zhúzi	竹子
bamboo shoot	zhúsǔn	竹笋
bambooware	zhúbiān	竹编
banana	xiāngjiāo	香蕉
band (music group)	yuèduì	乐队
band (radio)	bōduàn	播段
Band-Aid	zhǐxuè jiāobù	止血胶布
bandage (n)	bēngdài	绷带
Bangkok	Màngǔ	曼谷
bank (financial)	yínháng	银行
banquet	yànhuì	宴会
banquet manager	yànhuìtīng jīnglǐ	宴会厅经理
banyan tree	róngshù	榕树
bar (for drinks)	jiǔbā	酒吧
barber shop	lǐfà diàn	理发店
bargain prices	yìjià	议价
barley	dàmài, qīngkē	大麦,青稞
baseball	bàngqiú	棒球
basin (land)	péndì	盆地
basketball	lánqiú	兰球
bat	biānfú	蝙蝠
bath towel	yùjīn	浴巾
bathhouse	zǎotáng	澡堂
bathroom (for baths)	yùshì	浴室
bathroom (toilet)	cèsuǒ	厕所
bathtub	yùchí	浴池
batik	làrǎn	蜡染
battery	diànchí	电池

bayberry, red	yángméi	杨梅
be	shì	是
bean	dòuzi	豆子
bean paste	dòushā	豆沙
bean sauce, hot	dòubàn jiàng	豆瓣酱
bean sprout	dòuyá	豆芽
beancurd	dòufu	豆腐
bear (n)	xióng, gǒuxióng	熊，狗熊
beautiful	měilì, piàoliàng	美丽，漂亮
beauty salon	fàláng	发廊
beaver	hǎilí	海狸
because	yīnwéi	因为
bed	chuáng	床
bedroom	wòshì	卧室
bedtime	shuìjiào shíjiān	睡觉时间
beef	niúròu	牛肉
beefsteak	niúpái	牛排
beer	píjiǔ	啤酒
beet	tiáncài	甜菜
before	yǐqián	以前
before meals	fànqián	饭前
before sleep	shuìqián	睡前
beggar	qīgài	乞丐
begin	kāishǐ	开始
begonia	qiūhǎitáng	秋海棠
Beijing Opera	jīngjù	京剧
Belgium	Bǐlìshí	比利时
believe (faith)	xiāngxìn	相信
believe (opinion)	rènwéi	认为
bell (ancient)	gǔzhōng	古钟
bell captain	xíngli lǐngbān	行李领班
bell tower	zhōnglóu	钟楼
belong to	shǔyú	属于
below	zài...xiàmiàn	在……下面
Berlin	Bólín	柏林
berth	chuángwèi	床位
best	zuìhǎo	最好
better	gènghǎo	更好
bicycle	zìxíngchē	自行车
big	dà	大
bill (money notes)	piàozi	票子
bill (payment due)	zhàngdān	帐单
billiards	táiqiú	台球
billion	shíyì	十亿
biology	shēngwùxué	生物学
bird	niǎo	鸟
birthday	shēngrì	生日
biscuit	bǐnggàn	饼干

bite (v)	yǎo	咬
bitter	kǔ	苦
bitter gourd	kǔguā	苦瓜
black	hēi	黑
black mushroom	xiānggū, dōnggū	香菇, 冬菇
black tea	hóngchá	红茶
black-and-white	hēibái	黑白
blackboard	hēibǎn	黑板
bland	dàn	淡
blank tape	kòngbái dài	空白带
blanket (n)	tǎnzi	毯子
bleed	liúxuè	流血
blister	pào	疱
blocked (stopped up	dǔsè	堵塞
blonde	jīnfà	金发
blood	xuèyè	血液
blood pressure	xuèyā	血压
blood type	xuèxíng	血型
blouse	nǚ chènshān	女衬衫
blow dry	chuīgān	吹干
blow dryer	chuīfēngjī	吹风机
blue	lán	蓝
blunt (dull)	dùn	钝
board game	qísài	棋赛
boarding pass	dēngjī pái	登机牌
boat	chuán, zhōu	船, 舟
boat ride	chéngchuán	乘船
body (human)	shēntǐ	身体
boil (v)	shāokāi, zhǔ	烧开, 煮
boiled dumplings	shuǐjiǎo	水饺
boiled egg	zhǔ jīdàn	煮鸡蛋
boiled water	kāishuǐ	开水
bok choy	báicài	白菜
bon voyage	yílù shùnfēng	一路顺风
bone	gǔtou	骨头
Bonn	Bō'ēn	波恩
bonsai	pénjǐng	盆景
bonus	jiǎngjīn	奖金
book (n)	shū	书
booking office	dìngpiào chù	订票处
bookkeeper	kuài jì	会计
bookstore	shūdiàn	书店
boring	kūzào	枯燥
borrow	jiè	借
Boston	Bōshìdùn	波士顿
bottle (n)	píngzi	瓶子
bottle opener	pínggài qǐzi	瓶盖起子
bourgeois	zīchǎn jiējí	资产阶级

bowel movement	dàbiàn	大便
bowels	chángzi	肠子
bowl (n)	wǎn	碗
bowling	bǎolíngqiú	保龄球
bowling alley	bǎolíng qiúchǎng	保龄球场
box (carton)	hézi	盒子
box office	shòupiàochù	售票处
boxing	quánjī	拳击
boy	nánhái	男孩
boyfriend	nán péngyǒu	男朋友
bracelet	shǒuzhuó	手镯
brakes	zhá, shāchē	闸,刹车
brandy	báilándì	白兰地
brass instrument	tóngguǎn yuèqì	铜管乐器
Bravo!	Hǎo!	好!
bread	miànbāo	面包
breakdancing	pīlì wǔ	霹雳舞
breakfast	zǎofàn	早饭
breathe	hūxī	呼吸
brick	zhuāntóu	砖头
brick tea	zhuānchá	砖茶
bridge (n)	qiáo	桥
bright	liàng, xiānyàn	亮,鲜艳
brightness	liàngdù	亮度
bring	dài, ná	带,拿
Britain	Yīngguó	英国
broad bean	cándòu	蚕豆
broadcasting station	guǎngbō diàntái	广播电台
brocade	zhījǐn	织锦
broccoli, Chinese	gàilán	芥蓝
broken (out of order)	huài le	坏了
broken (severed)	duànle	断了
bronchitis	zhī qìguǎn yán	支气管炎
bronze chariot	tóng zhànchē	铜战车
broom	tiáozhou	笤帚
broth	qīngtāng	清汤
brother (older)	gēge	哥哥
brother (younger)	dìdi	弟弟
brown	zōngsè	棕色
brown paper	niúpí zhǐ	牛皮纸
brown sauce (braised in)	hóngshāo	红烧
brush	shuāzi	刷子
Brussels	Bùlǔsài'ěr	布鲁塞尔
bubble gum	pàopaotáng	泡泡糖
buddha	fó	佛
buddhism	fójiào	佛教
building (n)	lóufáng, jiànzhù	楼房,建筑
bull	gōngniú	公牛

Bund (Shanghai)	Wàitān	外滩
bureau (organization)	jú	局
bureau director	júzhǎng	局长
burial grounds	mùdì	墓地
Burma	Miǎndiàn	缅甸
burn (n)	shāoshāng	烧伤
bus (n)	qìchē	汽车
bus driver	sījī	司机
bus map	qìchē xiànlù tú	汽车线路图
bus station	qìchē zǒngzhàn	汽车总站
bus stop	qìchē zhàn	汽车站
bushel	pǔshì'ěr	蒲式耳
business	shēngyì	生意
business management	qǐyè guǎnlǐ	企业管理
business person	shāngrén	商人
busy	máng	忙
busy line (phone)	zhànxiàn	占线
but	dànshì	但是
butcher shop	ròudiàn	肉店
butter	huángyóu	黄油
buttocks	pìgu	屁股
button (for clothing)	kòuzi	扣子
button (pushbutton)	ànniǔ	按纽
buy	mǎi	买
CAAC	Zhōngguó mínháng	中国民航
cabbage	yáng báicài	洋白菜
cabbage heart	càixīn	菜心
cabbage, Chinese	dà báicài	大白菜
cabin (ship)	cāng, chuáncāng	舱，船舱
cable TV	bìlù diànshì	闭路电视
cable address	diànbào guàhào	电报挂号
cadre	gànbù	干部
cadre's jacket	zhōngshān zhuāng	中山装
cafe	kāfēiguǎn	咖啡馆
cake	dàngāo	蛋糕
calendar	rìlì	日历
California	Jiāzhōu	加州
call (to beckon)	jiào	叫
call (to telephone)	gěi…dǎdiànhuà	给……打电话
calligrapher	shūfǎjiā	书法家
calligraphy	shūfǎ	书法
calligraphy brush	máobǐ	毛笔
camel	luòtuo	骆驼
camelia	cháhuā	茶花
camera	zhàoxiàngjī	照像机
camphor tree	zhāngshù	樟树
can (know how to)	huì	会

can (possible to)	néng	能
can (tin, jar)	guàntou	罐头
can opener	guàntou qǐzi	罐头起子
Canada	Jiānádà	加拿大
canal	yùnhé	运河
cancel	qǔxiāo	取消
cancer	áizhèng	癌症
candied haws	bīngtáng húlu	冰糖葫芦
candy	táng, tángguǒ	糖，糖果
canoe	dúmùzhōu	独木舟
Canon	Jiā néng	佳能
Cantonese opera	yuèjù	粤剧
capital (city)	shǒudū	首都
capital (money)	zījīn, zīběn	资金，资本
capitalist	zīběnjiā	资本家
capon	yānjī	阉鸡
capsule	jiāonáng	胶囊
caption	zìmù	字幕
car	qìchē, xiǎojiàochē	汽车，小轿车
car sick	yùnchē	晕车
cardiac failure	xīnlì shuāijié	心力衰竭
cardiology	xīnzàngbìng xué	心脏病学
cards (playing)	Pùkè pái	扑克牌
career	shìyè	事业
careful	xiǎoxīn	小心
careless	mǎdàhā	马大哈
carpenter	mùjiàng, mùgōng	木匠
carpet	dìtǎn	地毯
carrot	húluóbo	胡萝卜
carry	xiédài	携带
carry-on luggage	shǒutí xíngli	手提行李
cart (n)	tuīchē	推车
cartoon (film)	dònghuà piàn	动画片
cartoon (print)	mànhuà	漫画
carving (n)	diāokè	雕刻
cash (n)	xiànjīn	现金
cash (v)	duìhuàn	兑换
cash advance	xiànjīn yùfù	现金预付
cashew nut	yāoguǒ	腰果
cashier	chū nà yuán	出纳员
cashier's booth	shōukuǎnchu	收款处
cashmere	kāishìmǐ	开士米
casserole	shāguō	沙锅
cassette (sound tape)	cídài	磁带
cassia	guìhuā	桂花
cassia wine	guìhuā jiǔ	桂花酒
casual	suíbiàn	随便
cat	māo	猫

catch (v)	zhuāzhù	抓住
cathartic	xièyào	泻药
cattle	shēngkou	牲口
cauliflower	càihuā	菜花
cave	shāndòng	山洞
CCTV English Service	diànshì yīngyǔ jiémù	电视英语节目
ceiling	tiānhuābǎn	天花板
celery	qíncài	芹菜
cellophane tape	tòumíng jiāodài	透明胶带
cement (concrete)	shuǐní	水泥
center (middle)	zhōngjiān	中间
centigrade	shèshì	摄氏
centimeter	límǐ	厘米
Central America	Zhōngměizhōu	中美洲
century	shìjì	世纪
ceramics	táocí	陶瓷
certain	yídìng	一定
certificate	zhèngmíng	证明
chain	liàntiáo, liànzi	链条, 链子
chair (n)	yǐzi	椅子
chairman	zhǔxí	主席
Chairman Mao	Máo zhǔxí	毛主席
chamber music	shìnèi yuè	室内乐
champagne	xiāngbīnjiǔ	香槟酒
champion	guànjūn	冠军
chance (opportunity)	jīhuì	机会
change (coins, small bills)	língqián	零钱
change (to replace, exchange)	huàn	换
change (transfer)	diào	调
change (transformation)	biànhuà	变化
channel (TV)	píndào	频道
character (role)	juésè	角色
characteristic	tèdiǎn	特点
charcoal drawing	tànhuà	炭画
charge d'affaires	lǐngshì	领事
charming	mírén	迷人
cheap	piányi	便宜
cheapest	zuìpiányi	最便宜
check, bank	zhīpiào	支票
check in (for flight)	bàn chéngjī shǒuxù	办乘机手续
check in (register)	dēngjì	登记
check out (from a hotel)	tuìfáng	退房
checkers, Chinese	tiàoqí	跳棋
Cheers!	Gānbēi!	干杯!
cheese	nǎilào	奶酪
chef	chúshī	厨师
chemical (adj)	huàxué	化学

chemist's (drugstore)	yàodiàn	药店
chemistry	huàxué	化学
chemotherapy	huàliáo	化疗
cheongsam (gown)	qípáo	旗袍
cherry	yīngtáo	樱桃
chess	guójì xiàngqí	国际象棋
chess, Chinese	xiàngqí	象棋
chest pain	xiōngkǒu tòng	胸口疼
chestnut	lìzi	栗子
chewing gum	kǒuxiāngtáng	口香糖
Chicago	Zhījiāgē	芝加哥
chicken	jī	鸡
child	xiǎohái	小孩
Children's Palace	shàonián gōng	少年宫
children's clothing	tóngzhuāng	童装
chilli pepper (dried)	gān làjiāo	干辣椒
China	Zhōngguó	中国
China Central Television (CCTV)	Zhōngyāng diànshì tái	中央电视台
Chinese (language)	hànyǔ	汉语
Chinese character	hànzì	汉字
Chinese meal	zhōngcān	中餐
Chinese Menu	zhōngcān càipǔ	中餐菜谱
Chinese New Year	chūnjié	春节
chives, Chinese	jiǔcài	韭菜
chocolate	qiǎokèlì	巧克力
choice	xuǎnzé	选择
cholera	huòluàn	霍乱
choose	xuǎn, tiāo	选，挑
chop (seal)	yìnzhāng shí, túzhāng	印章石，图章
chopsticks	kuàizi	筷子
chorus	héchàng	合唱
Christmas	Shèngdànjié	圣诞节
chronic	mànxìng	慢性
chrysanthemum	júhuā	菊花
chrysolite (jade)	fěicuì	翡翠
church	jiàotáng	教堂
cigarette	xiāngyān	香烟
cinema	diànyǐng yuàn	电影院
circle (n)	quān	圈
circus	mǎxì	马戏
citizen	gōngmín	公民
city	chéngshì	城市
city gate	chéngmén	城门
city map	chéngshì jiāotōng tú	城市交通图
city tour	yóulǎn shìróng	游览市容
civil	mínyòng	民用
clams	gélí	蛤蜊

clap (applaud)	gǔzhǎng	鼓掌
class (social)	jiējí	阶级
class (students)	bān	班
classic	gǔdiǎn	古典
classroom	jiàoshì, kètáng	教室，课堂
clay	niántǔ	粘土
clay figure	nírén	泥人
clean (adj)	gānjìng	干净
clean (v)	dǎsǎo	打扫
cleaning solution	xiāodú yè	消毒液
clear (distinct)	qīngchǔ	清楚
cliff	xuányá	悬崖
climb	pá	爬
clinic	yīwùshì	医务室
cloakroom	yīmàojiān	衣帽间
clock	zhōng	钟
cloisonne	jǐngtàilán	景泰蓝
cloisonne vase	jǐngtàilán huāpíng	景泰蓝花瓶
close (to shut)	guān	关
closed (business)	guānmén	关门
closed (not public)	bù kāifàng	不开放
closet	yīguì	衣柜
cloth	bù, liàozi	布，料子
clothespin	yīfujiā	衣服夹
clothing	yīfu	衣服
clothing store	fúzhuāng diàn	服装店
cloud	yún	云
cloudy (weather)	yīn, duōyún	阴，多云
clown	xiǎochǒu	小丑
club (recreation)	jùlèbù	俱乐部
coach (bus)	qìchē, lǚyóuchē	汽车，旅游车
coach (sports)	jiàoliàn	教练
coal	méi	煤
coat	shàngyī, dàyī	上衣，大衣
coat hanger	yījià	衣架
Coca-Cola	kěkǒu kělè	可口可乐
cocaine	kěkǎyīn	可卡因
cock's comb (flower)	jīguānhuā	鸡冠花
cockroach	zhāngláng	蟑螂
cocoa	kěkě	可可
coconut	yēzi	椰子
cocoon	cánjiǎn	蚕茧
coffee	kāfēi	咖啡
coffee shop	kāfēi diàn	咖啡店
cola	kělè	可乐
cold (adj)	lěng	冷
cold (illness)	gǎnmào, zháoliáng	感冒，着凉
cold drink	lěngyǐn	冷饮

cold drinking water	liángbáikāi	凉白开
cold milk	lěng niúnǎi	冷牛奶
cold platter	lěngpán	冷盘
cold water (from tap)	lěngshuǐ	冷水
cold water wash	lěngshuǐ xǐ	冷水洗
cold wave (perm)	lěngtàng	冷烫
collect (gather)	shōují	收集
collect (phon_ call)	duìfāng fùkuǎn	对方付款
college	xuéyuàn, dàxué	学院，大学
color (n)	yánsè	颜色
color TV	cǎidiàn	彩电
colored	cǎisè	彩色
column (pillar)	zhùzi	柱子
coma	hūnmí	昏迷
comb (n)	shūzi	梳子
come	lái	来
comedy	xǐjù	喜剧
comfortable	shūfu	舒服
commemorative stamp	jìniàn yóupiào	纪念邮票
common	pǔtōng	普通
commune	gōngshè	公社
communist party	gòngchǎndǎng	共产党
compact disc	jīguāng chàngpiàn	激光唱片
company (business)	gōngsi	公司
company account	gōngsi zhànghù	公司帐户
complain	bàoyuàn	抱怨
completely	wánquán	完全
composer (music)	zuòqǔjiā	作曲家
composition (music)	zuòpǐn	作品
composition (painting)	gòutú	构图
comprehensive	zōnghé	综合
computer	jìsuànjī, diànnǎo	计算机，电脑
computer programmer	diànnǎo chéngxùyuán	电脑程序员
comrade	tóngzhì	同志
concerning	guānyú	关于
concert	yīnyuèhuì	音乐会
concert hall	yīnyuè tīng	音乐厅
concierge (hotel)	jiēdàiyuán	接待员
concubine	fēizi, qiè	妃子，妾
condition	tiáojiàn, qíngkuàng	条件，情况
conditioner (for hair)	hùfàsù	护发素
conductor (bus)	shòupiàoyuán	售票员
conductor (music)	zhǐhuī	指挥
conductor (train)	chéngwùyuán	乘务员
conference room	huìyìshì	会议室
confirm	quèdìng	确定
connect	jiē	接
connecting flight	xiánjiē hángbān	衔接航班

connection (relation)	guānxi	关系
conscience	liángxin	良心
consider	kǎolǜ	考虑
consomme	qīngtāng	清汤
constipation	biànbì	便秘
Constitution	xiànfǎ	宪法
construction	jiànshè	建设
contact lens	yǐnxíng yǎnjìng	隐形眼镜
contact prints (photo)	xiǎoyàng	小样
contagious	jiēchù chuánrǎn	接触传染
container	róngqì	容器
contemporary (adj)	dāngdài	当代
continent	dàlù	大陆
contraceptives	bìyùn yòngpǐn	避孕用品
contrast (n)	duìbǐ	对比
convenient	fāngbiàn	方便
convulsion	jìngluán	痉挛
cook (n)	chúshī, dà shīfù	厨师, 大师傅
cook (prepare meals)	zuòfàn	做饭
cookie	bǐnggān	饼干
cooking	pēngtiáo	烹调
cool (adj)	liáng, liángkuài	凉, 凉快
copy (n)	fùběn	副本
corduroy	dēngxīn róng	灯芯绒
coriander	xiāngcài	香菜
cork carving	ruǎnmù diāo	软木雕
corkscrew	píngsāi qǐzi	瓶塞起子
corn	yùmǐ	玉米
cornet, Chinese	suǒnà	锁呐
corporation	gōngsī	公司
correct (yes)	duì	对
costume	xìzhuāng	戏装
cot	zhédié chuáng	折叠床
cottage (thatched)	cǎofáng	草房
cotton	mián	棉
cotton-padded jacket	miányī	棉衣
cotton-padded shoes	miánxié	棉鞋
cough	késòu	咳嗽
cough drops	hánpiàn	含片
cough syrup	zhǐké tángjiāng	止咳糖浆
country (nation)	guójiā	国家
country (rural)	xiāngcūn	乡村
country music	xiāngcūn yīnyuè	乡村音乐
countryside	nóngcūn	农村
county	xiàn	县
courtyard	yuànzi	院子
cover (n)	gàizi	盖子
cow	nǎiniú	奶牛

crab	pángxiè	螃蟹
crabapple, Chinese	hǎitáng	海棠
craft	gōngyì	工艺
craftsman	gōngjiàng	工匠
cramp	chōujīn	抽筋
crane	hè	鹤
crayons	làbǐ	蜡笔
cream (dairy)	nǎiyóu	奶油
creator	chuàngzào zhě	创造者
credit card	xìnyòngkǎ	信用卡
crepe (pancake)	jiānbǐng	煎饼
crispy	cuì	脆
crispy duck	xiāngsū yā	香酥鸭
critical condition	qíngkuàng wēijí	情况危急
crop (n)	nóngzuòwù	农作物
cross (pass)	guò	过
cross talk (comedy routine)	xiàngsheng	相声
crosswalk	rénxíng héngdào	人行横道
cruise (v)	yóu	游
cruise boat	yóutǐng	游艇
cry (sob)	kū	哭
cub	yòuzǎi	幼仔
cucumber	huángguā	黄瓜
Cultural Revolution	wéngé	文革
cultural exchange	wénhuà jiāoliú	文化交流
cultural relic	wénhuà gǔjì	文化古迹
culture (arts, customs)	wénhuà	文化
cup	bēi, bēizi	杯, 杯子
curler (for hair)	fàjuǎn	发卷
curling iron	měifà qì	美发器
curly	juǎnqū shì	卷曲式
curry	gālí	咖喱
curtain (theater)	mù	幕
curtain (window)	chuānglián	窗帘
cushion	diànzi	垫子
custom (tradition)	fēngsú	风俗
custom-made	dìngzuò de	订做的
customer	gùkè	顾客
Customs	hǎiguān	海关
customs declaration	hǎiguān shēnbào dān	海关申报单
customs duty	guānshuì	关税
cut (v)	jiǎn, qiè	剪, 切
cuttlefish	mòdǒuyú, wūzéi	墨斗鱼, 乌贼
cycling	qí zìxíngchē	骑自行车
cymbals	chǎ	钗
cypress tree	bǎishù	柏树
daily (newspaper)	rìbào	日报

Dalai Lama	Dálài Lǎma	达赖喇嘛
dam	dībà	堤坝
damaged	nònghuài le	弄坏了
damp	shī	湿
dance (n)	wǔdǎo	舞蹈
dance (v)	tiàowǔ	跳舞
dance drama	wǔjù	舞剧
dance hall	wǔtīng	舞厅
dance party	wǔhuì	舞会
dance troupe	wǔdǎo tuán	舞蹈团
dancer	wǔdǎo yǎnyuán	舞蹈演员
danger	wēixiǎn	危险
dark	hēi	黑
darkroom	ànshì	暗室
date (appointment)	yuēhuì	约会
date (fruit)	zǎo	枣
dating (courtship)	tán liàn'ài	谈恋爱
daughter	nǚ'ér	女儿
day	rì, tiān	日,天
day after tomorrow	hòutiān	后天
day-lily bud	jīnzhēn	金针
daytime	báitiān	白天
deaf	lóng	聋
December	shí'èryuè	十二月
decide	juédìng	决定
declare (at Customs)	shēnbào	申报
decongestant	bítōng	鼻通
decoration	zhuāngshì	装饰
deep	shēn	深
deep-fried	zhá	炸
deer	lù	鹿
degree (temperature)	dù	度
delicatessen	shúshí diàn	熟食店
delicious	hǎochī	好吃
democracy	mínzhǔ	民主
demonstration (in street)	yóuxíng	游行
Denmark	Dànmài	丹麦
dentist	yákē yīshēng	牙科医生
dentist's office	yákē zhěnsuǒ	牙科诊所
depart	líkāi	离开
department	bùmén, kē	部门,科
department store	bǎihuò shāngdiàn	百货商店
departure time (planes)	qǐfēi shíjiān	起飞时间
deposit (bank)	chǔxù	储蓄
deposit (pledge)	yājīn	押金
depressed (mood)	qíngxù bù hǎo	情绪不好
dermatologist	pífūkē yīshēng	皮肤科医生
dermatology department	pífūkē	皮肤科

descend	xià	下
descend (planes)	jiàngluò	降落
describe	xíngróng	形容
desert	shāmò	沙漠
design (v)	shèjì	设计
designer	shèjìshī	设计师
designer (name brand)	míngpái	名牌
desk	shūzhuō	书桌
dessert	diǎnxin	点心
detergent	qùwūfěn	去污粉
detour	wānlù	弯路
develop (film)	chōng, chōngxǐ	冲，冲洗
diabetes	tángniàobìng	糖尿病
diagnosis	zhěnduàn	诊断
dial (v)	bō	拨
dialog (theater)	duìbái	对白
diamond	zuànshí	钻石
diaphragm (camera)	guàngquān	光圈
diarrhea	lā dùzi	拉肚子
diced meat or vegetable	dīng	丁
die (v)	sǐ, qùshì	死，去逝
diet (foods eaten)	yǐnshí	饮食
diet (weight loss)	jiǎnféi	节食
dietician	yíngyǎng yīshī	营养医师
different	bù yíyàng	不一样
difficulty	kùnnán	困难
dig	wā	挖
dignified	yǒu qìpài	有气派
diligent	qínfèn	勤奋
dim sum	diǎnxin	点心
dining car	cānchē	餐车
dining room	cāntīng	餐厅
dinner (supper)	wǎnfàn	晚饭
dip (v)	zhàn	蘸
diplomat	wàijiāoguān	外交官
diplomatic	wàijiāo	外交
director (artistic)	dǎoyǎn	导演
director (of an organization)	zhǔrèn	主任
dirty	zāng	脏
disastrous	zāogāo	糟糕
disco	dísīkē	迪斯科
discomfort	bù shūfu	不舒服
discount (n)	zhékòu	折扣
discover	fāxiàn	发现
discussion	tǎolùn	讨论
dish (plate, tray)	pán	盘
dishwashing liquid	xǐdíjì	洗涤剂

disinfectant	xiāodú jì	消毒剂
disk film	pán shì jiāopiàn	盘式胶片
disperse	sàn	散
distance	jùlí	距离
district	qū	区
disturb	dǎrǎo, gānrǎo	打扰，干扰
divide	fēn	分
divorce	líhūn	离婚
dizzy	tóuyūn	头晕
do (be occupied with)	zuò	做
do business	zuò shēngyì	做生意
Do not...	bié, búyào...	别，不要·····
dock (n)	mǎtóu	码头
doctor	yīshēng, dàifu	医生，大夫
documentary (film)	jìlù piàn	记录片
doesn't work	bù xíng	不行
dog	gǒu	狗
dollar	yuán	元
domestic (national)	guónèi	国内
don't mind (object to)	bú zàihu	不在乎
Donald Duck	Tánglǎoyā	唐老鸭
door	mén	门
door god	ménshén	门神
dormitory	sùshè	宿舍
double (adj)	shuāng	双
double bed	shuāngrén chuáng	双人床
double happiness	shuāngxǐ	喜
double-sided embroidery	shuāngmiàn xiù	双面绣
dough figure	miànrén	面人
down	xià	下
downstairs	lóuxià	楼下
downtown	shìzhōngxīn	市中心
dragon	lóng	龙
Dragon Well tea	Lóngjǐngchá	龙井茶
dragon dance	lóngwǔ	龙舞
drain (n)	xiàshuǐdào	下水道
drama	xìjù	戏剧
drawing	túhuà	图画
dress rehearsal	cǎipái	彩排
dresser	yīchú	衣橱
dressing room	huàzhuāng shì	化装室
dried bean curd	dòufu gān	豆付干
dried shrimps	hǎimǐ	海米
drink	hē	喝
drive (v)	kāichē	开车
driver (bus, taxi)	sījī	司机
driver's license	jiàshǐ zhízhào	驾驶执照
drop (n)	dī	滴

drop (v)	diào	掉
drug	yào	药
drug (narcotic)	dúpǐn	毒品
drugstore	yàodiàn	药店
drum (n)	gǔ	鼓
drum tower	gǔlóu	鼓楼
dry	gàn	干
dry clean	gānxǐ	干洗
dry white wine	gàn bái pútao jiǔ	干白葡萄酒
dubbed film	yìzhì piàn	译制片
duck	yāzi	鸭子
duet (instrumental)	èrchóngzòu	二重奏
duet (vocal)	èrchóngchàng	二重唱
dulcimer	yángqín	扬琴
dull (uninteresting)	dāndiào, méi yìsi	单调, 没意思
dumb (mute)	yǎ	哑
dumplings	jiǎozi, bāozi	饺子, 包子
duplication machine	fùyìn jī	复印机
during	zài...zhōng	在······中
dustpan	bòji	簸箕
dusty	huīchén duō	灰尘多
dynasty	cháodài	朝代
dysentery	lìji	痢疾
each	měi, měigè	每, 每个
each time	měicì	每次
ear	ěrduo	耳朵
ear-nose-throat specialist	ěr-bí-hóu kē dàifu	耳鼻喉科大夫
early	zǎo	早
earn	zhèng	挣
earth (planet)	dìqiú	地球
east	dōng	东
East China Sea	Dōnghǎi	东海
easy	róngyì	容易
eat	chī	吃
Economic Daily	Jīngjì Rìbào	经济日报
economics	jīngjìxué	经济学
economy	jīngjì	经济
economy class	pǔtōng cāngwèi	普通舱位
edge	biān	边
editor	biānjí	编辑
education	jiàoyù	教育
eel	shànyú	鳝鱼
effect	xiàoguǒ	效果
efficiency	xiàolù	效率
egg	jīdàn	鸡旦
egg white	dànbái, dànqīng	旦白, 旦清
egg-drop soup	dànhuātāng	旦花汤

eggplant	qiézi	茄子
Egypt	Āijí	埃及
eight	bā	八
eight precious rice	bābǎofàn	八宝饭
eighty	bāshí	八十
ejaculation	shèjīng	射精
elbow	zhǒu	肘
election	xuǎnjǔ	选举
electrical equipment	diànqì	电器
electricity	diàn	电
electronic	diànzǐ	电子
electrotherapy	diànliáo	电疗
elephant	dàxiàng	大象
elevator	diàntī	电梯
elm tree	yúshù	榆树
embarrassed	bù hǎo yìsi	不好意思
embassy	dàshǐguǎn	大使馆
embroidery	cìxiù	刺绣
emergency	jǐnjí qíngkuàng	紧急情况
emergency room	jízhěn shì	急诊室
emetic	cuītùjì	催吐剂
emperor	huángdì	皇帝
employee	gùyuán	雇员
empress	huánghòu, nǚhuáng	皇后，女皇
empress dowager	tàihòu	太后
empty (adj)	kōng	空
enamel	tángcí	搪瓷
encephalitis	nǎoyán	脑炎
Encore!	Zài lái yí gè!	再来一个!
end (v)	jiéshù	结束
energy (spirit)	jīnglì	精力
engine	fādòngjī	发动机
engineer	gōngchéngshī	工程师
England	Yīngguó	英国
English (language)	yīngyǔ	英语
engraving	diāokè	雕刻
enjoy	xǐhuan	喜欢
enlargement	fàngdà	放大
enough	zúgòu	足够
ensemble (instrumental)	hézòu	合奏
enter	jìn	进
entrance	rùkǒu, jìnkǒu	入口，进口
entrepreneur	qǐyè jiā	企业家
entry visa	rùjìng qiānzhèng	入境签证
envelope	xìnfēng	信封
episode	chāqǔ	插曲
equal (adj)	píngděng, yíyàng	平等，一样
equal (v)	děngyú	等于

eraser	xiàngpí	橡皮
escalator	zìdòng fútī	自动扶梯
especially	tèbié	特别
et cetera	děng	等
eunuch	tàijiàn	太监
Europe	Ōuzhōu	欧洲
even (more)	gèng	更
evening	wǎnshang	晚上
everyday	měitiān	每天
everyone	dàjiā	大家
everything	yíqiè	一切
everywhere	dàochù	到处
evil	huài	坏
example	lìzi	例子
exceed	chāoguò	超过
excellent	fēicháng hǎo	非常好
excellent (slang)	bàng	棒
exchange (ideas)	jiāoliú	交流
exchange (money)	duìhuàn	兑换
exchange rate	duìhuàn lǜ	兑换率
exciting	lìngrén jīdòng	令人激动
excuse me (make way)	láojià	劳驾
excuse me (pardon)	duìbuqǐ	对不起
exercise (physical)	duànliàn	锻炼
exhibition	zhǎnlǎn	展览
exit (n)	chūkǒu	出口
exit visa	chūjìng qiānzhèng	出境签证
expectation	qīwàng	期望
expense	fèiyòng	费用
expensive	guì	贵
experience (n)	jīngyàn	经验
experiment	shìyàn	试验
expert	zhuānjiā	专家
expertise	zhuāncháng	专长
explain	jiěshì	解释
export goods	chūkǒu huò	出口货
export license	chūkǒu xǔkě zhèng	出口许可证
express (speed)	tèkuài	特快
express (to convey)	biǎodá	表达
extension (phone)	fēnjī	分机
extension cord	diànxiàn	电线
external use	wàiyòng	外用
extra (surplus)	fùyù de	富余的
extra large	tèdà hào	特大号
extra small	tèxiǎo hào	特小号
extract a tooth	báyá	拔牙
extremely	jí	极
eye (n)	yǎnjīng	眼睛

eye drops	yǎn yàoshuǐ	眼药水
face (n)	liǎn	脸
face cream	miànshuāng	面霜
facial (n)	měiróng	美容
factory	gōngchǎng	工厂
Fahrenheit	huáshì	华氏
faint	tóuhūn	头昏
fake	màopái	冒牌
fall (v)	shuāidǎo, diào	摔倒, 掉
false	jiǎ de	假的
family	jiā, jiātíng	家, 家庭
family members	jiātíng chéngyuán	家庭成员
fan, electric	diànshàn	电扇
fan, folding	zhéshàn	折扇
fan, hand-held	shànzi	扇子
Fantastic!	Juéle!	绝了!
far	yuǎn	远
fare (bus, taxi, or train)	chēfèi	车费
farm	nóngchǎng	农场
farmer	nóngmín	农民
farmer's home	nóngjiā	农家
fast (speed)	kuài	快
fast food	kuàicān	快餐
fat (adj)	pàng	胖
fat (n)	zhīfáng	脂肪
father	fùqin	父亲
faucet	lóngtóu	龙头
FAX	chuánzhēn	传真
feature film	gùshì piān	故事片
February	èryuè	二月
fee	fèi	费
feel (sense)	juéde	觉得
female (animals)	cí, mǔ	雌, 母
female (people)	nǚ	女
fencing	jījiàn	击剑
fertilizer	féiliào	肥料
fever	fāshāo	发烧
few	hěnshǎo, bù duō	很少, 不多
fiction	xiǎoshuō	小说
fiddle, Beijing Opera	jīnghú	京胡
fiddle, two-stringed	èrhú	二胡
field (farm)	tián	田
field (for athletics)	yùndòng chǎng	运动场
fifty	wǔshí	五十
fig	wúhuāguǒ	无花果
fill a tooth	bǔyá	补牙
fill in (a form)	tián	填

film (for camera)	jiāojuǎn	胶卷
film (movie)	diànyǐng	电影
film festival	diànyǐng jié	电影节
film studio	diànyǐng chǎng	电影厂
final (adj)	zuìhòu	最后
finally	zhōngyú	终于
find (v)	zhǎo	找
fine (delicate)	jīngzhì	精致
fine (good)	hěnhǎo, tǐnghǎo	很好，挺好
fine arts	yìshù	艺术
finger	shǒuzhǐ	手指
fingernail polish	zhǐjia yóu	指甲油
finish (v)	wánchéng	完成
finished	wán le	完了
Finland	Fēnlán	芬兰
fire (n)	huǒ	火
fire equipment	mièhuǒ qì	灭火器
fire escape	ānquán tī	安全梯
fire exit	tàipíng mén	太平门
fire fighter	xiāofáng duìyuán	消防队员
first (beforehand)	xiān	先
first, the	dìyī	第一
first-aid station	jíjiù zhàn	急救站
first class (seat)	tóuděng cāng	头等舱
first run (bus or train)	shǒu bān chē, tóu bān chē	首班车，头班车
fish	yú	鱼
fish maw	yúchì	鱼翅
fisherfolk	yúmín	渔民
fishing	diàoyú	钓鱼
fishing village	yúcūn	渔村
five	wǔ	五
Five-grain liquor	wǔliángyè	五粮液
fix (repair)	xiūlǐ	修理
flag (n)	qí	旗
flash (camera)	shǎnguāng dēng	闪光灯
flashlight	shǒudiàntǒng	手电筒
flask	hú	壶
flight (airline)	hángbān	航班
flight schedule	fēixíng shíkèbiǎo	飞行时刻表
floor (of a room)	dìbǎn	地板
floor (story)	céng, lóu	层，楼
flour	miànfěn	面粉
flower	huā	花
flu	liúgǎn	流感
fluent	liúlì	流利
flute, bamboo	dízi	笛子
fly (insect)	cāngying	苍蝇
fly (v)	fēi	飞

Flying Pigeon (bike)	Fēigē	飞鸽
fog	wù	雾
folder	jiāzi	夹子
folk dance	mínjiān wǔdǎo	民间舞蹈
folk music	mínjiān yīnyuè	民间音乐
folk tale	mínjiān gùshì	民间故事
folklore	mínjiān chuánshuō	民间传说
follow	gēn	跟
food	shípǐn, shíwù	食品, 食物
food poisoning	shíwù zhòng dú	食物中毒
foot (12 inches)	yīngchǐ	英尺
foot (body)	jiǎo, zú	脚, 足
football (American)	gǎnlǎnqiú	橄榄球
footlight	jiǎodēng	脚灯
for example	bǐrú, bǐfang shuō	比如, 比方说
Forbidden City (Palace Museum)	Gùgōng	故宫
foreign	wàiguó	外国
foreign affairs office	wàishì bàngōngshì	外事办公室
foreign exchange certificate	wàihuìquàn, wàihuì	外汇券, 外汇
foreign exchange desk	wàibì duìhuàn tai	外币兑换台
foreign expert	wàiguó zhuānjiā	外国专家
foreign guest	wàibīn	外宾
foreign policy	wàijiāo zhèngcè	外交政策
foreign student	liúxuéshēng	留学生
foreigner	wàiguórén	外国人
forest	sēnlín	森林
Forever (bike)	Yǒngjiǔ	永久
forget	wàngjì	忘记
forgive	yuánliàng	原谅
fork	chāzi	叉子
fork (road)	chà lù kǒu	叉路口
form (printed sheet)	biǎogé	表格
forty	sìshí	四十
forward (sports)	qiánfēng	前锋
four	sì	四
fox	húli	狐狸
fracture	gǔzhé	骨折
fragile	yìsuì	易碎
fragrant	xiāng	香
franc	fǎláng	法郎
France	Fǎguó	法国
free (no charge)	miǎnfèi	免费
free market	zìyóu shìchǎng	自由市场
freedom	zìyóu	自由
freelancer	zìyóu zhíyè zhě	自由职业者
freeze	dòng	冻

freezing	bīngdòng	冰冻
fresh	xīnxiān	新鲜
Friday	xīngqī wǔ	星期五
fried, deep	zhá	炸
fried, lightly	jiān	煎
fried crisp chicken	xiāngsū jī	香酥鸡
fried cruller	yóutiáo	油条
fried dumplings (pot-stickers)	guōtiē	锅贴
fried egg	jiān jīdàn	煎鸡蛋
fried noodles	chǎomiàn	炒面
fried rice	chǎofàn	炒饭
fried sesame twists	máhuā	麻花
friend	péngyǒu	朋友
friendship	yǒuyì	友谊
Friendship Store	Yǒuyì Shāngdiàn	友谊商店
fries, potato	zhá tǔdòu	炸土豆
frog	qīngwā	青蛙
front	qián	前
front door	qiánmén	前门
front section (seating)	qiánpái	前排
front yard	qiányuàn	前院
fruit	shuǐguǒ	水果
fuel	ránliào	燃料
Fuji	Fùshì	富士
full	mǎn	满
full (after meal)	bǎo le	饱了
fun	yǒuqù, hǎowán	有趣, 好玩
funny (amusing)	kě xiào, dòu	可笑, 逗
fur	qiúpí, pímáo	裘皮, 皮毛
furnace	gāolú, lúzi	高炉, 炉子
furniture	jiājù	家俱
fuse (n)	bǎoxiǎnsī	保险丝
gallon	jiālún	加仑
game	yóuxì	游戏
game room	yóuyì shì	游艺室
garbage can	lājī xiāng	拉圾箱
garden	huāyuán	花园
garlic	suàn	蒜
gas (coal)	méiqì	煤气
gas (vapor)	qì, qìtǐ	气, 气体
gas station	jiāyóu zhàn	加油站
gas stove	méiqìlú	煤气炉
gas tank	yóuxiāng	油箱
gasoline	qìyóu	汽油
gastric	wèi	胃
gastric perforation	wèi chuānkǒng	胃穿孔

gastritis	wèiyán	胃炎
gate	mén	门
gear (driving)	dǎng	档
gear (part)	chǐlún	齿轮
general anesthesia	quánshēn mázuì	全身麻醉
Geneva	Rìnèiwǎ	日内瓦
geranium	xiùqiú	绣球
Germany	Déguó	德国
gesture	dòngzuò	动作
get (obtain)	dé	得
get off (a vehicle)	xiàchē	下车
get off work	xiàbān	下班
get on (a vehicle)	shàng chē	上车
giant panda	dàxióngmāo	大熊猫
gift	lǐwù	礼物
gin (liquor)	dùsōngzi jiǔ	杜松子酒
ginger	shēngjiāng	生姜
ginkgo	yínxìng, báiguǒ	银杏, 白果
ginkgo tree	báiguǒ shù	白果树
ginseng	rénshēn	人参
girl	nǚhái	女孩
girlfriend	nǚ péngyǒu	女朋友
give	gěi	给
give away	sòngdiào	送掉
give up hope	xièqì	泻气
glass (cup)	bōli bēi	玻璃杯
glasses (optical)	yǎnjìng	眼镜
glassware	bōli zhìpǐn	玻璃制品
glaucoma	qīngguāng yǎn	青光眼
glucose	pútáo táng	葡萄糖
glue (mucilage)	jiāoshuǐ	胶水
glue (paste)	jiànghu	浆糊
glutinous rice cake	niángāo	年糕
go (board game)	wéiqí	围棋
go (v)	qù	去
go around (an obstacle)	ràokāi	绕开
Go! (sports)	Jiā yóu!	加油!
goalie (sports)	shǒuményuán	守门员
goat	shānyáng	山羊
gold	jīn	金
golden-haired monkey	jīnsīhóu	金丝猴
goldfish	jīnyú	金鱼
golf	gāo'ěrfū	高尔夫
gong	luó	锣
good	hǎo	好
good luck	hǎo yùnqi	好运气
good morning	zǎochén hǎo	早晨好
good-bye	zàijiàn	再见

good-looking	hǎokàn	好看
goods (stock)	huò	货
goose	é	鹅
gorge	xiá	峡
government	zhèngfǔ	政府
grade school	xiǎoxué	小学
graduate (v)	bìyè	毕业
grain (crop)	liángshi	粮食
grain coupon	liángpiào	粮票
gram	kè	克
grammar	yǔfǎ	语法
Grand Canal	Dàyùnhé	大运河
granddaughter	sūnnǚ, wài sūnnǚ	孙女, 外孙女
grandfather (maternal)	lǎoyé, wàigōng	老爷, 外公
grandfather (paternal)	yéye	爷爷
grandmother (maternal)	lǎolao, wàipó	姥姥, 外婆
grandmother (paternal)	nǎinai	奶奶
grandson	sūnzi, wàisūn	孙子, 外孙
grape	pútáo	葡萄
grasp (v)	zhuā	抓
gray	huīsè	灰色
Great Hall of the People	Rénmín Dàhuìtáng	人民大会堂
Great Wall	Chángchéng	长城
Great!	Zhēn bàng!	真棒!
Greece	Xīlà	希腊
green	lǜ	绿
green onion	dàcōng	大葱
green tea	lǜchá	绿茶
greeting card	jìniàn kǎ	纪念卡
grilled	kǎo	烤
groceries	shípǐn	食品
grocery store	shípǐn diàn	食品店
grotto	shíkū	石窟
ground (n)	dì	地
ground meat	ròumò	肉末
group (people)	tuántǐ, qún	团体, 群
group visa	jítǐ qiānzhèng	集体签证
grow (plant)	zhòng	种
guarantee	bǎozhèng	保证
guard (sports)	hòuwèi	后卫
guesthouse	bīnguǎn, zhāodàisuǒ	宾馆, 招待所
guide (person)	dǎoyóu	导游
guidebook	dǎoyóu shū	导游书
guitar	jíta	吉他
guitar, 3-string	sānxián qín	三弦琴
gun	qiāng	枪
gymnasium	tǐyùguǎn	体育馆
gymnastics	tǐcāo	体操

| gynecologist | fùkē yīshēng | 妇科医生 |
| gynecology department | fùkē | 妇科 |

habit (custom)	xíguàn	习惯
hair	tóufa	头发
hair oil	fàyóu	发油
hairbrush	fàshuā	头刷
haircut	lǐfà	理发
hairspray	dìngxíng yè	定型液
half	yíbàn, bànge	一半, 半个
half a day	bàntiān	半天
half-price	bànjià	半价
halt	zhànzhù	站住
ham	huǒtuǐ	火腿
hammer	chuízi	锤子
hand (n)	shǒu	手
hand carry-on	suíshēn xínglǐ	随身行李
hand towel	shǒujīn	手巾
hand wash	shǒu xǐ	手洗
handball	shǒuqiú	手球
handicapped person	cánjí rén	残疾人
handicraft	shǒugōngyì pǐn	手工艺品
handkerchief	shǒujuàn	手绢
handlebar (bike)	chēbǎ	车把
handmade	shǒugōng zhìzuò	手工制作
happen	fāshēng	发生
happiness	xìngfú	幸福
happiness (symbol)	xǐ	喜
harbor	gǎng	港
hard-seat	yìngzuò	硬座
hard-sleeper	yìngwò	硬卧
harvest (n)	shōuhuò	收获
hat	màozi	帽子
hate	hèn	恨
have	yǒu	有
haw	shānzhā	山楂
Hawaii	Xiàwēiyí	夏威夷
hay fever	huāfěn rè	花粉热
he	tā	他
head	tóu	头
headache	tóuténg	头疼
headlight	qiándēng	前灯
health	jiànkāng	健康
health care	bǎojiàn	保健
health club	jiànshēn fáng	健身房
health declaration	jiànkāng biǎo	健康表
heart	xīnzàng, xīn	心脏, 心
heart attack	xīnzàngbìng fāzuò	心脏病发作

heat (energy)	rèliàng, rè	热量,热
heat (radiator)	nuǎnqì	暖气
heat (v)	jiārè	加热
heavy	chén, zhòng	沉,重
heavy (taste)	nóng	浓
hectare	gōngqīng	公顷
hedge rose	qiángwēi	蔷薇
height	gāodù	高度
hello	nǐhǎo	你好
help (n)	bāngzhù	帮助
help (v)	bāng	帮
Helsinki	Hè'ěrxìnjī	赫尔辛基
hemorrhage	chūxuè	出血
Henan Opera	yùjù	豫剧
hepatitis	gānyán	肝炎
her	tāde	她的
herbal medicine	cǎoyào	草药
here	zhèlǐ, zhèr	这里,这儿
hero	yīngxióng	英雄
heroin	hǎiluòyīn	海洛因
heroine	nǚ yīngxióng	女英雄
hesitation	yóuyù	犹豫
hey	wèi	喂
high	gāo	高
high school	zhōngxué	中学
highest	zuìgāo	最高
highland	gāoyuán	高原
highway	gōnglù	公路
hill	shān	山
Hilton	Xī'ěrdùn	希尔顿
Himalayas	Xǐmǎlāyǎ shān	喜玛拉雅山
hip	kuà	胯
hire (a person)	gù	雇
hire (charter)	bāo	包
hired car	bāochē	包车
his	tāde	他的
history	lìshǐ	历史
history museum	lìshǐ bówùguǎn	历史博物馆
hold (embrace)	bào	抱
hold (take)	ná	拿
holder	jiàzi	架子
holiday	jiérì	节日
Holland	Hélán	荷兰
Hollywood	Hǎoláiwù	好莱坞
home	jiā	家
home-style	jiācháng	家常
homemaker	zhǔfù	主妇
Honda	Běntián	本田

honey crystalized apples	bāsī píngguǒ	拔丝苹果
Hong Kong	Xiānggǎng	香港
Hong Kong dollar	gǎngbì	港币
honor	róngxìng	荣幸
hook (n)	gōuzi	钩子
hope	xīwàng	希望
horrible	kěpà	可怕
hors d'oeuvre	lěngpán	冷盘
horse	mǎ	马
hospital	yīyuàn	医院
hospitality	hàokè, zhāodài	好客, 招待
host (person)	zhǔrén	主人
host organization	jiēdài dānwèi	接待单位
hostel	lǚshè	旅社
hot	rè	热
hot (spicy)	là	辣
hot-and-sour soup	suānlà tāng	酸辣汤
hot pot	huǒguǒ	火锅
hot sauce	làjiàng	辣酱
hot spring	wēnquán	温泉
hot water (from tap)	rèshuǐ	热水
hotel	lǚguǎn, fàndiàn	旅馆, 饭店
hour	xiǎoshí	小时
house	fángzi	房子
housekeeping department	kèfáng bù	客房部
how	zěnme	怎么
how far	duōyuǎn	多远
how long (length)	duōcháng	多长
how long (time)	duōjiǔ	多久
how many	jǐ gè, duōshǎo	几个, 多少
how much	duōshǎo	多少
how old (person)	duōdà	多大
humid	cháoshī	潮湿
humor	yōumò	幽默
humor, sense of	yōumò gǎn	幽默感
hundred	bǎi	百
hundred million	yì	亿
hunting	dǎliè	打猎
hurry up	gǎnkuài	赶快
hurt	téng	疼
husband	zhàngfu, àirén	丈夫, 爱人
Hyatt	Kǎiyuè	凯乐
hypertension	gāo xuèyā	高血压
hypodermic	píxià	皮下
hypotension	dī xuèyā	低血压
I	wǒ	我
ice	bīng	冰

ice cream	bīngqílín	冰淇淋
ice hockey	bīngqiú	冰球
ice water	bīngshuǐ	冰水
idea	zhúyì, xiǎngfǎ	主意, 想法
idiom	chéngyǔ	成语
if	rúguǒ	如果
illness	bìng	病
image	xíngxiàng	形象
imitate	mófǎng	模仿
immediately	mǎshàng	马上
immigrant	yímín	移民
immigration checkpoint	yímín jiǎnchá zhàn	移民检查站
implement (a policy)	zhíxíng	执行
import	jìnkǒu	进口
import goods	jìnkǒu huò	进口货
import license	jìnkǒu xǔkězhèng	进口许可证
important	zhòngyào	重要
impression (thought)	yìnxiàng	印象
inch (n)	yīngcùn	英寸
increase	zēngjiā	增加
India	Yìndù	印度
indigestion	xiāohuà bù liáng	消化不良
individual	gèrén, gètǐ	个人, 个体
industry	gōngyè, chǎnyè	工业, 产业
inexpensive	búguì	不贵
infection	fāyán	发炎
infectious	chuánrǎn	传染
inflammation	fāyán	发炎
information (knowledge)	zhīshi	知识
information (news)	xiāoxi	消息
information desk	wènxún chù	问询处
injection	zhùshè, dǎzhēn	注射, 打针
ink (for calligraphy)	mòzhī	墨汁
ink (for fountain pen)	mòshuǐ	墨水
ink painting, Chinese	shuǐmò huà	水墨画
ink slab	yàntai	砚台
ink stick	mò	墨
Inner Mongolia	Nèiměnggǔ	内蒙古
inpatient department	zhùyuàn chù	住院处
inquire	xúnwèn	询问
insect	kūnchóng	昆虫
inside	lǐ	里
insignia (badge)	huīzhāng	徽章
insomnia	shīmián	失眠
instrumental music	qìyuè	器乐
insure	bǎoxiǎn	保险
intellectual	zhīshi fènzǐ	知识分子
intelligent	cōngming	聪明

interesting	yǒu yìsi	有意思
intermission	mùjiān xiūxi	幕间休息
intern	shíxí shēng	实习生
internal	nèi	内
international	guójì	国际
interpreter	fānyì	翻译
intersection (crossroad)	shízì lùkǒu	十字路口
intravenous injection	jìngmài zhùshè	静脉注射
introduction	jièshào	介绍
inventor	fāmíngzhě	发明者
investigate	diàochá	调查
invitation card	qǐngtiě	请帖
iron (for clothing)	yùndǒu	熨斗
iron (metal)	tiě	铁
iron (v)	yùn, tàng	熨, 烫
Iron Goddess of Mercy tea	Tiěguānyin chá	铁观音茶
iron openwork	tiěhuā	铁花
is	shì	是
isolation ward	gélí bìngfáng	隔离病房
It	tā	它
It's a pity	hěn yíhàn	很遗憾
It's nothing	méi guānxi	没关系
Italian opera	Yìdàlì gējù	意大利歌剧
Italy	Yìdàlì	意大利
itch	yǎng	痒
itinerary	rìchéng	日程
ivory	xiàngyá	象牙
Ivory carving	yádiāo	牙雕
jacket	jiákè	夹克
jade	yù	玉
jade carving	yùdiāo	玉雕
jade carving factory	yùdiāo chǎng	玉雕厂
Jail	jiānyù	监狱
jam (jelly)	guǒjiàng	果酱
January	yīyuè	一月
Japan	Rìběn	日本
Japanese yen	rìyuán	日元
jar	píng, guàn	瓶, 罐
jasmine tea	mòlì huāchá	茉莉花茶
jaw	xiàba	下巴
jaywalking	luàn chuān mǎlù	乱穿马路
jazz music	juéshiyuè	爵士乐
jeep	jípǔchē	吉普车
jellyfish	hǎizhé	海蜇
jetlag	shíchà fǎnyìng	时差反应
jewel (precious)	zhūbǎo	珠宝
jewelry (ornamental)	shǒushì	首饰

job	gōngzuò	工作
join	cānjiā	参加
joints (body)	guānjié	关节
joke (v)	kāi wánxiào	开玩笑
journal (diary)	rìjì	日记
journal (periodical)	qīkān, kānwù	期刊,刊物
journalism	xīnwén gōngzuò	新闻工作
journalist (reporter)	jìzhě	记者
judge (n)	fǎguān	法官
judge (v)	pànduàn	判断
judo	róudào	柔道
juice (fruit)	guǒzhī	果汁
July	qīyuè	七月
jump	tiào, bèng	跳,蹦
jumprope (n)	tiàoshéng	跳绳
June	liùyuè	六月
just	jiù	就
just now	cái, gāngcái	才,刚才
karst	yánróng	岩溶
Keemun tea	Qímén hóngchá	祁门红茶
keep	bǎoliú	保留
ketchup (catsup)	fānqié jiàng	蕃茄酱
key (n)	yàoshi	钥匙
keyboard instrument	jiànpán yuèqì	键盘乐器
kick (v)	tī	踢
kidney	shèn	肾
kidney bean	yúndòu	云豆
kidskin	xiǎoshànyáng pí	小山羊皮
Kiev	Jīfǔ	基辅
kill (v)	shā	杀
kilogram	gōngjīn	公斤
kilometer	gōnglǐ	公里
kind (personality)	shànliáng	善良
kindergarten	yòu'éryuán	幼儿园
kiss (n)	qīn, wěn	亲,吻
kitchen	chúfáng	厨房
kite	fēngzheng	风筝
knee	xīgài	膝盖
knife	dāozi	刀子
knit	zhī	织
know (a fact)	zhīdao	知道
know (a person)	rènshi	认识
know how to	huì	会
knowledge	zhīshi	知识
Kodak	Kēdá	柯达
Korea	Cháoxiǎn	朝鲜
Kowloon	Jiǔlóng	九龙

Kublai Khan	Hūbìliè	忽必烈
kumquat	jīnjú	金桔
Kunshan Opera	kūnqǔ	昆曲
Kyoto	Jīngdū	京都
label (n)	biāoqiān	标签
labor union	gōnghuì	工会
laboratory	huàyàn shì	化验室
lacquer, carved	diāoqī	雕漆
lacquerware	qīqì	漆器
lake	hú	湖
lamasery	lǎmasì	喇嘛寺
lamb (mutton)	yángròu	羊肉
lambskin	xiǎoyáng pí	小羊皮
lamp	dēng	灯
land (earth)	tǔdì	土地
landscape	fēngjǐng	风景
lane	hútong, xiàng	胡同, 巷
language	yǔyán	语言
large	dà	大
largest	zuìdà	最大
last (final)	zuìhòu	最后
last month	shàng ge yuè	上个月
last one	zuìhòu yígè	最后一个
last run (bus or train)	mòbān chē	末班车
last week	shàng ge xīngqī	上个星期
last year	qùnián	去年
later (afterwards)	hòulái	后来
later (in a while)	yìhuìr	一会儿
laundry (clean)	xǐ wán de yīfu	洗完的衣服
laundry (dirty)	yào xǐ de yīfu	要洗的衣服
laundry bag	xǐyīdài	洗衣袋
laundry detergent	xǐyīfěn	洗衣粉
law	fǎlǜ	法律
lawyer	lǜshī	律师
layered	duōcéng	多层
lazy	lǎn	懒
lead (v)	dài, lǐng	带, 领
lead actor (or actress)	zhǔyǎn	主演
leader	lǐngdǎo	领导
leads to (street)	tōngxiàng	通向
leaf	shùyè	树叶
leak (v)	lòu	漏
lean (thin)	shòu	瘦
leopard	bào	豹
learn	xué	学
leather	pígé	皮革
leather shoes	píxié	皮鞋

leave (behind)	liú	留
leave (depart)	líkāi	离开
leave (set out)	chūfā	出发
leave a message (spoken)	liú huà	留话
leave a note	liú tiáo	留条
lecture (n)	jiǎngzuò	讲座
left (direction)	zuǒ	左
leg	tuǐ	腿
lemon	níngméng	柠檬
lemonade	níngméng shuǐ	柠檬水
length	chángdù	长度
Leningrad	Lièníngélè	列宁格勒
lens (camera)	jìngtóu	镜头
less	shǎo	少
lesser panda	xiǎoxióngmāo	小熊猫
lesson (class)	kè	课
lesson (moral)	jiàoxùn	教训
let	ràng	让
letter (mail)	xìn	信
lettuce	wōjù	莴苣
level (degree)	shuǐpíng	水平
Li River	Líjiāng	漓江
liberalism	zìyóuhuà	自由化
library	túshūguǎn	图书馆
license plate	chēpái	车牌
lie down	tǎng xià	躺下
life	shēnghuó	生活
light (in color, density)	qiǎn, dàn	浅，淡
light (lamp)	dēng	灯
light (to kindle)	diǎn	点
light (weight)	qīng	轻
light meter	cèguāng biǎo	测光表
lighting	zhàomíng	照明
lighting design	dēngguāng shèjì	灯光设计
like (v)	xǐhuān	喜欢
like this (this way)	zhèyàng	这样
lilac	dīngxiāng	丁香
line (n)	xiàn	线
linen	yàmá bù	亚麻布
linguistics	yǔyánxué	语言学
lion	shīzi	狮子
lion dance	shīzi wǔ	狮子舞
liquor	jiǔ	酒
lira	lǐlā	里拉
listen to	tīng	听
listen to music	tīng yīnyuè	听音乐
liter	shēng	升
literature	wénxué	文学

lithograph	shíbǎnhuà	石版画
little (small)	xiǎo	小
live (reside)	zhù	住
live telecast	xiànchǎng zhíbò	现场直播
liver	gàn	肝
living	huózhe	活着
living room	kètīng	客厅
lobby (n)	xiūxishì	休息室
lobster	lóngxiā	龙虾
local (place)	dìfāng	地方
local (slow bus or train)	mànchē	慢车
local (within a city)	běndì, dāngdì	本地，当地
local anesthesia	júbù mázui	局部麻醉
local guide	dìpéi·	地陪
local money, Chinese	rénmínbì	人民币
local opera	dìfāng xì	地方戏
located at	zài	在
location	dìdiǎn	地点
lock	suǒ	锁
lock (ship)	chuánzhá	船闸
locust tree	huáishù	槐树
London	Lúndūn	伦敦
lonely	jìmò	寂寞
long (adj)	cháng	长
long bean, green	jiāngdòu	江豆
long-distance	chángtú	长途
long-distance bus	chángtú qìchē	长途汽车
long live...	...wànsuì	···万岁
longan fruit	lóngyǎn	龙眼
longevity	chángshòu	长寿
longevity (symbol)	shòu	寿
look	kàn	看
loose	sōngsǎn	松散
loquat	pípá	枇杷
Los Angeles	Luòshānjī	洛杉矶
lose	diūshī	丢失
lost (an object)	diū le	丢了
lost (the way)	mílù	迷路
lost-and-found office	shīwù zhǎolǐng chù	失物领招处
lotus flower	liánhuā, héhuā	莲花，荷花
lotus root	ǒu	藕
lotus seed	liánzǐ	莲子
loud	dàshēng	大声
love (n)	àiqíng	爱情
love (v)	ài	爱
love wine	dīngxiāng jiǔ	丁香酒
low	dī	低
lowest	zuìdī	最低

luck	yùnqi	运气
luck (symbol)	fú	福
luggage (see baggage)	xíngli	行李
luggage rack	xíngli jià	行李架
lumbago	yāoténg	腰疼
lunch (n)	wǔfàn	午饭
lung	fèi	肺
lute, 4-string	pípá	琵琶
lychee (litchi)	lìzhī	荔枝
lynx	shēli	猞猁
lyrics (song)	gēcí	歌词
Macao	Àomén	澳门
machine	jīqì	机器
Madríd	Mǎdélǐ	马德里
magazine (reading)	zázhì	杂志
magic	móshù	魔术
magician	móshùshī	魔术师
mah-jongg	májiàng	麻将
mail (letters)	xìn	信
mail (v)	jì	寄
mailbox	yóutǒng	邮筒
main	zhǔyào	主要
main character	zhǔjué	主角
main desk	zǒngtái	总台
maitre d'	zǒngguǎn	总管
make	zuò	做
make progress	yǒu jìnzhǎn	有进展
make-up (cosmetics)	huàzhuāng	化妆
malaria	nüèji	疟疾
male (animals)	gōng, xióng	公，雄
male (people)	nán	男
man	nánrén	男人
management	guǎnlǐ	管理
manager	jīnglǐ	经理
Manchurian jasper	xiùyù	岫玉
mandarin ducks	yuānyang	鸳鸯
mandarin orange	gānzi	柑子
mandolin, 4-string	yuèqín	月琴
mango	mángguǒ	芒果
manicure	xiū zhǐjia	修指甲
manual transmission (car)	shǒudòng huàndǎng	手动换档
manufacture (produce)	shēngchǎn	生产
many	hǎo duō	好多
Mao cap	jūnmào	军帽
Mao jacket	jūnbiànfú	军便服
Maotai liquor	Máotái	茅台
map (n)	dìtú	地图

marble	dàlǐshí	大理石
March	sānyuè	三月
Marco Polo	Mǎkě Bōluó	马可·波罗
marijuana	dàmá	大麻
marine (military)	hǎijūn lùzhànduì	海军陆战队
marionette	tíxiàn mù'ǒu	提线木偶
mark (currency)	mǎkè	马克
marriage	hūnyīn	婚姻
marry	jiéhūn	结婚
marten	diāo	貂
martial arts	wǔshù	武术
martial arts performer	wǔshù biǎoyǎnzhě	武术表演者
martyr	lièshì	烈士
mashed potatos	tǔdòu ní	土豆泥
mask	miànjù	面具
massage	ànmó, tuīná	按摩, 推拿
masses (people)	qúnzhòng	群众
master worker	shīfu	师傅
matches	huǒchái	火柴
maternity ward	chǎnkē bìngfáng	产科病房
mathematics	shùxué	数学
matter (affair)	shìqing	事情
mausoleum	líng	陵
Maxwell House	Màishì	麦氏
May	wǔyuè	五月
maybe	yěxǔ	也许
me	wǒ	我
meaning	yìsi	意思
measles	mázhěn	麻疹
measure (v)	cèliáng	测量
meatball	ròu wánzi	肉丸子
medical science	yīxué	医学
medicine	yīyào	医药
medicine, traditional Chinese	zhōngyī, zhōngyào	中药
medium (size)	zhōng hào	中号
meet (a person)	jiàn	见
meeting (n)	huì	会
Melbourne	Mò'ěrběn	墨尔本
melon, Hami	hāmìguā	哈蜜瓜
member (of a group)	chéngyuán	成员
memorial arch	páilóu	牌楼
memorial hall	jìniàntáng	纪念堂
memory	jìyì	记忆
men's bike	nánchē	男车
mend	bǔ	补
meningitis	nǎomó yán	脑膜炎
menstruation	yuèjīng	月经

mental	jīngshén	精神
menu	càidān	菜单
Mercedes Benz	Bēnchí	奔驰
merchandise	shāngpǐn	商品
metal	jīnshǔ	金属
meter (metric)	mǐ	米
meter (taxi)	jìjiàqì	计价器
method	fāngfǎ	方法
metric ton	gōngdūn	公吨
Mickey Mouse	Mǐlǎoshǔ	米老鼠
microphone	huàtǒng	话筒
midnight	bànyè	半夜
mile	yīnglǐ	英里
military	jūnshì	军事
military band	jūnyuèduì	军乐队
milk	niúnǎi	牛奶
Milky Way	Yínhé	银河
milliliter	háoshēng	毫升
millimeter	háomǐ	毫米
million	bǎiwàn	百万
mind (brain)	tóunǎo	头脑
mine (my)	wǒde	我的
mineral water	kuàngquán shuǐ	矿泉水
Ming Tombs	Shísānlíng	十三陵
mini-bus	miànbāochē	面包车
miniature bottle painting	bíyānhú	鼻烟壶
miniature carving	wēidiāo	微雕
mink	shuǐdiāo	水貂
Minolta	Měinéngdá	美能达
minorities' dance	mínzú wǔdǎo	民族舞蹈
minority nationality	shǎoshù mínzú	少数民族
minute (n)	fēnzhōng	分钟
mirror (n)	jìngzi	镜子
miscellaneous	záwù, záshì	杂务, 杂事
mischievous	táoqì	淘气
Miss	xiǎojiě	小姐
mistake (n)	cuòwù	错误
mistake (v)	nòngcuò, gǎocuò	弄错, 搞错
Mitsubishi	Sānlíng	三菱
model (of an object)	móxíng	模型
model (person)	mótèr	模特儿
modern (advanced)	xiàndài	现代
modern (style)	xiàndàipài	现代派
modernization	xiàndàihuà	现代化
monastery	sì, sìyuàn	寺, 寺院
Monday	xīngqī yī	星期一
money	qián	钱
money order	huìpiào	汇票

Mongolian hot pot	shuànyángròu	涮羊肉
monk	héshàng	和尚
monkey	hóuzi	猴子
monster	móguǐ, guàiwù	魔鬼，怪物
month	yuè	月
monthly ticket (bus, subway)	yuèpiào	月票
monument	jìniànbēi	纪念碑
moon	yuèliang, yuè	月亮，月
mop (n)	tuōbǎ	拖把
mop (v)	tuōdì	拖地
more	duō	多
morning	zǎochen, shàngwǔ	早晨，上午
morphine	mǎfēi	吗啡
Moscow	Mòsīkē	莫斯科
Moslem	qīngzhēn	清真
mosque	qīngzhēn sì	清真寺
mosquito	wénzi	蚊子
most (comparative)	zuì	最
most (majority of)	dà duōshù	大多数
mother	mǔqin	母亲
motor	mǎdá	马达
Mount Everest	Zhūmùlǎngmǎ fēng	珠穆朗玛峰
mountain	shān	山
mountaineering	dēngshān	登山
mounting	zhuāngbiǎo	装裱
mouth	zuǐ	嘴
mouth organ, Chinese	shēng	笙
mouthwash	shùkǒu jì	漱口剂
move aside (objects)	bānkāi	搬开
move aside (people)	ràngkāi	让开
movement (music)	yuèzhāng	乐章
movie	diànyǐng	电影
movie camera	diànyǐng shèxiàngjī	电影摄像机
movie star	yǐngxīng	影星
Mr.	xiānsheng	先生
Mrs.	tàitai, fūrén	太太，夫人
Ms.	nǚshì	女士
MSG	wèijīng	味精
much	duō	多
mug	bēizi	杯子
mulberry tree	sāngshù	桑树
multiply	chéng	乘
mung bean	lǜdòu	绿豆
mural	bìhuà	壁画
muscle	jīròu	肌肉
museum	bówùguǎn	博物馆
mushroom	mógu	蘑菇

music	yīnyuè	音乐
musical (show)	gēwǔ jù	歌舞剧
musical instrument	yuèqì	乐器
musical staff, 5-line	wǔxiàn pǔ	五线谱
must	bìxū	必须
mustard (condiment)	jièmo	芥末
mustard, leaf	jiècài	芥菜
musty	fāméi	发霉
mutton	yángròu	羊肉
my	wǒde	我的
My God!	Wǒde tiān!	我的天!
nail (hardware)	dīngzi	钉子
name (n)	míngzi	名字
napkin, paper	cānjīn zhǐ	餐巾纸
narcissus	shuǐxiān	水仙
narrow	xiázhǎi	狭窄
nasal congestion	bízi bù tōng	鼻子不通
national (adj)	guójiā	国家
national anthem	guógē	国歌
national defense	guófáng	国防
national emblem	guóhuī	国徽
national flag	guóqí	国旗
national guide	quánpéi	全陪
nationality (ethnic)	mínzú	民族
native place (ancestral)	lǎojiā	老家
natural	zìrán	自然
nature (character)	xìnggé	性格
nature (outdoors)	dà zìrán	大自然
nauseous	ěxīn	恶心
navy	hǎijūn	海军
near	jìn	近
nearest	zuìjìn	最近
neck	bózi	脖子
necklace	xiàngliàn	项链
need	xūyào, yào	需要, 要
needle	zhēn	针
needle and thread	zhēnxiàn	针线
needlework	zhēnxiàn huó	针线活
negative (film)	dǐpiàn	底片
neighbor	línjū	邻居
Neolithic era	xīn shíqì shídài	新石器时代
Nepal	Níbó'ěr	尼泊尔
nerve	shénjīng	神经
nervous (mood)	jǐnzhāng	紧张
Nescafe	Quècháo	雀巢
neurology	shénjīng bìngxué	神经病学
neurosis	shénjīngzhì	神经质

never	yǒng bù	永不
never again	zài yě bù	再也不
never have	cóng méi	从没
new	xīn	新
New Wave	xīncháo	新潮
New Year	xīnnián, yuándàn	新年，元旦
New Year painting	niánhuà	年画
New York	Niǔyuē	纽约
New Zealand	Xīnxīlán	新西兰
New Zealand dollar	Xīnxīlán yuán	新西兰元
news	xīnwén, xiāoxi	新闻，消息
news program	xīnwén jiémù	新闻节目
newspaper	bàozhǐ	报纸
newsstand	bàotíng, bàotàn	报亭，报摊
next (forthcoming)	xiàyígè, xiàmiàn de	下一个，下面的
next stop	xiàzhàn	下站
next time	xià cì	下次
next to (at the side of)	zài...pángbiān	在……旁边
next year	míngnián	明年
nice	hǎo, bú cuò	好，不错
night	yèwǎn	夜晚
night bus	yèbān chē	夜班车
night market	yèshì	夜市
night shift	yèbān	夜班
nightlife	yè shēnghuó	夜生活
nightstand	chuángtóuguì	床头柜
Nikon	Níkāng	尼康
nine	jiǔ	九
ninety	jiǔshí	九十
Nissan	Nísāng	尼桑
noisy	chǎo	吵
nonstaple food	fùshí pǐn	副食品
noodles	miàntiáo	面条
noon	zhōngwǔ	中午
north	běi	北
North America	Běiměizhōu	北美洲
North Pole	Běijí	北极
North Star	Běijí xīng	北极星
nose	bízi	鼻子
not	bù, méi	不，没
not bad	bú cuò	不错
novel (n)	xiǎoshuō	小说
November	shíyīyuè	十一月
now	xiànzài	现在
nuclear	hé	核
numb	má	麻
number (numeral)	hàomǎ	号码
number (quantity)	shùzì	数字

nurse (n)	hùshì	护士
nursery school	tuō'érsuǒ	托儿所
o'clock	diǎnzhōng	点钟
oatmeal	màipiàn	麦片
object (thing)	dōngxi	东西
observation ward	guānchá shì	观察室
ocean	hǎiyáng	海洋
October	shíyuè	十月
of course	dāngrán	当然
office	bàngōngshì	办公室
often	jīngcháng	经常
Oh well (forget it)	suànle	算了
oil	yóu	油
oil (petroleum)	shíyóu	石油
oil painting	yóuhuà	油画
ointment	ruǎngāo	软膏
okay	xíng	行
old (aged)	lǎo	老
old (used)	jiù	旧
old age	lǎonián	老年
old man	lǎo dàye	老大爷
old town (section of a city)	lǎochéng, jiùchéng	老城，旧城
oleander	jiāzhútáo	夹竹桃
olive	gǎnlǎn	橄榄
Olympic Games	Àoyùnhuì	奥运会
omelet	dànjiǎo	蛋饺
one	yī	一
one-child policy	dúshēng zǐnǚ zhèngcè	独生子女政策
one-way street	dānxíng xiàn	单行线
one-way ticket	dānchéng piào	单程票
onion	cōngtóu	葱头
only	zhǐ	只
oolong tea	wūlóng chá	乌龙茶
open	kāi	开
open for business	kāimén	开门
open-dated ticket	bú dìngqī piào	不定期票
opera	gējù	歌剧
opera mask	xìjù liǎnpǔ	戏剧脸谱
opera singer (Chinese opera)	xìjù yǎnyuán	戏剧演员
opera singer (Western opera)	gējù yǎnyuán	歌剧演员
operation room	shǒushù shì	手术室
operator (phone)	zǒngjī	总机
opinion	yìjiàn	意见
opium	yāpiàn	鸦片
opportunity	jīhuì	机会

opthamologist	yǎnkē yīshēng	眼科医生
opthamology department	yǎnkē	眼科
or	huòzhě, háishì	或者，还是
orange (color)	júhuáng	桔黄
orange (fruit)	gānjú, guǎnggān	柑桔，广柑
orange juice	júzi zhī	桔子汁
orange soda	júzi shuǐ	桔子水
orchestra	jiāoxiǎng yuèduì	交响乐队
orchestra, traditional Chinese	mínzú yuèduì	民族乐队
orchid	lánhuā	兰花
order (command)	mìnglìng	命令
order (for purchase)	dìnggòu	订购
order (sequence)	cìxù	次序
order food	diǎncài	点菜
original (n)	yuánzuò, yuánjiàn	原作，原件
ornament	zhuāngshì	装饰
other	biéde	别的
otter	shuǐtǎ	水獭
ounce	àngsī	盎司
our	wǒmende	我们的
outlet (electrical)	chāzuò	插座
outside	wài	外
outstanding	chūsè	出色
overcoat	dàyī	大衣
overpass	tiānqiáo	天桥
overseas Chinese	huáqiáo	华侨
overseas edition	hǎiwài bǎn	海外版
overture (music)	xùqǔ	序曲
overworked (tired)	láolèi	劳累
owe	qiàn	欠
own	yǒu	有
ox	niú	牛
oxygen	yǎngqì	氧气
oyster	háo	蚝
oyster sauce	háoyóu	蚝油
Pacific Ocean	Tàipíngyáng	太平洋
pack (v)	zhuāng	装
pack suitcases	dǎ xíngli	打行李
package (n)	bāoguǒ	包裹
packaging tape	mìfēng jiāodài	密封胶带
pagoda	tǎ	塔
paid	yǐfù	已付
pain (physical)	téng	疼
pain-killer	zhǐténg yào	止疼药
paint (a picture)	huàhuà	画画
painter (artist)	huàjiā	画家

painting (art)	huìhuà	绘画
painting, traditional Chinese	guóhuà	国画
pajama	shuìyī	睡衣
palace	gōngdiàn	宫殿
palpitation	xīntiào	心跳
pancake (for Peking Duck)	báobǐng	薄饼
panda	xióngmāo	熊猫
pantomime	yǎjù	哑剧
pants	kùzi	裤子
paper	zhǐ	纸
paper clip	zhǐjiā	纸夹
papercut (folk art)	jiǎnzhǐ	剪纸
parade (military)	yuèbīng	阅兵
parasol tree, Chinese	wútóngshù	梧桐树
parcel	bāoguǒ	包裹
pardon (an offense)	ráoshù	饶恕
parents	fùmǔ	父母
Paris	Bālí	巴黎
park (a vehicle)	tíng	停
park, public	gōngyuán	公园
parking lot (bikes)	cúnchē chù	存车处
part (not whole)	bùfen	部分
partner	huǒbàn	伙伴
party (gathering)	jùhuì	聚会
party (political)	dǎng	党
party member	dǎngyuán	党员
pass (go beyond)	guò	过
passion	gǎnqíng	感情
passport	hùzhào	护照
past, in the	guòqù	过去
patience	nàixīn	耐心
patient (sick person)	bìngrén	病人
pattern (decorative)	tú'àn	图案
pattern (standard)	guīgé	规格
pavilion	tíngzi	亭子
pay (v)	fùqián	付钱
pea	wāndòu	豌豆
pea-flour cake	wāndòuhuáng	豌豆黄
peace	hépíng	和平
peach	táozi	桃子
peanut	huāshēng	花生
pear	lí	梨
pearl	zhēnzhū	珍珠
Pearl River	Zhūjiāng	珠江
pearl cream	zhēnzhū shuāng	珍珠霜
peasant	nóngmín	农民
pedal (n)	jiǎotàbǎn	脚踏板

peddler	xiǎofàn	小贩
pedestrian	xíngrén	行人
pediatrician	érkē yīshēng	儿科医生
pediatrics department	érkē	儿科
peel (n)	pí	皮
peel (v)	xiāopí	削皮
Peking duck	Běijīng kǎoyā	北京烤鸭
pen (ball-point)	yuánzhūbǐ	圆珠笔
pen (fountain)	gāngbǐ	钢笔
pencil	qiānbǐ	铅笔
penicillin	qīngméisù	青霉素
peony	mǔdān	牡丹
people (of a nation)	rénmín	人民
People's Daily	Rénmín Rìbào	人民日报
pepper (ground)	hújiāo fěn	胡椒粉
pepper, green	qīngjiāo	青椒
pepper, hot	làjiāo	辣椒
percent	bǎi fēn zhī...	百分之……
percussion instrument	dǎjī yuèqì	打击乐器
performer	biǎoyǎnzhě	表演者
perhaps	yěxǔ	也许
permanent wave	tàngfà	烫发
permission	xǔkě, yǔnxǔ	许可, 允许
persimmon	shìzi	柿子
person	rén	人
person-to-person (phone)	jiàorén	叫人
personal effects	sīrén cáichǎn	私人财产
personality	xìnggé	性格
petroleum	shíyóu	石油
Peugeot	Báirú	白茹
pharmacist	yàojì shī	药剂师
pharmacy	yàofáng	药房
Philadelphia	Fèichéng	费城
Philippines	Fēilǜbīn	菲律宾
phoenix	fènghuáng	凤凰
phone (see telephone)	diànhuà	电话
photo album	yǐngjí, xiàngcè	影集, 像册
photograph (n)	zhàopiàn	照片
photograph (v)	zhàoxiàng	照相
photographer	shèyǐng shī	摄影师
photography	shèyǐng	摄影
physics	wùlǐ	物理
piano	gāngqín	钢琴
pick (select)	tiāo	挑
pick up (get)	qǔ	取
pick up (meet)	jiē	接
pick up (retrieve from ground)	jiǎn	捡

pickled cabbage, hot	là báicài	辣白菜
pickled cucumber	suān huánggua	酸黄瓜
pickled mustard tuber, hot	zhàcài	榨菜
pickled vegetables	pàocài	泡菜
pictorial (magazine)	huàbào	画报
picture	túhuà	图画
picture book	huàcè	画册
piece (n)	kuài, jiàn, gè	块,件,个
pig	zhū	猪
pigeon	gēzi	鸽子
pill	yàowán	药丸
pillar	zhùzi	柱子
pillow	zhěntou	枕头
pillowcase	zhěntou tào	枕头套
pilose antler	lùróng	鹿茸
pilot (airplane)	fēixíngyuán	飞行员
pin (straight pin)	dàtóuzhēn	大头针
pine (tree)	sōngshù	松树
pineapple	bōluó	菠萝
ping-pong	pīngpāng qiú	乒乓球
Pingju Opera	píngjù	评剧
pink	fěnsè	粉色
pint	pǐntuō	品脱
place (n)	dìfang	地方
place of interest	kěkàn de dìfang	可看的地方
plains	píngyuán	平原
plan	jìhuà, dǎsuàn	计划,打算
plane	fēijī	飞机
plant (botanical)	zhíwù	植物
plaster (medicated)	gāoyào	膏药
plate (dish)	pánzi	盘子
plateau	gāoyuán	高原
platform	píngtái	平台
platform (train station)	yuètái	月台
play (a game)	wán	玩
play (sports: hit)	dǎ	打
play (sports: kick)	tī	踢
play (theater)	huàjù	话剧
player (in a game)	xuǎnshǒu	选手
player (sports team)	duìyuán	队员
playground	cāochǎng	操场
playwright	jùzuò jiā	剧作家
please...	qǐng...	请⋯⋯
pleased	hěn gāoxìng	很高兴
pliers	qiánzi	钳子
plot (story)	qíngjié	情节
plug (n)	chātóu	插头
plum	lǐzi	李子

plum blossom	méihuā	梅花
pneumonia	fèiyán	肺炎
poached egg	wòjīdàn, shuǐpūdàn	卧鸡蛋，水浦蛋
pocket	dōu, kǒudài	兜，口袋
pocket-size	xiùzhēn	袖珍
poet	shīrén	诗人
poetry	shī	诗
poker (game)	pūkè	扑克
Polaroid camera	yīcì chéngxiàng jī	一次成相机
Polaroid film	Pāilìdé xiàngzhǐ	拍立得相纸
police	jǐngchà	警察
police station	pàichūsuǒ	派出所
policy	zhèngcè	政策
polite	yǒu lǐmào	有礼貌
political bureau	zhèngzhìjú	政治局
politics	zhèngzhì	政治
polo	mǎqiú	马球
polyester (fiber)	qínglún	晴纶
pomegranate	shíliu	石榴
pomelo (grapefruit)	yòuzi	柚子
poor (not good)	bù hǎo	不好
poor (not rich)	qióng	穷
popular music	liúxíngqǔ	流行曲
porcelain	cíqì	瓷器
pork	zhūròu	猪肉
pork chop	zhūpái	猪排
porridge	zhōu	粥
port city	gǎngwān chéngshì	港湾城市
portable	biànxiéshì	便携式
porter	xíngli yuán	行李员
portrait	xiàoxiàng	肖像
portray	sùzào	塑造
possibility	kěnéng xìng	可能性
possible	kěnéng	可能
post (to mail)	jì	寄
post office	yóujú	邮局
postcard	míngxìnpiàn	明信片
poster	zhāotiēhuà	招贴画
pot (pan)	guō	锅
Potala Palace	Bùdálā gōng	布达拉宫
potato	tǔdòu	土豆
pottery	táoqì	陶器
pound (weight)	bàng	磅
pound sterling	yīngbàng	英磅
powder	fěnmò	粉末
power (authority)	quánlì	权力
power (energy)	néngyuán	能源
power (force)	lìliàng	力量

practical (realistic)	shíjì	实际
practical (useful)	shíyòng	实用
practice (v)	liànxí	练习
prawn	dàxiā	大虾
pray	qídǎo	祈祷
prefer	gèng xǐhuān	更喜欢
pregnant	huáiyùn	怀孕
premier	zǒnglǐ	总理
prepare	zhǔnbèi	准备
prescription	yàofāng	药方
present (current)	mùqián	目前
president (corporate)	zǒngcái	总裁
president (national)	zǒngtǒng	总统
press (clothing)	tàng	烫
press (push down)	àn	按
pretty	piàoliàng	漂亮
pride	zìháo, jiāo'ào	自豪, 骄傲
principal (school)	xiàozhǎng	校长
print (art)	bǎnhuà	版画
print (photo)	xiàngpiàn	相片
print (v)	yìn	印
printed matter	yìnshuā pǐn	印刷品
private	sīrén	私人
probably	dàgài	大概
problem	wèntí	问题
process (n)	guòchéng	过程
producer	shēngchǎnzhě	生产者
product	chǎnpǐn	产品
production	shēngchǎn	生产
profession	zhíyè, hángyè	职业, 行业
professor	jiàoshòu	教授
program (event)	jiémù	节目
program (theater handout)	jiémù dān	节目单
prohibited	jìnzhǐ	禁止
promise (n)	nuòyán	诺言
promise (v)	dāying	答应
prop (stage accessory)	dàojù	道具
province	shěng	省
provincial museum	shěng bówùguǎn	省博物馆
prune	lǐzi pǔ	李子脯
psychiatrist	jīngshénbìng yīshēng	精神病医生
psychologist	xīnlǐxuéjiā	心理学家
psychology	xīnlǐxué	心理学
psychosis	jīngshénbìng	精神病
pub	jiǔguǎn	酒馆
public	gōnggòng	公共
Public Security Bureau	gōng'ānjú	公安局
public bus	gōnggòng qìchē	公共汽车

public relations	gōnggòng guānxì	公共关系
public square	guǎngchǎng	广场
Puer tea	Pǔ'ěr chá	普洱茶
pull	lā	拉
pullover	tàotóu shān	套头衫
pulse	màibó	脉搏
punk	péngkè	朋客
puppet show	mù'ǒu xì	木偶戏
pure	chún	纯
purple	zǐsè	紫色
purpose	mùdì	目的
purse	qiánbāo	钱包
push	tuī	推
put	fàng	放
put away (in place)	fànghǎo	放好
Qin Emperor	Qínshǐhuáng	秦始皇
quail	ānchún	鹌鹑
quality	zhìliàng	质量
quantity	shùliàng	数量
quarantine	jiǎnyì	检疫
quart	kuātuō	夸脱
quarter (one-fourth)	sìfēn zhīyī	四分之一
quarter hour	kè, kèzhōng	刻, 刻钟
quartet	sìchóngzòu	四重奏
question (n)	wèntí	问题
question (v)	tíwèn	提问
quick	kuài	快
quiet	ānjìng	安静
quilt	bèizi	被子
quinine	kuíníng	奎宁
quite	xiāngdāng	相当
quota	dìng'é	定额
rabbit	tùzi	兔子
racket (paddle)	qiúpāi	球拍
radiator	nuǎnqì	暖气
radio (broadcast)	guǎngbō	广播
radio (machine)	shōuyīnjī	收音机
radio program	guǎngbō jiémù	广播节目
radiologist	fàngshèkē yīshī	放射科医师
radish	xiǎo luóbo	小罗卜
railroad	tiělù	铁路
railway station	huǒchēzhàn	火车站
rain (n)	yǔ	雨
rain (v)	xiàyǔ	下雨
rain poncho	yǔpī	雨披
rainbow	cǎihóng	彩虹

raincoat	yǔyī	雨衣
raise (lift up)	tái qǐlai	抬起来
raisin	pútáo gān	葡萄干
ram	yáng, shānyáng	羊, 山羊
ramie	zhùmá	苎麻
rape (vegetable)	yóucài	油菜
rash (on skin)	pízhěn	皮疹
rat	lǎoshǔ	老鼠
rate (price)	jiàgé	价格
rather (prefer to)	nìngyuàn	宁愿
ratio	bǐlì	比例
ravioli (boiled dumplings)	jiǎozi	饺子
rayon	rénzào sī	人造丝
razor	tìdāo	剃刀
razor blade	dāopiàn	刀片
read	dú, kàn	读, 看
read aloud	niàn	念
read books	kàn shū	看书
real	zhēn	真
real estate agent	dìchǎn jīngjìrén	地产经纪人
really	zhēn	真的
reason (cause)	yuányīn	原因
reason (logic)	dàoli	道理
receipt (sales slip)	fāpiào	发票
receive (goods)	shōu	收
recently	jìnlái	近来
reception	jiēdài	接待
reception desk	jiēdài chù	接待处
reception personnel	jiēdài rényuán	接待人员
reception room	jiēdài shì	接待室
recipe (cooking)	shípǔ	食谱
recipient	shōujiàn rén, duìfāng	收件人, 对方
recite	bèi	背
recommend	tuījiàn	推荐
record store	yīnxiǎng ménshìbù	音响门市部
recreation room	yúlè shì	娱乐室
red	hóng	红
red-crowned crane	dāndǐnghè	丹顶鹤
red paste (for seals)	yìnní	印泥
red wine	hóngjiǔ	红酒
reference (for study)	cānkǎo	参考
reform	gǎigé	改革
refreshment (cold drinks)	lěngyǐn	冷饮
refreshment (snacks)	xiǎochī	小吃
refreshment stand	xiǎochī tān	小吃摊
refrigerator	bīngxiāng	冰箱
refund	péicháng, péi	赔偿, 赔
region	dìqū	地区

register	dēngjì	登记
registered (mail)	guàhào	挂号
registration desk	dēngjì chù	登记处
registration office (hospital)	guàhào chù	挂号处
regret	hòuhuǐ	后悔
regulation	guīdìng	规定
rehearsal	páiliàn	排练
relative (kin)	qīnqī	亲戚
relatives (kinfolk)	qīnshǔ	亲属
relevance	guānxi	关系
relief (sculpture)	fúdiāo	浮雕
remain (stay)	liú	留
remember	jìde	记得
Renault	Léinuò	雷诺
rent (v)	zū	租
rental fee	zūjīn	租金
repair	xiūlǐ	修理
repeat	chóngfù	重复
reprint (v)	jiāyìn	加印
reproduction (replica)	fùzhìpǐn	复制品
request	yāoqiú	要求
reroute	gǎihuàn	改换
research institute	yánjiūsuǒ	研究所
resemble	xiàng	象
reservations desk	yùdìng chù	预订处
reserve (v)	yùdìng	预订
reside	zhù	住
residence permit	jūliú zhèng	居留证
respect	zūnjìng	尊敬
rest (relax)	xiūxi	休息
restaurant	fànguǎn, cāntīng	饭馆，餐厅
result	jiéguǒ	结果
retail	língshòu	零售
retired worker	tuìxiū gōngrén	退休工人
return (come back)	huí	回
return (give back)	huán	还
return (merchandise)	tuì	退
reunion	tuánjù	团聚
review (critique)	pínglùn	评论
review (study again)	fùxí	复习
revolution	gémìng	革命
rheumatism	fēngshī bìng	风湿病
rib (n)	lèigǔ	肋骨
rice (cooked)	mǐfàn	米饭
rice (crop)	dàozi	稻子
rice congee	xīfàn	稀饭
rice paper	xuānzhǐ	宣纸

rich (prosperous)	fù	富
ride (a bicycle)	qí	骑
ride (a car)	zuò	坐
ride (an animal)	qí	骑
right (correct)	duì	对
right (direction)	yòu	右
right away	mǎshàng	马上
ring (jewelry)	jièzhi	戒指
riot	bàoluàn	暴乱
rise (go up, increase)	shàngshēng	上升
river	hé, jiāng	河, 江
road	lù, mǎlù	路, 马路
roadside	lùbiān	路边
roast (v)	kǎo	烤
roast pork bun	chāshāo bāo	叉烧包
roast suckling pig	rǔzhū	乳猪
rock-and-roll	yáogǔn yuè	摇滚乐
roll (n)	juǎn	卷
Rome	Luómǎ	罗马
roof	fángdǐng	房顶
room (in a building)	fángjiān	房间
room number	fánghào	房号
roommate	tóngwū	同屋
rooster	gōngjī	公鸡
rope skipping (Chinese)	tiào píjīn	跳皮筋
rose (flower)	méiguihuā	玫瑰花
rose, Chinese	yuèjì	月季
rough	cūcāo	粗糙
round (shape)	yuán	圆
round-trip ticket	láihuí piào	来回票
route	lu	路
row (column, line)	pái	排
rowboat	huátǐng	小船
rowing (sport)	huáchuán	划船
rubbing alcohol	yīyòng jiǔjīng	医用酒精
rude	cūbào	粗暴
rug	dìtǎn	地毯
ruins	yízhǐ	遗址
ruler (measuring stick)	chǐzi	尺子
runny nose	liú bíti	流鼻涕
rural	nóngcūn	农村
rush service	jiājí fúwù	加急服务
Russian (language)	Éyǔ	俄语
rusty	xiù le	锈了
sable	zǐdiāo	紫貂
Sacred Way	shéndào	神道
safety pin	biézhēn	别针

salad	shālā	沙拉
salary	gōngzī	工资
sales counter	shòuhuò tái, guìtái	售货台，柜台
sales manager	xiāoshòu jīnglǐ	销售经理
salesperson	tuīxiāoyuán	推销员
saline solution	shēnglǐ yánshuǐ	生理盐水
saliva	kǒushuǐ	口水
salt	yán	盐
salted duck egg	xián yādàn	咸鸭蛋
salty	xián	咸
same	yíyàng	一样
sample good	yàngpǐn	样品
San Francisco	Jiùjīnshān	旧金山
sand	shāzi	沙子
sandals	liángxié	凉鞋
sandalwood fan	tánxiāng shàn	檀香扇
sandwich	sānmíngzhì	三明治
sanitary napkin	wèishēng jīn	卫生巾
Santana	Sāngtǎnà	桑塔纳
satellite	wèixīng	卫星
satisfied	mǎnyì	满意
satisfy	mǎnzú	满足
Saturday	xīngqī liù	星期六
sauce	jiàng	酱
sausage	xiāngcháng	香肠
sauteed	chǎo	炒
say	shuō	说
scallion	cōng	葱
scallop	gànbèi	干贝
scarf	wéijīn	围巾
scarlet fever	xīnghóngrè	猩红热
scenery	fēngjǐng	风景
schedule (timetable)	shíkè biǎo	时刻表
schizophrenia	jīngshén fēnliè zhèng	精神分裂症
school	xuéxiào	学校
school (of thought)	liúpài	流派
science	kēxué	科学
scientist	kēxuéjiā	科学家
scissors	jiǎndāo	剪刀
scrambled eggs	chǎo jīdàn	炒鸡蛋
screen (n)	píngfēng	屏风
screw (n)	luósīdīng	螺丝钉
screwdriver	luósīdāo	螺丝刀
script (play or film)	jiǎoběn	脚本
sculptor	diāosù jiā	雕塑家
sculpture	diāosù	雕塑
sea	hǎi	海
sea cucumber	hǎishēn	海参

seafood	hǎixiān	海鲜
season (n)	jìjié	季节
seat (n)	zuòwèi	座位
seat number	zuòhào	座号
seatbelt	ānquándài	安全带
second (fraction of time)	miǎo	秒
secret	mìmì	秘密
secretariat	shūjìchù	书记处
secretary, office	mìshū	秘书
security guard	ānquán rényuán	安全人员
see	kànjiàn	看见
see off	sòng	送
See you later	huítóujiàn	回头见
seems	hǎoxiàng	好象
self	zìjǐ, zìgěr	自己，自个儿
self-portrait	zìhuàxiàng	自画像
self-timer (camera)	zìpāi	自拍
sell	mài	卖
seminar	yántǎohuì	研讨会
send a telegram	fā diànbào	发电报
send a telex	fā diànchuán	发电传
senior citizen	lǎoniánrén	老年人
sentence (n)	jùzi	句子
Seoul	Hànchéng	汉城
September	jiǔyuè	九月
serious (earnest)	rènzhēn	认真
serious (grave)	yánzhòng	严重
servant	púrén	仆人
service	fúwù	服务
service attendant	fúwùyuán	服务员
service desk	fúwùtái	服务台
service fee	fúwùfèi	服务费
service, religious	lǐbài	礼拜
sesame biscuit	shāobǐng	烧饼
sesame oil	máyóu	麻油
set (matching pieces)	tào	套
set (theater)	bùjǐng	布景
set design	bùjǐng shèjì	布景设计
settle the bill	jiézhàng	结帐
seven	qī	七
seventy	qīshí	七十
several	hǎo jǐgè	好几个
sew	féng	缝
sex	xìng	性
shadow	yǐng	影
shadow puppet	píyǐng	皮影
shake hands	wòshǒu	握手
shampoo	xiāngbō	香波

Shanghai Opera	hùjù	沪剧
Shangri-La	Xiānggélǐlā	香格里拉
Shaoxing Opera	yuèjù, shàoxīng xì	越剧, 绍兴戏
Shaoxing rice wine	Shàoxīng jiāfàn jiǔ	绍兴加饭酒
share (an expense)	fēntān	分摊
shark's fin soup	yúchì tāng	鱼翅汤
sharp (edge)	fēnglì	锋利
shattered	suì le	碎了
shave	guāliǎn	刮脸
shaver, electric	diàn tìdāo	电剃刀
she	tā	她
sheep	yáng	羊
sheet (of paper)	zhāng	张
sheets (linen)	chuángdān	床单
shelf	jiàzi	架子
shell mosaic	bèidiāohuà	贝雕画
Sheraton	xǐláidēng	喜来登
shiny	shǎnguāng	闪光
ship (n)	chuán	船
ship (v)	hǎiyùn	海运
shipping company	hángyùn gōngsī	航运公司
shirt	chènshān	衬衫
shiver	fādǒu	发抖
shock (n)	xiūkè	休克
shoe	xié	鞋
shoe polish	xiéyóu	鞋油
shoehorn	xiébázi	鞋拔子
shoelaces	xiédài	鞋带
shooting (sport)	shèjī	射击
shop (n)	shāngdiàn, pùzi	商店, 铺子
shopping	mǎi dōngxi	买东西
short (height)	ǎi	矮
short (length)	duǎn	短
should	yīnggāi	应该
shoulder (n)	jiānbǎng	肩膀
shoulder bag	bēibāo	背包
show (performance)	biǎoyǎn, yǎnchū	表演, 演出
show (to demonstrate)	shìfàn	示范
shower	línyù	淋浴
shower cap	línyù mào	淋浴帽
shredded dried meat	ròusōng	肉松
shrimp	xiā	虾
shrine	jìtán	祭坛
shut	guān, bì	关, 闭
shutter (camera)	kuàimén	快门
Siberia	Xībólìyà	西伯利亚
sickness	bìng	病
side (body)	cèlèi	侧肋

side (margin)	biān	边
sidewalk	rénxíngdào	人行道
sightsee	guānguāng, yóulǎn	观光,游览
sign (notice board)	páizi	牌子
sign (symbol)	biāojì	标记
signature	qiānmíng	签名
silent	wúshēng	无声
silk (pure)	zhēnsī	真丝
Silk Road	sīchóu zhīlù	丝绸之路
silk and brocade factory	sīzhī chǎng	丝织厂
silk cocoon factory	sāosī chǎng	缫丝厂
silk fabric	sīchóu	丝绸
silk mill	sīchóu chǎng	丝绸厂
silk products shop	sīchóu shāngdiàn	丝绸商店
silkworm	cán	蚕
silver	yín	银
simulate	mónǐ	模拟
sing	chànggē	唱歌
Singapore	Xīnjiāpō	新加坡
singer	gēchàng jiā	歌唱家
single room	dānjiān	单间
sink	shuǐchízi	水池子
sister (older)	jiějie	姐姐
sister (younger)	mèimei	妹妹
sit	zuò	坐
six	liù	六
sixty	liùshí	六十
size (measurement)	chǐcùn, guīgé	尺寸,规格
size (number)	hào	号
sketch (art)	sùxiě	速写
sketch (design draft)	cǎotú	草图
skiing	huáxuě	滑雪
skill	jìqiǎo	技巧
skin	pífū	皮肤
skirt	qúnzi	裙子
sky	tiānkōng	天空
sky-diving	tiàosǎn	跳伞
sleep (v)	shuìjiào	睡觉
sleeping pill	ānmián yào	安眠药
slice (n)	piàn	片
slide (photo)	huàndēng piàn	幻灯片
slide film	fǎnzhuǎn piàn	反转片
slide mount	huàndēngpiàn kuàng	幻灯片框
slip (petticoat)	chènqún	衬裙
slippers	tuōxié	拖鞋
slow	màn	慢
small	xiǎo	小
smell (n)	wèidao, wèi	味道,味

smell (v)	wén	闻
smile	wēixiào	微笑
smoke cigarettes	chōuyān	抽烟
smoked fish	xūnyú	熏鱼
snack	xiǎochī, diǎnxin	小吃,点心
snake	shé	蛇
snow (n)	xuě	雪
snow (v)	xiàxuě	下雪
snow mountain	xuěshān	雪山
snow peas	xuědòu	雪豆
snuff bottle	bíyānhú	鼻烟壶
snuff box	bíyānhé	鼻烟盒
so (therefore)	suǒyǐ	所以
so-so	yìbān, mǎmǎhūhū	一般,马马虎虎
soap (n)	féizào	肥皂
soccer	zúqiú	足球
soccer match	zúqiú bǐsài	足球比赛
social dancing	jiāojì wǔ	交际舞
sociology	shèhuìxué	社会学
socket (electrical)	chāzuò	插座
socks	wàzi	袜子
soda pop	qìshuǐ	汽水
soda water	sūdá shuǐ	苏打水
sofa	shāfā	沙发
soft-seat	ruǎnxí	软席
soft-sleeper	ruǎnwò	软卧
softball	lěiqiú	垒球
soil (n)	tǔ, tǔrǎng	土,土壤
soldier	shìbīng, jūnrén	士兵,军人
solo (dance)	dúwǔ	独舞
solo (instrumental)	dúzòu	独奏
solo (vocal)	dúchàng	独唱
solution (method)	bànfǎ	办法
solve	jiějué	解决
some	yìxiē	一些
sometimes	yǒushí	有时
son	érzi	儿子
sonata	zòumíngqǔ	奏鸣曲
song	gēqǔ	歌曲
song-and-dance	gēwǔ	歌舞
song-and-dance troupe	gēwǔ tuán	歌舞团
Sony	Suǒní	索尼
soon	mǎshàng, yìhuǐr	马上,一会儿
sore (ache)	fāsuān, suān	发酸,酸
sore throat	hóulóng téng	喉咙疼
soreness	suānténg	酸疼
sorghum	gāoliáng	高粱
sound (n)	shēngyīn	声音

sound effect	yīnxiǎng	音响
soup	tāng	汤
soup noodles	tāngmiàn	汤面
sour	suān	酸
south	nán	南
South America	Nánměizhōu	南美洲
South China Sea	Nánhǎi	南海
Soviet Union	Sūlián	苏联
soy sauce	jiàngyóu	酱油
soybean	huángdòu	黄豆
soybean milk	dòujiāng	豆浆
space	kōngjiān	空间
space shuttle	hángtiān fēijī	航天飞机
spare time	yèyú shíjiān	业余时间
sparerib	páigǔ	排骨
speak	jiǎng	讲
special delivery (mail)	kuàidì	快递
speed limit	xiànsù	限速
spend	huā	花
spicy (hot)	là	辣
spinach	bōcài	菠菜
spine	jǐzhuī	脊椎
splinter (n)	cì	刺
spoke (wheel)	chētiáo	车条
spoon	sháozi	勺子
sporting goods	tǐyù yòngpǐn	体育用品
sports	yùndòng	运动
sports event	yùndòng xiàngmù	运动项目
spotlight	jùguāngdēng	聚光灯
spouse	pèi'ǒu	配偶
sprained	niǔshāng	扭伤
spring (season)	chūntiān	春天
spring roll	chūnjuǎn	春卷
square (area measure)	píngfāng	平方
square (shape)	fāng	方
square meter	píngfāng mǐ	平方米
squid	yóuyú	鱿鱼
stadium	tǐyùchǎng	体育场
stage (n)	wǔtái	舞台
stage (of progress)	jiēduàn	阶段
stainless steel	búxiùgāng	不锈钢
stairs	lóutī	楼梯
stale	bù xīnxiān	不新鲜
stamp (postage)	yóupiào	邮票
stamp collecting	jíyóu	集邮
stand (n)	jiàzi	架子
stand (v)	zhàn	站
standard	biāozhǔn	标准

standing committee	chángwù wěiyuánhuì	常务委员会
star (celebrity)	míngxīng	明星
star (n)	xīngxing	星星
state council	guówùyuàn	国务院
station (depot)	zhàn	站
station-to-station (phone)	jiàohào	叫号
stationery (writing paper)	xìnzhǐ	信纸
statue	sùxiàng, diāoxiàng	塑像，雕像
stay (live, spend time)	dāi	呆
steak (beef)	niúpái	牛排
steam (v)	zhēng	蒸
steamed bun	mántou	馒头
steamed dumpling	baozi	包子
steamed twisted roll	huājuǎn	花卷
steel	gāng	钢
steep (in hot water)	pào	泡
steering wheel	fāngxiàngpán	方向盘
stele	shíbǎn, shízhù	石板，石柱
step (footstep)	bù	步
stereo system	zǔhé yīnxiǎng	组合音响
stew (v)	dùn	炖
stiff	jiāngyìng	僵硬
still (further)	hái	还
still (motionless)	bú dòng, tíngzhǐ	不动，停止
still (yet)	yīrán, réngrán	依然，仍然
still life painting	jìngwù huà	静物画
stir-fry	chǎo	抄
Stockholm	Sīdégē'ěrmó	斯德哥尔摩
stockings	chángtǒng wà	长筒袜
stocks (shares)	gǔpiào	股票
stomach	wèi, dùzi	胃，肚子
stomachache	wèiténg	胃疼
stone (n)	shítou	石头
Stone Forest	Shílín	石林
stone rubbing	tàpiàn	拓片
stop (station)	zhàn	站
stop (v)	tíng	停
store (put away)	cúnfàng	存放
store (shop)	diàn, shāngdiàn	店，商店
storyteller	shuōshū rén	说书人
storytelling	shuōshū	说书
straight	zhí	直
straits (waterway)	hǎixiá	海峡
strange	qíguài	奇怪
stranger (person)	mòshēng rén	陌生人
strawberry	cǎoméi	草莓
street	jiē	街
strength	lìliang, lìqi	力量，力气

strict	yán	严
string (n)	shéngzi	绳子
string bean	sìjìdòu	四季豆
string instrument	xián yuèqì	弦乐器
string quartet	xiányuè sìchóngzòu	弦乐四重奏
striped	yǒu tiáowén de	有条纹的
stroke (paralysis)	zhòngfēng	中风
strong	qiángliè	强烈
struggle	dòuzhēng	斗争
stuck	dǔzhù le	堵住了
student	xuéshēng	学生
study (v)	xué	学
study abroad	liúxué	留学
stuffy (unventilated)	mèn	闷
stupid	bèn, chǔn	笨,蠢
sturdy	jiēshi	结实
style	fēnggé	风格
suburb	jiāoqū	郊区
subway	dìtiě	地铁
subway station	dìtiě chēzhàn	地铁车站
success	chénggōng	成功
sugar	táng	糖
sugar cane	gānzhe	甘蔗
suit (clothing)	xīzhuāng	西装
suitcase	xiāngzi	箱子
suite (room)	tàojiān	套间
sulfa	huáng'ān	磺胺
summer	xiàtiān	夏天
Summer Palace	Yíhéyuán	颐和园
sun	tàiyang	太阳
Sun Yat-sen	Sūn Zhōngshān	孙中山
Sunday	xīngqī rì	星期日
sunlight	yángguāng	阳光
sunrise	rìchū	日出
sunset	rìluò	日落
sunstroke	zhòngshǔ	中暑
supervisor	jiāndū rén	监督人
support (an endeavor)	zhīchí	支持
surface mail	píngxìn	平信
surgeon	wàikē yīshēng	外科医生
surgery	shǒushù	手术
surgery department	wàikē	外科
surprised	jīngyà	惊讶
sutra	fójīng	佛经
swallow (v)	yàn	咽
sweat (n)	hàn	汗
sweat (v)	chūhàn	出汗
sweater	máoyī	毛衣

sweatpants	róngkù	绒裤
sweatshirt	róngyī	绒衣
Sweden	Ruìdiǎn	瑞典
sweep	sǎo	扫
sweet	tián	甜
sweet-and-sour	tángcù	糖醋
sweet-and-sour pork	gǔlǎo ròu	古老肉
sweet potato	báishǔ, shānyù	白薯，山芋
swelling	zhǒngzhàng	肿胀
swim	yóuyǒng	游泳
swimming pool	yóuyǒngchí	游泳池
swimsuit	yóuyǒngyī	游泳衣
swing (playground)	qiūqiān	秋千
switchboard operator	zǒngjī	总机
Switzerland	Ruìshì	瑞士
sword bean	dāodòu	刀豆
Sydney	Xīní	悉尼
symbol	biāozhì	标志
symbolize	xiàngzhěng	象征
sympathetic	tóngqíng	同情
symphony	jiāoxiǎng yuè	交响乐
symphony orchestra	jiāoxiǎng yuèduì	交响乐队
symptom	zhèngzhuàng	症状
synthetic (fiber)	huàxiān	化纤
syrup	tángjiāng	糖浆
system	xìtǒng	系统
T-intersection	dīngzì lukou	丁字路口
T-shirt	duǎnxiù shān	短袖衫
table (n)	zhuōzi	桌子
tablecloth	táibù, zhuōbù	台布，桌布
tablespoon	tāngchí	汤匙
table tennis	pīngpāngqiú	乒乓球
tablet	yàopiàn	药片
taillight	wěidēng	尾灯
tailor (n)	cáifeng	裁缝
Taipei	Táiběi	台北
Taiwan	Táiwǎn	台湾
take (hold)	ná	拿
take (medication)	fúyào	服药
take a picture	zhào zhāng xiàng	照张相
take away	názǒu	拿走
take interest in	duì...gǎn xìngqù	对···感兴趣
take off (flights)	qǐfēi	起飞
talk (converse)	tánhuà, jiāotán	谈话，交谈
tamer	xùnshòu yuán	驯兽员
tampon	wèishēng shuān	卫生栓
Tang figurine (tri-colored)	tángsāncǎi	唐三彩

tangerine	júzi	橘子
tango	tàngē	探戈
Taoism	dàojiào	道教
tap (faucet)	shuǐ lóngtóu	水龙头
tape (cellophane)	tòumíng jiāodài	透明胶带
tape (sound)	lùyīn cídài	录音磁带
tape measure	juǎnchǐ	卷尺
tape recorder	lùyīnjī	录音机
tapestry	bìtǎn	壁毯
taro	yùtou	芋头
taste (n)	wèidao	味道
taste (v)	cháng	尝
tax (n)	shuì	税
taxi (n)	chūzū qìchē	出租汽车
tea	chá	茶
tea plantation (factory)	cháchǎng	茶场
tea set	chájù	茶具
tea shop	cháyè diàn	茶叶店
teach	jiāo	教
teacher	lǎoshī, jiàoshī	老师,教师
teacup	chábēi	茶杯
teapot	cháhú	茶壶
teaspoon	cháchí	小铜勺
technician	jìshùyuán	技术员
telegram	diànbào	电报
telephone (n)	diànhuà	电话
telephone (v)	dǎ diànhuà	打电话
telephone number	diànhuà hàomǎ	电话号码
television	diànshì	电视
television set	diànshìjī	电视机
television station	diànshì tái	电视台
telex	diànchuán	电传
telex call number	diànchuán guàhào	电传挂号
telex machine	diànchuánjī	电传机
tell	gàosù	告诉
temperature (general)	wēndù	温度
temperature (of body)	tǐwēn	体温
temple (Buddhist)	sì, miào	寺,庙
temple (Daoist)	guàn	观
Temple of Heaven	Tiāntán	天坛
ten	shí	十
ten thousand	wàn	万
tendon	jīn	筋
tennis	wǎngqiú	网球
terracotta figure	bīngmǎyǒng	兵马俑
terrible	kěpà, zāogāo	可怕,糟糕
test (exam)	kǎoshì	考试
tetanus	pòshāngfēng	破伤风

textile	fǎngzhī pǐn	纺织品
Thailand	Tàiguó	泰国
thank you	xièxie	谢谢
that	nà	那
that one	nàge, nèige	那个
theater	jùchǎng	剧场
theater troupe	jùtuán	剧团
their	tāmende	他们的
them	tāmen	他们
there	nàli, nàr	那里, 那儿
therefore	yīncǐ	因此
thermal pants	miánmáo kù	棉毛裤
thermal shirt	miánmáo shān	棉毛衫
thermometer	wēndù biǎo	温度表
thermos	nuǎnshuǐpíng	暖水瓶
these	zhèxiē	这些
they	tāmen	他们
thick (coarse)	cū	粗
thick (dense)	nóng	浓
thick (layer)	hòu	厚
thin (layer)	báo	薄
thin (slender)	shòu, xì	瘦, 细
thin (sparse)	xī	稀
thing	dōngxi	东西
think (believe)	rènwéi	认为
thirsty	kě	渴
thirty	sānshí	三十
this	zhè	这
this one	zhège, zhèige	这个
this year	jīnnián	今年
those	nàxiē, nèixiē	那些
thousand	qiān	千
thousand-year egg	pídàn, sōnghuādàn	皮蛋, 松花蛋
thread (n)	xiàn	线
three	sān	三
Three Gorges	Sānxiá	三峡
three delicacies soup	sānxiān tāng	三鲜汤
three-dimensional	lìtǐ	立体
three-prong plug	sānxiàng chātóu	三相插头
throat	hóulóng	喉咙
throw	rēng	扔
throw away	rēng diào	扔掉
thunder	léi	雷
Thursday	xīngqī sì	星期四
Tibet	Xīzàng	西藏
ticket	piào	票
ticket office	shòupiào chù	售票处
ticket seller	shòupiàoyuán	售票员

tie (necktie)	lǐngdài	领带
tie up	kǔn qǐlai	捆起来
tiger	lǎohǔ	老虎
tiger balm	qīngliángyóu	清凉油
tight	jǐn	紧
tile (n)	wǎ	瓦
timber	mùliào	木料
time (n)	shíjiān	时间
time (occasion)	cì	次
time period (historic)	niándài	年代
timer	jìshí qì	计时器
timetable	shíkè biǎo	时刻表
tip (gratuity)	xiǎofèi	小费
tire (wheel)	chētāi	车胎
tired	lèi	累
toast (bread)	kǎo miànbāo	烤面包
today	jīntiān	今天
toe	jiǎozhǐ	脚趾
toilet	cèsuǒ	厕所
toilet paper	wèishēng zhǐ	卫生纸
Tokyo	Dōngjīng	东京
tomato	xīhóngshì, fānqié	西红柿,番茄
tomato sauce	fānqié jiàng	番茄酱
tomb	fénmù	坟墓
tombs, imperial	líng	陵
tomorrow	míngtiān	明天
ton	dūn	吨
tongue	shétou	舌头
tonight	jīnwǎn	今晚
too (also)	yě	也
too (excessive)	tài	太
tool	gōngjù	工具
tooth	yá	牙
toothache	yáténg	牙疼
toothbrush	yáshuā	牙刷
toothpaste	yágāo	牙膏
toothpick	yáqiān	牙签
top (height)	dǐng	顶
torn	pòle	破了
Toronto	Duōlúnduō	多伦多
tortoise	wūguī	乌龟
touch-me-not	fèngxiānhuā	凤仙花
tour escort	lǐngduì	领队
tour group	lǚyóu tuán	旅游团
tourist	lǚkè	旅客
tournament	bǐsài	比赛
toward	wǎng, xiàng	往,向
towel	máojīn	毛巾

town	zhèn	镇
township	xiāng	乡
toy	wánjù	玩具
toy store	wánjù diàn	玩具店
Toyota	Fēngtián	丰田
track and field	tiánjìng	田径
tractor	tuōlājī	拖拉机
trade (business)	màoyì	贸易
traditional	chuántǒng	传统
traffic	jiāotōng	交通
traffic circle	jiāotōng huándǎo	交通环岛
traffic jam	dǔchē	堵车
traffic light	hónglǜdēng	红绿灯
tragedy	bēijù	悲剧
train (railroad)	huǒchē	火车
train station	huǒchē zhàn	火车站
training	xùnliàn	训练
tranquilizer	zhènjìngjì	镇静剂
transfer (bus, train)	dǎo, huàn	倒，换
transformer (voltage)	biànyāqì	变压器
transit visa	guòjìng qiānzhèng	过境签证
translate	fānyì	翻译
translator	fānyì	翻译
transparent	tòumíng	透明
travel	lǚxíng	旅行
travel permit	lǚyóu xǔkězhèng	旅游许可证
travel service (agency)	lǚxíngshè	旅行社
traveler's check	lǚxíng zhīpiào	旅行支票
traveling bag	lǚxíng bāo	旅行包
tree	shù	树
tribe	bùluò, jiāzú	部落，家族
trick (v)	piàn	骗
tricycle (child's)	értóng chē	儿童车
tricycle (pedicab)	sānlún chē	三轮车
trim	xiūjiǎn	修剪
trio (instrumental)	sānchóngzòu	三重奏
trip (travel)	lǚxíng	旅行
tripod	sānjiǎojià	三角架
trolley	wúguǐ diànchē	无轨电车
truck (n)	kǎchē	卡车
true	zhēn	真
trunk (car)	xínglǐ xiāng	行李箱
trunk (luggage)	píxiāng	皮箱
truth	zhēnlǐ	真理
try	shì yíxià	试一下
tuberculosis	fèi jiéhé	肺结核
Tuesday	xīngqī èr	星期二
tug of war	báhé	拔河

turn (a corner)	guǎiwān	拐弯
turn around (head back)	diàotóu, huízhuǎn	调头，回转
turn off (to shut off)	guān	关
turn on (to switch on)	kāi	开
turnip	luóbo	萝卜
turtle	wūguī	乌龟
twenty	èrshí	二十
twin bed	dānrén chuáng	单人床
twin room	shuāngrén fángjiān	双人房间
two (the number)	èr	二
two (the quantity)	liǎng	两
two-prong plug (flat prongs)	píngjiǎo chātóu	平角插头
two-prong plug (round prongs)	yuánjiǎo chātóu	圆角插头
type (kind)	zhǒnglèi	种类
typewriter	dǎzìjī	打字机
typhoid	shānghán	伤寒
typhoon	táifēng	台风
typhus	bānzhěn shānghán	斑疹伤寒
typist	dǎzìyuán	打字员
ugly	chǒu, nánkàn	丑，难看
ulcer	kuìyáng	溃疡
umbrella	yǔsǎn	雨伞
uncle (see Appendix H)	shūshu	叔叔
under	zài...xiàmiàn	在···下面
underground (adj)	dìxià	地下
underpass	dìxià guòdào	地下通道
understand	dǒng	懂
underwear	nèiyī	内衣
uniform	zhìfú	制服
unit (organization)	dānwèi	单位
united	liánhé	联合
United Nations	Liánhéguó	联合国
United States	Měiguó	美国
university	dàxué	大学
until	dào...wéizhǐ	到···为止
up	shàng	上
upstairs	lóushàng	楼上
urban	chéngshì	城市
urinate	xiǎobiàn	小便
US dollar	měiyuán	美元
use (n)	zuòyòng	作用
use (v)	yòng	用
useful	yǒu yòng	有用
usually	tōngcháng, jīngcháng	通常，经常

vacation (n)	jiàqī, jià	假期，假
vacation, spend a	dùjià	度假
vaccination certificate	fángyì zhèng	防疫证
vacuum cleaner	xīchén qì	吸尘器
vague	móhu	模糊
valley	shāngǔ	山谷
valuable object	guìzhòng wùpǐn	贵重物品
value (n)	jiàzhí	价值
van (mini-bus)	miànbāochē	面包车
Vancouver	Wēngēhuá	温哥华
vase	huāpíng	花瓶
vegetable	shūcài	蔬菜
vegetarian food	sùshí	素食
ventilation	tōngfēng	通风
vermicelli (dried)	guàmiàn	挂面
vertical flute (bamboo)	xiāo	箫
very	hěn	很
vest	bèixīn	背心
vice-president (national)	fù zǒngtǒng	副总统
video camera	shèxiàng jī	摄像机
video cassette recorder	lùxiàng jī	录像机
videotape	lùxiàng cídài	录像磁带
Vietnam	Yuènán	越南
view (scenery)	jǐngsè	景色
viewfinder	qǔjǐngqì	取景器
village	cūnzhuāng	村庄
village fair	jíshì	集市
villain	ègùn	恶棍
vinegar	cù	醋
violin	xiǎotíqín	小提琴
visa	qiānzhèng	签证
visa office (PSB)	gōng'ānjú wàiguǎnchù	公安局外管处
visit	cānguān, fǎngwèn	参观，访问
visit relatives	tànqīn	探亲
vocabulary	cíhuì liàng	词汇量
vodka	fútèjiā	伏特加
voice (n)	sǎngzi	嗓子
volleyball	páiqiú	排球
voltage	diànyā	电压
voltage converter	biànyāqì	变压器
volts, 110	yìbǎi yīshí fú	110 伏
volts, 220	èrbǎi èrshí fú	220 伏
volume (book)	juàn	卷
volume (sound)	yīnliàng	音量
vomit	ǒutù	呕吐
wage (salary)	gōngzī	工资
waist	yāo	腰

waist drum	yāogǔ	腰鼓
wait	děng	等
waiter or waitress	fúwùyuán	服务员
waiting lounge	hòukè shì	候客室
wake up (self)	xǐnglái	醒来
wake up (someone else)	jiàoxǐng	叫醒
walk	zǒu, sànbù	走,散步
Walkman (personal stereo)	dānfàng jī	单放机
wall	qiáng	墙
wallet	píjiāzi	皮夹子
walnut	hétao	核桃
waltz (dance)	huá'ěrzī	华尔兹
waltz (music)	yuánwǔqǔ	圆舞曲
want (v)	yào	要
war	zhànzhēng	战争
warm (adj)	nuǎnhuo	暖和
warm (personality)	rèqíng	热情
wash (v)	xǐ	洗
washcloth	xǐliǎn jīn	洗脸巾
Washington DC	Huáshèngdùn Tèqù	华盛顿特区
waste (v)	làngfèi	浪费
wastebasket	zhǐlǒu	纸篓
watch (v)	kàn	看
watch (wristwatch)	shǒubiǎo	手表
watchband	biǎodài	表带
water (n)	shuǐ	水
water caltrop	língjiǎo	菱角
water chestnut	bíqì	荸荠
water lily	shuǐfúlián	水浮莲
water polo	shuǐqiú	水球
water-skiing	huáshuǐ yùndòng	划水运动
watercolors	shuǐcǎi	水彩
waterfall	pùbù	瀑布
watermelon	xīguā	西瓜
wavy	bōlàngshì	波浪式
way (direction)	fāngxiàng	方向
way (method)	fāngfǎ	方法
we	wǒmen	我们
weak	ruò	弱
wealth	cáifù	财富
wealth (symbol)	lù	禄
wear	chuān, dài	穿,戴
weasel	huángshǔláng	黄鼠狼
weather	tiānqì	天气
weather forecast	tiānqì yùbào	天气预报
weaver	biānzhī gōngrén	编织
weaving (n)	zhīpǐn	织品
wedding	hūnlǐ	婚礼

Wednesday	xīngqī sān	星期三
week	xīngqī	星期
weekend	zhōumò	周末
weekly (magazine)	zhōubào	周报
weight-lifting	jǔzhòng	举重
welcome	huānyíng	欢迎
well (adv)	hǎo	好
well (n)	jǐng	井
west	xī	西
West Germany	Xīdé	西德
West Lake	Xīhú	西湖
Western meal	xīcān	西餐
Western menu	xīcān càipǔ	西餐菜谱
Western toilet	zuòshì cèsuǒ	坐式厕所
wet (adj)	shī	湿
what	shénme	什么
wheat	màizi	麦子
wheel	lúnzi	轮子
wheelchair	lúnyǐ	轮椅
when	shénme shíhòu	什么时候
where	nǎlǐ, nǎr	哪里，哪儿
which	nǎge, něige	哪个
whiskey	wēishìjì	威士忌
white	bái	白
White Peony tea	Shòuméi chá	寿眉茶
white edible fungus	yín'ěr	银耳
white liquor, Chinese	báijiǔ	白酒
white wine	bái pútáo jiǔ	白葡萄酒
who (question)	shéi	谁
whole	zhěnggè	整个
wholesale	pīfā	批发
why	wèi shénme	为什么
wide	kuān	宽
width	kuāndù	宽度
wife	qīzi, fūrén, àirén	妻子，夫人，爱人
wildlife preserve	zìrán bǎohù qū	自然保护区
will (determination)	yìzhì	意志
will (future tense)	yào	要
willow tree	liǔshù	柳树
win	yíng	赢
wind (n)	fēng	风
wind instrument (music)	guǎn yuèqì	管乐器
window	chuānghu	窗户
windshield	dǎngfēng bōlí	挡风玻璃
windsurfing	fānbǎn yùndòng	帆板运动
windy	yǒufēng	有风
wine	pútáo jiǔ	葡萄酒
wine glass	jiǔbēi	酒杯

winter melon	dōngguā	冬瓜
wipe	cā	擦
wish (n)	yuànwàng	愿望
wishing you…	zhù nǐ…	祝你……
within	zài…yǐnèi	在…以内
wok	chǎocài guō	炒菜锅
woman	fùnǚ	妇女
women's bike	nǚchē	女车
wonderful	fēicháng jīngcǎi	非常精彩
wonton	húntún	馄饨
wood	mùtou	木头
woodcut	mùbǎn huà	木版画
wool	yángmáo	羊毛
word	zì	字
work (art, literature)	zuòpǐn	作品
work (job)	gōngzuò	工作
work quota	gōngzuò liàng	工作量
work unit	dānwèi	单位
worker	gōngrén	工人
worker's cap	yàshémào	鸭舌帽
workshop	chējiān	车间
world	shìjiè	世界
World War II	èr cì dàzhàn	二次大战
worry	dānxīn	担心
worse	gènghuài, gèngzāo	更坏, 更糟
would like to	xiǎngyào	想要
wound (n)	shāngkǒu	伤口
wrap	bāo	包
wrapping paper	bāozhuāng zhǐ	包装纸
wrench (hardware)	bānshǒu	搬手
wrestling	shuāijiāo	摔跤
wrist	shǒuwàn	手腕
write	xiě	写
write down	xiě xià	写下
writer	zuòjiā	作家
writing brush, Chinese	máobǐ	毛笔
wrong	cuò le, bú duì	错了, 不对
X-ray	X-guāng	X 光
xerox (see duplication)	fùyìn	复印
yak	máoniú	牦牛
Yangtze River	Chángjiāng	长江
yard (3 feet)	mǎ	码
year	nián	年
years old (age)	suì	岁
yellow	huáng	黄
yellow croaker	huánghuāyú	黄花鱼

Yellow River	Huánghé	黄河
Yellow Sea	Huánghǎi	黄海
yen	Rìyuán	日元
yesterday	zuótiān	昨天
yet	hái	还
yogurt	suānnǎi	酸奶
you	nǐ	你
you (plural)	nǐmen	你们
you (polite form)	nín	您
young	niánqīng, xiǎo	年青, 小
young man	xiǎo huǒzi	小伙子
young people	qīngnián	青年
young woman	niánqīng nǚrén	年青女人
your	nǐde	你的
your (plural)	nǐménde	你们的
yurt	měnggǔbāo	蒙古包
zebra crosswalk	bānmǎ xiàn	斑马线
zero	líng	零
zipper	lāliàn	拉链
zither, 25-string	sè	瑟
zither, 7-string	gǔqín	古琴
zither, many-stringed	zhēng	筝
zoo	dòngwùyuán	动物园

Chinese-English Dictionary

This part of the dictionary aims at providing English definitions of Chinese vocabulary that travelers to China may hear during their visit in the country. The vocabulary in this dictionary, therefore, consists of words and expressions commonly used in places such as hotel, restaurant, hospital, plane, train and shopping center. With this dictionary, you may be able to understand replies to your questions like *Zhè shì shénme?* (What's this?) and *Yào mǎi shénme?* (What do you want to buy?)

Pinyin	Chinese	English
ǎi	矮	short
ài	爱	love
àihào	爱好	hobby
àizībìng	爱滋病	AIDS
ānchún	鹌鹑	quail
ānmián yào	安眠药	sleeping pill
ànmó	按摩	massage
Àodàlìyà	澳大利亚	Australia
āsīpǐlín	阿斯匹林	aspirin
āyí	阿姨	auntie
bàba	爸爸	father
bābǎofàn	八宝饭	eight-treasure rice
bǎi	百	hundred
bái	白	white
báicài	白菜	bok choy; cabbage
báiguǒ	白果	ginkgo
bǎihuò shāngdiàn	百货商店	department store
báijiǔ	白酒	Chinese white liquor
bǎishù	柏树	cypress tree
báiyángshù	白杨树	aspen tree
Bālí	巴黎	Paris
bàn	半	half
bàng	磅	pound

bàngōngshì	办公室	office
bǎnhuà	版画	print
bānzhěn shānghán	斑疹伤寒	typhus
bāo	包	bag
bāochē	包车	hired car
bāoguǒ dān	包裹单	parcel form
bàoyú	鲍鱼	abalone
bàozhǐ	报纸	newspaper
bāozi	包子	steamed stuffed bun
básī píngguǒ	拔丝苹果	honey crystalized apples
báyá	拔牙	extract a tooth
bēi	杯	cup
bēijù	悲剧	tragedy
běnshì	本市	this city
bǐ	笔	pen; pencil
biànbì	便秘	constipation
biànfàn	便饭	a simple meal
biānpào	鞭炮	firecrackers
biǎo	表	watch
biǎoqíng	表情	expression
biǎoyǎn	表演	perform
bìlù diànshì	闭路电视	cable TV
bǐnggān	饼干	biscuit
bǐnglún	丙纶	acrylic
bīngqiú	冰球	ice hockey
bīngtáng húlu	冰糖葫芦	candied haws
bīnguǎn	宾馆	guesthouse; hotel
bíqì	荸荠	water chestnut
bǐsài	比赛	competition; match
bítōng	鼻通	decongestant
bìyùn yòngpǐn	避孕用品	contraceptives
bízi	鼻子	nose
bōcài	菠菜	spinach
bōluó	菠萝	pineapple

bùliào	布料	cloth
bùxié	布鞋	cloth shoe
búxiùgāng	不锈钢	stainless steel
bǔyá	补牙	fill a tooth
càidòu	菜豆	kidney bean
càihuā	菜花	cauliflower
càixīn	菜心	cabbage heart
cán	蚕	silkworm
cándòu	蚕豆	broad bean
cāntīng	餐厅	dining room; restaurant
cǎoyào	草药	herbal medicine
chéngshì	城市	city
cèsuǒ	厕所	toilet
chá	茶	tea
cháhuā	茶花	camelia
Chángchéng	长城	the Great Wall
Chángjiāng	长江	the Yangtze River
chángshòu	长寿	longevity
chángzi	肠子	bowels
chǎnkē bìngfáng	产科病房	maternity ward
chāshāobāo	叉烧包	roast pork bun
chē	车	train; bus; bike
chējiān	车间	workshop
chéngmén	城门	city gate
chéngqiáng	城墙	city wall
chéngyǔ	成语	idiom
chēpiào	车票	(bus or train) ticket
chī	吃	eat
chídào	迟到	be late
chōujīn	抽筋	cramp
chuán	船	ship; boat
chuáng	床	bed
chuāng	窗	window
chuánrǎn	传染	infection
chuánshuō	传说	legend

chuánzhá	船闸	ship lock
chuánzhēn	传真	Fax
chūfā	出发	set off
chúfáng	厨房	kitchen
chūkǒu shāngpǐn	出口商品	export goods
Chūn Jié	春节	Chinese New Year
chūnjuǎn	春卷	spring roll
chūntiān	春天	spring
chúxī	除夕	New Year's Eve
chūxuè	出血	hemorrhage
chūzū chē	出租车	taxi
cídài	磁带	cassette tape
cídiǎn	词典	dictionary
cōng	葱	scallion
cōngtóu	葱头	onion
cù	醋	vinegar
cuītùjì	催吐剂	emetic
dà	大	big
dà báicài	大白菜	Chinese cabbage
dàbiàn	大便	bowel movement
dàifu	大夫	doctor
dàjiā	大家	everybody
dàlǐshí	大理石	marble
dàmài	大麦	barley
dāndǐnghè	丹顶鹤	red-crowned crane
dàngāo	蛋糕	cake
dànhuātāng	蛋花汤	egg-drop soup
dānwèi	单位	work unit; organization
dānxíng xiàn	单行线	one-way street
dānyuán	单元	housing unit
dāodòu	刀豆	sword bean
dǎoyóu	导游	tourist guide
dàxiā	大虾	prawn
dàxiàng	大象	elephant
dàxué	大学	university

dàxuéshēng	大学生	college student
dēngjì chù	登记处	registration desk
dēngjīpái	登机牌	boarding pass
dī	低	low
diǎn	点	point
diànbào	电报	telegram
diànbào guàhào	电报挂号	cable address
diànchuán	电传	telex
diànhuà	电话	telephone
diànhuàfèi	电话费	telephone charge
diànliáo	电疗	electrotherapy
diànshì	电视	TV set
diǎnxīn	点心	dessert
diǎnxuèfǎ	点穴法	acupressure
diànyǐng	电影	film; movie
diāo	貂	marten
dìdi	弟弟	younger brother
dìfāng	地方	place
dìng'é	定额	quota
dīngxiāng	丁香	lilac
dīngxiāng jiǔ	丁香酒	clove wine
dīngzì lùkǒu	丁字路口	T-intersection
dìtiě	地铁	subway
dìtú	地图	map
dízi	笛子	bamboo flute
dōng	东	east
dōnggū	冬菇	black mushroom
dōngguā	冬瓜	winter melon
dōngtiān	冬天	winter
dùzi	肚子	belly; abdomen
dòubàn jiàng	豆瓣酱	hot bean sauce
dòufu	豆腐	beancurd
dòufu gān	豆腐干	dried beancurd
dòujiāng	豆浆	soybean milk
dòushā	豆沙	sweetened bean paste

dòuyá	豆芽	bean sprout
dòuzi	豆子	bean
duìhuàndān	兑换单	exchange slip
duì	对	correct
duìbuqǐ	对不起	excuse me; sorry
duìhuàn	兑换	exchange
duìhuànlǜ	兑换率	exchange rate
dùjuānhuā	杜鹃花	azalea
duōshǎo	多少	how many
duànluò	段落	paragraph
è	饿	hungry
ěr-bí-hóu kē	耳鼻喉科	ear-nose-throat department
èrhú	二胡	2-string fiddle
érkē	儿科	pediatrics department
érzi	儿子	son
ěxīn	恶心	nauseous
fādǒu	发抖	shiver
Fǎguó	法国	France
fàn	饭	rice
fàndiàn	饭店	hotel; restaurant
fāngfǎ	方法	method
fángjiān	房间	room
fàngshèkē	放射科	radiology department
fànguǎn	饭馆	restaurant
fángyì zhèngshū	防疫证书	vaccination certificate
fángzi	房子	house
fànhòu	饭后	after meals
fànqián	饭前	before meals
fānqié	蕃茄	tomato
fāyán	发炎	inflammation; infection
Fǎyǔ	法语	French
fèi	肺	lung
féi	肥	fat
fèi jiéhé	肺结核	tuberculosis
fěicuì	翡翠	jadeite

fēijī	飞机	aeroplane
fēijīchǎng	飞机场	airport
fèiyán	肺炎	pneumonia
fèiyòng	费用	expenditure
fēn	分	cent
fēng	风	wind
fēngjǐng	风景	scenery
fēngshī bìng	风湿病	rheumatism
fēngsú	风俗	custom
fēngwèi	风味	local flavour
fèngxiānhuā	凤仙花	touch-me-not
fénmù	坟墓	tomb
fójiào	佛教	Buddhism
fú	福	symbol for luck
fùkē	妇科	gynecology department
fùshí pǐn	副食品	nonstaple food
fúwùfèi	服务费	service fee
fúwùyuán	服务员	service attendant
fùxiè	腹泻	diarrhea; loose bowels
fùzhìpǐn	复制品	reproduction
gàicài	芥菜	leaf mustard
gàilán	芥蓝	Chinese broccoli
gālí jī	咖喱鸡	curry chicken
gān	干	dry
gān	肝	liver
gānbèi	干贝	scallop
Gānbēi!	干杯	Cheers!
gāngqín	钢琴	piano
gānjìng	干净	clean
gǎnkuài	赶快	hurry
gǎnlǎn	橄榄	olive
gǎnmào	感冒	have a cold
gǎnxiè	感谢	thank
gānyán	肝炎	hepatitis
gānzi	柑子	mandarin orange

gāo	高	high; tall
gāo'ěrfū	高尔夫	golf
gāoliang	高粱	sorghum
gāoxìng	高兴	happy
gāoyào	膏药	medicated plaster
gāoyuán	高原	highland
gèdì	各地	different places
gēge	哥哥	elder brother
gěli	蛤蜊	clams
géli bìngfáng	隔离病房	isolation ward
gèshì gèyàng	各式各样	various kinds of
gēzi	鸽子	pigeon
gōng'ānjú	公安局	Public Security Bureau
gōngchéngshī	工程师	engineer
gōngchǐ	公尺	meter
gōngjīn	公斤	kilogram
gōnglǐ	公里	kilometer
gōnglù	公路	highway
gōngqǐng	公顷	hectare
gōngyì měishù	工艺美术	arts and crafts
gōngyìpǐn	工艺品	handicraft article
gōngyù	公寓	apartment
gōngyuán	公园	park
gōngzī	工资	salary
gōngzuò	工作	work
gǒu	狗	dog
guàmiàn	挂面	vermicelli
guānchá shì	观察室	observation ward
guānjié	关节	joints
guānjié yán	关节炎	arthritis
guānxì	关系	connection; relation
gǔdài	古代	ancient
gǔdū	古都	ancient capital
Gùgōng	故宫	Imperial Palace; Palace Museum

guì	贵	expensive
guīdìng	规定	regulation
guìhuā	桂花	cassia
guìhuā jiǔ	桂花酒	cassia wine
gǔlóu	鼓楼	drum tower
guō	锅	pot; wok
guóhuà	国画	traditional Chinese painting
guójiā	国家	country
guǒjiàng	果酱	jam
guòmǐn zhèng	过敏症	allergy
guōtiē	锅贴	fried dumplings
guówùyuàn	国务院	state council
gǔqín	古琴	7-string zither
gùshi	故事	story
gútou	骨头	bone
hǎibiān	海边	seaside
hǎibīn	海滨	beach
hǎiguān shēnbào dān	海关申报单	customs declaration form
hǎilí	海狸	beaver
hǎimǐ	海米	dried shrimps
hǎishēn	海参	sea cucumber
hǎitáng	海棠	Chinese crabapple
hǎixiān	海鲜	seafood
hǎizhé	海蜇	jellyfish
háizi	孩子	child
hāmìguā	哈密瓜	Hami melon
hàn	汗	sweat
hángkōng	航空	aviation
hánpiàn	含片	throat lozenges
hǎo	好	good
háo	蚝	oyster
hǎochī	好吃	delicious
hǎokàn	好看	good-looking

Hǎoláiwū	好莱坞	Hollywood
hàomǎ	号码	number
háoyóu	蚝油	oyster sauce
hé	盒	box
hè	鹤	crane
héhuā	荷花	lotus
hēi	黑	black
hējiǔ	喝酒	drink wine
hēshuǐ	喝水	drink water
hétao	核桃	walnut
hóng	红	red
hóngchá	红茶	black tea
hónglǜdēng	红绿灯	traffic light
hóngshāo	红烧	braised in brown sauce
hóngshǔ	红薯	sweet potato
hòubiān	后边	at the back; behind
hòujīshì	候机室	airport waiting room
hóulóng	喉咙	throat
hóuzi	猴子	monkey
huàbào	画报	pictorial
huācài	花菜	cauliflower
huāfěn rè	花粉热	hay fever
huài	坏	bad
huáishù	槐树	locust tree
huáiyùn	怀孕	pregnant
huàjiā	画家	painter
huàliáo	化疗	chemotherapy
huáng'ān	黄胺	sulfa
huángdòu	黄豆	soybean
huángguā	黄瓜	cucumber
huánghuāyú	黄花鱼	yellow croaker
huángshǔláng	黄鼠狼	weasel
huángyóu	黄油	butter
huānyíng	欢迎	welcome
huāpíng	花瓶	vase

huáqiáo	华侨	overseas Chinese
huāshēng	花生	peanut
huáxuě	滑雪	skiing
huàzhǎn	画展	painting exhibition
Hūbìliè	忽必烈	Kublai Khan
hùjù	沪剧	Shanghai Opera
húntún	馄饨	wonton
hūnmí	昏迷	coma
huǒ	火	fire
huǒguō	火锅	hot pot
huòluàn	霍乱	cholera
huǒtuǐ	火腿	ham
húpō	湖泊	lake
hútòng	胡同	lane; alley
hùzhào	护照	passport
jī	鸡	chicken
jiā	家	family
jiājí	加急	urgent
jiājù	家俱	furniture
Jiānádà	加拿大	Canada
jiānbǐng	煎饼	crepe; egg pancake
jiǎndān	简单	simple
jiǎndāo	剪刀	scissors
jiāngdòu	豇豆	green long bean
jiǎngjīn	奖金	bonus
jiàngyóu	酱油	soy sauce
jiàngjià	降价	price reduction
jiànkāng	健康	healthy
jiànměi cāo	健美操	aerobics
jiǎnpiào	检票	ticket-check
jiǎnpǔ	简谱	numbered music notation
jiǎnyì	检疫	quarantine
jiànzhù	建筑	architecture
jiǎo	脚	foot
jiàoshī	教师	teacher

jiàoshì	教室	classroom
jiǎozi	饺子	boiled dumplings
jiàqī	假期	vacation
jiàqián	价钱	price
jiàshǐ zhízhào	驾驶执照	driver's license
jiāxiāng	家乡	hometown
Jiāyóu!	加油	Come on!
jiāzhútáo	夹竹桃	oleander
jīchǎng fèi	机场费	airport departure tax
jīdàn	鸡蛋	egg
jiēdào	街道	neighborhood
jièguāng	借光	excuse me; make way
jiéhūn	结婚	marry
jiějie	姐姐	elder sister
jièmo	芥末	mustard
jiémù	节目	program
jiérì	节日	festival
jiézhàng	结帐	settle the bill
jīguānhuā	鸡冠花	cock's comb
jīhuì	机会	chance
jíjiù zhàn	急救站	first-aid station
jīn	斤	a Chinese unit of weight (=1/2 kilogram)
jīn	筋	tendon
jīnghú	京胡	Beijing Opera fiddle
Jīngjì Rìbào	经济日报	Economic Daily
Jīngjù	京剧	Beijing Opera
jìngluán	痉挛	convulsion
jìngmài zhùshè	静脉注射	intravenous injection
jīngshén fēnliè	精神分裂	schizophrenia
jīngshénbìng	精神病	psychosis
jīnjú	金桔	kumquat
jìnkǒu huò	进口货	import goods
jīnnián	今年	this year
jīnsīhóu	金丝猴	golden-haired monkey

jǐngsè	景色	scenery
jǐngtàilán	景泰蓝	cloisonné
jīntiān	今天	today
jīnyú	金鱼	goldfish
jīnzhēn	金针	day-lily bud
jīròu	肌肉	muscle
jíshì	集市	village fair
jiǔ	酒	wine
jiǔ	九	nine
jiǔbēi	酒杯	wine cup
jiǔcài	韭菜	Chinese chives
jiǔjīng	酒精	alcohol
Jiùjīnshān	旧金山	San Francisco
jìyì	记忆	memory
jíyóu	集邮	stamp collecting
jízhěn shì	急诊室	emergency room
jìzhù	记住	remember
jǐzhuī	脊椎	spine
júbù mázuì	局部麻醉	local anesthesia
jùchǎng	剧场	theatre
juésè	角色	role; part
júhuā	菊花	chrysanthemum
jùhuì	聚会	get-together; party
jùlèbù	俱乐部	club
jūliúzhèng	居留证	residence permit
jūnduì	军队	army
jǔxíng	举行	hold
kāfēi	咖啡	coffee
kāishuǐ	开水	boiled water
kāiwánxiào	开玩笑	kidding; joking
kāiyǎn	开演	(of a movie, a play, etc.) begin
kàngshēngsù	抗生素	antibiotic
kǎoyā	烤鸭	roast duck
kě	渴	thirsty

kèqi	客气	polite
késòu	咳嗽	cough
kètīng	客厅	living room
kōng	空	empty
kōngqì	空气	air
kōngtiáojī	空调机	air-conditioner
kǒushuǐ	口水	saliva
kuài	快	quick
kuàilè	快乐	happy
kǔguā	苦瓜	bitter gourd
kuíníng	奎宁	quinine
kuìyáng	溃疡	ulcer
kùn	困	sleepy
Kūnqǔ	昆曲	Kunshan Opera
là	辣	hot; spicy
lā dùzi	拉肚子	diarrhea; loose bowels
làjiàng	辣酱	hot sauce
làjiāo	辣椒	chilli pepper
làméi	腊梅	allspice
lǎnchē	缆车	cable car
lánhuā	兰花	orchid
lánqiú	蓝球	basketball
lánsè	蓝色	blue
lǎohǔ	老虎	tiger
láojià	劳驾	excuse me; make way
lǎojiā	老家	ancestral place
làròu	腊肉	dried minced meat
lèi	累	be tired
lèigǔ	肋骨	rib
lěng	冷	cold
lí	梨	pear
lǐ	里	a Chinese unit of length (=1/2 kilometer)
liǎn	脸	face
liàng	亮	bright

liángkuài	凉快	cool
liángpiào	粮票	grain coupon
liánhuā	莲花	lotus
liánzǐ	莲子	lotus seed
liáotiān	聊天	chat
lièshì	烈士	martyr
lǐfà guǎn	理发馆	barber's; hairdresser's
lìji	痢疾	dysentery
líng	铃	ring
língjiǎo	菱角	water caltrop
língqián	零钱	coins; small bills
língshòu	零售	retail
lìshǐ	历史	history
liúgǎn	流感	flu
Liúlíchǎng	琉璃厂	Liuli Chang (lit. Colored Glaze Factory, a culture street in Beijing)
liǔshù	柳树	willow tree
lǐwù	礼物	gift
lìzhī	荔枝	lychee
lǐzi	李子	plum
lìzi	栗子	chestnut
Lóngjǐngchá	龙井茶	Dragon Well tea
lóngxiā	龙虾	lobster
lóngyǎn	龙眼	longan fruit
lóu	楼	building
lùxiàn	路线	route
lù	禄	symbol for wealth
lù	鹿	deer
lù	路	road
lǜ	绿	green
lǜchá	绿茶	green tea
lǜdòu	绿豆	mung bean
lǚguǎn	旅馆	hotel
lùkǒu	路口	intersection; crossroad

Lúndūn	伦敦	London
luóbo	萝卜	turnip
Luòshānjī	洛杉矶	Los Angeles
lùróng	鹿茸	pilose antler
lǚshè	旅社	hostel
lǚtú	旅途	journey; trip
lùxiàngjī	录像机	VCR
lǚxíngshè	旅行社	travel service
lǚxíng zhīpiào	旅行支票	traveler's cheques
lùyīnjī	录音机	tape recorder
mǎ	马	horse
máfan	麻烦	trouble
mǎfēi	吗啡	morphine
máhuā	麻花	fried sesame twists
màibó	脉搏	pulse
mǎi dōngxi	买东西	shopping
màizi	麦子	wheat
májiàng	麻将	mah-jong
Mǎkě Bōluó	马可·波罗	Marco Polo
māma	妈妈	mother
màn	慢	slow
mǎnǎo	玛瑙	agate
mànchē	慢车	slow train
máng	忙	busy
mángguǒ	芒果	mango
mántou	馒头	steamed bread
mànxìng	慢性	chronic
mǎnyì	满意	satisfaction
māo	猫	cat
màozi	帽子	hat
máoniú	牦牛	yak
máotái	茅台	Maotai (Moutai) liquor
mǎshàng	马上	immediately
máyóu	麻油	sesame oil
mázhěn	麻疹	measles

mázuì	麻醉	anesthesia
méiguānxì	没关系	It doesn't matter.
méiguìhuā	玫瑰花	rose
Měiguó	美国	U. S. A.
méihuā	梅花	plum blossom
měilì	美丽	beautiful
mèimei	妹妹	younger sister
měishùguǎn	美术馆	art gallery
mǐ	米	metre
mián	棉	cotton
miànbāo	面包	bread
miǎnfèi	免费	free of charge
miànjī	面积	area
miàntiáo	面条	noodles
mǐfàn	米饭	rice
Mǐlǎoshǔ	米老鼠	Mickey Mouse
míngchēng	名称	name
míngshèng	名胜	scenic spots
míngtiān	明天	tomorrow
míngxìnpiàn	明信片	postcard
mìngyùn	命运	fate
míngzi	名字	name
mínzú	民族	nation
mò	墨	ink
mòbān chē	末班车	last run
mòdǒuyú	墨斗鱼	cuttlefish
mógu	蘑菇	mushroom
mòlìhuā chá	茉莉花茶	jasmine tea
mǔdān	牡丹	peony
mùdì	目的	purpose
mùdì	墓地	burial grounds
mùdìdì	目的地	destination
mùlù	目录	catalog
nán	男	male
nán	难	difficult

nán cèsuǒ	男厕所	men's room
nánfāng	南方	south
nánguò	难过	sad
nǎomó yán	脑膜炎	meningitis
nánshòu	难受	uncomfortable
nǎoyán	脑炎	encephalitis
nèn	嫩	tender
niángāo	年糕	glutinous rice cake
niánhuà	年画	New Year painting
niánjǐ	年纪	age
niǎo	鸟	bird
niú	牛	ox
niúnǎi	牛奶	milk
niúpái	牛排	beefsteak
niúròu	牛肉	beef
Niǔyuē	纽约	New York
nóng	浓	thick
nónglì	农历	lunar calendar
nǚ cèsuǒ	女厕所	lady's room
Nǚ·ér	女儿	daughter
nüèji	疟疾	malaria
ǒu	藕	lotus root
ǒutù	呕吐	vomit
pàichūsuǒ	派出所	police station
páiduì	排队	line up
páigǔ	排骨	sparerib
páilóu	牌楼	memorial arch
páiqiú	排球	volleyball
pāizhào	拍照	take photos
pán	盘	plate
pàng	胖	fat
pángbiān	旁边	beside
pángxiè	螃蟹	crab
pánníxīlín	盘尼西林	penicillin
pàocài	泡菜	pickled vegetables

péndì	盆地	land basin
pén	盆	basin
péngyǒu	朋友	friend
pénjǐng	盆景	bonsai
piányi	便宜	cheap
pídàn	皮蛋	preserved duck egg
pīfā	批发	wholesale
pífūkē	皮肤科	dermatology department
píjiǔ	啤酒	beer
pīlìwǔ	霹雳舞	breakdancing
píng	瓶	bottle
píngguǒ	苹果	apple
Píngjù	评剧	Pingju Opera
pīngpāngqiú	乒乓球	table tennis
píngyuán	平原	plains
pínxuè zhèng	贫血症	anemia
pípá	琵琶	4-string lute
pípá	枇杷	loquat
píxià	皮下	hypodermic
píxiāng	皮箱	suitcase
píxié	皮鞋	leather shoes
píyǐng	皮影	shadow puppet
pízhěn	皮疹	rash
pòshāngfēng	破伤风	tetanus
Pǔ'ěr chá	普洱茶	Puer tea
pútáo	葡萄	grape
pútáo gān	葡萄干	raisin
pútáo táng	葡萄糖	glucose
pǔtōngcāng	普通舱	economy class
pǔtōnghuà	普通话	standard Chinese
qiān	千	thousand
qián	钱	money
qiǎn	浅	shallow
qiánbiān	前边	front
qiángwēi	蔷薇	hedge rose

qiānkè	千克	kilogram
qiántiān	前天	the day before yesterday
qiānzhèng	签证	visa
qiáo	桥	bridge
qiáo	瞧	look
qìchē	汽车	automobile; bus; car
qǐchuáng	起床	get up (from sleep)
qìchuǎn	气喘	asthma
qiézi	茄子	eggplant
qìgōng	气功	*qigong*; a kind of breathing exercise
qìhòu	气候	climate
Qímén hóngchá	祁门红茶	Keemun tea
qíncài	芹菜	celery
qíng	晴	fine
qǐng	请	please
qīngguāng yǎn	青光眼	glaucoma
qīngjiāo	青椒	green pepper
qīngkē	青稞	barley
qīnglún	晴纶	polyester
qīngméisù	青霉素	penicillin
qíngrén	情人	lover
qīngwā	青蛙	frog
qīngzhēn	清真	Moslem
qìngzhù	庆祝	celebrate
qīnqī	亲戚	relatives
qípáo	旗袍	a close-fitting woman's dress with high neck and slit skirt
qìshuǐ	汽水	soda water
qítā	其他	others
qiūhǎitáng	秋海棠	begonia
qiúsài	球赛	ball game; match
qiūtiān	秋天	autumn
qìwēn	气温	temperature

qīzi	妻子	wife
qù	去	go
quān	圈	circle
quánjiā	全家	the whole family
quánshēn mázuì	全身麻醉	general anesthesia
rén	人	person
rénkǒu	人口	population
rénmín	人民	the people
Rénmín Rìbào	人民日报	*People's Daily*
rénmínbì	人民币	*renminbi* (Chinese currency)
rénshēn	人参	ginseng
rénzào sī	人造丝	rayon
rìbào	日报	daily newspaper
rìjì	日记	diary
rìlì	日历	calendar
róngshù	榕树	banyan tree
ròu	肉	meat
ròumò	肉末	minced meat
ròusōng	肉松	dried meat floss
ruǎn	软	soft
ruǎn	阮	Chinese banjo
ruǎngāo	软膏	ointment
ruǎnwò	软卧	softsleeper
ruǎnyǐnliào	软饮料	soft drink
ruǎnzuò	软座	soft seat
sànbù	散步	go for a walk
sāngshù	桑树	mulberry tree
sǎngzi	嗓子	throat; voice
sānmíngzhì	三明治	sandwich
sānxián qín	三弦琴	3-string guitar
sè	瑟	25-string zither
sèlā	色拉	salad
shāfā	沙发	sofa
shāguō dòufu	沙锅豆腐	beancurd casserole
shān	山	mountain

shāndǐng	山顶	mountaintop
shàng	上	up
shāngdiàn	商店	shop
Shànghǎi	上海	Shanghai
shānghán	伤寒	typhoid
shāngkǒu	伤口	wound
shàngwǔ	上午	morning
shānyáng	山羊	goat
shānyù	山芋	sweet potato
shànyú	鳝鱼	eel
shānzhā	山楂	haw
shāobǐng	烧饼	sesame pancake
shé	蛇	snake
shělì	猞猁	lynx
shèmén	射门	shoot at a goal
shèn	肾	kidney
shēn	深	deep
shēng	升	litre
shēng	生	raw
shēng	笙	Chinese mouth organ
shěng	省	province
shēngjiāng	生姜	ginger
shēngqì	生气	angry
shēngrì	生日	birthday
shénhuà	神话	fairy tales
shénjīngbìng xué	神经病学	neurology
shénjīngzhì	神经质	neurosis
shénme	什么	what
shēntǐ	身体	body
shíbǎnhuà	石版画	lithograph
shìbiǎo	试表	take one's temperature
shífēn	十分	very
shīfu	师父	master worker
shìjiè	世界	world
shíliu	石榴	pomegranate

shīmián	失眠	insomnia
shípǐn	食品	food
shípǐn diàn	食品店	food store
shìqū	市区	city proper
shítáng	食堂	canteen
shíwù zhòngdú	食物中毒	food poisoning
shīzi	狮子	lion
shìzi	柿子	persimmon
shòu	寿	symbol for longevity
shǒubān chē	首班车	first bus or train
shǒufēngqín	手风琴	accordion
shōukuǎnchù	收款处	cashier's booth
Shòuméichá	寿眉茶	White Peony tea
shòupiàochù	售票处	ticket office
shōushi	收拾	pack; get things ready
shǒushùshì	手术室	operation room
shǒutào	手套	gloves
shǒuxù	手续	formalities
shōuyīnjī	收音机	radio
shǒuzhuó	手镯	bracelet
shú(shóu)	熟	ripe
shuànyángròu	涮羊肉	Mongolian hot pot
shūdiàn	书店	bookstore
shūfu	舒服	comfortable
shuǐ	水	water
shuì	税	tax
shuǐdiāo	水貂	mink
shuǐfúlián	水浮莲	water lily
shuǐjiǎo	水饺	ravioli; boiled dumplings
shuìjiào	睡觉	sleep
shuǐtǎ	水獭	otter
shuǐxiān	水仙	narcissus
shǔjià	暑假	summer vacation
shūjichù	书记处	secretariat
shuōmíngshū	说明书	synopsis

shūshu	叔叔	uncle
sìhéyuàn	四合院	traditional Chinese courtyard
sìjìdòu	四季豆	string bean
sōngshù	松树	pine tree
sōnghuādàn	松花蛋	preserved duck egg
suān	酸	sore; sour
suàn	蒜	garlic
suānlàtāng	酸辣汤	hot-and-sour soup
suānnǎi	酸奶	yogurt
sùcài	素菜	vegetarian food
Sūn Zhōngshān	孙中山	Sun Yat-sen
suǒnà	唢呐	Chinese cornet
sùshè	宿舍	dormitory; housing
tǎ	塔	tower
táifēng	台风	typhoon
tàijiàn	太监	eunuch
tàiyáng	太阳	sun
tāng	汤	soup
tāng miàn	汤面	soup noodles
Tánglǎoyā	唐老鸭	Donald Duck
tángniàobìng	糖尿病	diabetes
táozi	桃子	peach
tèkuài	特快	express
téng	疼	pain
Tiān'ānmén	天安门	Tian'anmen
tiáncài	甜菜	beet
Tiānjīn	天津	Tianjin
tiānkōng	天空	sky
tiānqì	天气	weather
tiánshí	甜食	dessert
Tiāntán	天坛	Temple of Heaven
tiāntáng	天堂	heaven
tiáowèi zuóliao	调味作料	seasonings
tiàowǔ	跳舞	dance

tǐcāo	体操	gymnastics
Tiěguānyīn chá	铁观音茶	Iron Goddess of Mercy tea
tīngshuō	听说	hear of
tǐwēn	体温	body temperature
tǐyùchǎng	体育场	stadium
tǐyùguǎn	体育馆	gymnasium
tòngkǔ	痛苦	pain
tóngxué	同学	classmate
tóngzhì	同志	comrade
tóuděngcāng	头等仓	first class (in a plane)
tóuyūn	头晕	dizzy
tuīná	推拿	massage
tuìrè	退热	antipyreti
tuìxiū	退休	retire
tūnyàn	吞咽	swallow
tūrán	突然	suddenly
túshūguǎn	图书馆	library
tǔtèchǎn	土特产	local product
túzhāng	图章	seal; chop
tùzi	兔子	rabbit
wàibì	外币	foreign currency
wàibīn	外宾	foreign guest
wàidì	外地	parts of the country other than where one is
wàiguó	外国	foreign country
wàihuì	外汇	foreign exchange certificate (FEC)
wàikē	外科	surgery department
wàimiàn	外面	outside
wàiyòng	外用	external use
wǎn	晚	late
wǎn	碗	bowl
wàn	万	ten thousand
wāndòuhuáng	碗豆黄	pea-flour cake

wǎnfàn	晚饭	supper
wǎngqiú	网球	tennis
wǎnhuì	晚会	evening party
wèi	胃	stomach
wèichuānkǒng	胃穿孔	gastric perforation
wèidào	味道	taste
wēijí	危急	critical
wéiqí	围棋	go
wèitòng	胃痛	stomachache
wèiyán	胃炎	gastritis
wènxùnchù	问讯处	information desk
wénzi	蚊子	mosquito
wòshì	卧室	bedroom
wōsǔn	莴笋	asparagus lettuce
wūguī	乌龟	tortoise
wúguǐ diànchē	无轨电车	trolley bus
wúhuāguǒ	无花果	fig
Wǔliángyè	五粮液	Five-grain Liquor
Wūlóng chá	乌龙茶	Oolong tea
wǔshù	武术	martial arts
wǔtīng	舞厅	dance hall
wútóngshù	梧桐树	Chinese parasol tree
wǔxiàn pǔ	五线谱	5-line music notation
wūzéi	乌贼	cuttlefish
xǐ	喜	symbol for happiness
xǐ	喜喜	double happiness
xì	戏	play
xiā	虾	shrimp
xián	咸	salty
xiàn	县	county
xiāng	乡	township
xiàng	象	resemble
xiāngcài	香菜	coriander
xiāngcháng	香肠	sausage
Xiānggélǐlā	香格里拉	Shangri-La

xiānggū	香菇	black mushroom
xiàngqí	象棋	Chinese chess
xiàngshēng	相声	cross talk
xiāngsū jī	香酥鸡	crispy fried chicken
xiāngsū yā	香酥鸭	crispy fried duck
xiāngwèi	香味	fragrance
xiāngyóu	香油	sesame oil
xiānhuā	鲜花	fresh flowers
xiánjiē hángbān	衔接航班	connecting flight
xián yādàn	咸鸭蛋	salted duck egg
xiànzài	现在	now
xiāo	箫	vertical bamboo flute
xiǎo	小	small; little
xiāodú gāo	消毒膏	antiseptic cream
xiāohuà	消化	digestion
xiǎohuǒzi	小伙子	young fellow
xiǎolóng bāo	小笼包	small steamed dumpling
xiǎomàibù	小卖部	kiosk
xiǎoshānyáng pí	小山羊皮	kidskin
xiǎochīdiàn	小吃店	snack bar
xiǎoshuō	小说	novel
xiǎotíqín	小提琴	violin
xiǎoxīn	小心	be careful
xiǎoxióngmāo	小熊猫	lesser panda
xiǎoxué	小学	primary school
xiǎoyáng pí	小羊皮	lambskin
xiàtiān	夏天	summer
xiàwǔ	下午	afternoon
xiàyǔ	下雨	rain
xīcān	西餐	Western meal
xié	鞋	shoes
xièxie	谢谢	thanks
xièyào	泻药	cathartic
xīfàn	稀饭	porridge; congee
xīhóngshì	西红柿	tomato

xǐjù	喜剧	comedy
Xǐmǎlāyǎ shān	喜玛拉雅山	Himalayas
xīn	新	new
xìn	信	letter
xīn shíqì shídài	新石器时代	Neolithic era
xìng	杏	apricot
xìng	姓	surname
xìngfú	幸福	happiness
xīnghóngrè	猩红热	scarlet fever
xíngli	行李	luggage
xìngmíng	姓名	name
xīngqīliù	星期六	Saturday
xìngqù	兴趣	interest
xìngrén	杏仁	almond
xìngrén dòufu	杏仁豆腐	almond gelatin
xìngrénchá	杏仁茶	almond-flour tea
xīnjiǎotòng	心绞痛	angina pectoris
xīnlì shuāijié	心力衰竭	cardiac failure
xīnlǐxué	心理学	psychology
xīntiào	心跳	palpitation
xìnyòng kǎ	信用卡	credit card
xīnzàngbìng fāzuò	心脏病发作	heart attack
xióngmāo	熊猫	panda
xìpiào	戏票	opera ticket
xiùhuā chènyī	绣花衬衣	embroidered shirt
xiūkè	休克	shock
xiùqiú	绣球	geranium
xiūxi	休息	have a rest
xiùyù	岫玉	Manchurian jasper
xuānzhǐ	宣纸	rice paper
xǔduō	许多	many
xuě	雪	snow
xuè	血	blood
xuéxiào	学校	school
xuèxíng	血型	blood type

xuèyā	血压	blood pressure
xūnyú	熏鱼	smoked fish
yákē yīshēng	牙科医生	dentist
yàmá bù	亚麻布	linen
yān	烟	tobacco; cigarette
yàn	咽	swallow
yān huánggua	腌黄瓜	pickled cucumber
yáng	羊	goat; sheep
yǎng	痒	itch
yángmáo	羊毛	wool
yángméi	杨梅	red bayberry
yàngpǐn	样品	sample
yǎngqì	氧气	oxygen
yángqín	扬琴	dulcimer
yángròu	羊肉	mutton
yǎnjīng	眼睛	eye
yánjiūsuǒ	研究所	research institute
yǎnkē	眼科	opthamology department
yǎnjīng	眼睛	eye
vànqǐng	宴请	invite sb. to a meal
yánróng	岩溶	karst
yánsè	颜色	color
yàntai	砚台	ink slab
yǎnyàoshuǐ	眼药水	eye drops
yǎnyuán	演员	actor; actress
yào	药	medicine
yàofāng	药方	prescription
yàofáng	药房	pharmacy
yāogǔ	腰鼓	waist drum
yāoqǐng	邀请	invite
yāotòng	腰痛	lumbago
yàowán	药丸	pill
Yàyùncūn	亚运村	Asian Games Village
yāzi	鸭子	duck
yě	也 ·	too; also; either

yèbān chē	夜班车	night bus
yèxià	腋下	armpit
yèyú	业余	spare time
yēzi	椰子	coconut
yì	亿	hundred million
yìdiǎnr	一点儿	a little
yīfu	衣服	clothes
yīgòng	一共	altogether
yìhuǐr	一会儿	for a while
yǐjing	已经	already
yīlù píng·ān	一路平安	Have a nice trip!
yīlù shùnfēng	一路顺风	Have a nice trip!
yín·ěr	银耳	white edible fungus
yìng	硬	hard; solid
yīngbàng	英镑	pound sterling
yīnglǐ	英里	mile
yīngtáo	樱桃	cherry
Yīngwén	英文	English
yìngwò	硬卧	hardsleeper
yìngzuò	硬座	hardseat
yǐnliào	饮料	beverage
yìnní	印泥	red paste for seals
yīntiān	阴天	cloudy
yínxìng	银杏	ginkgo
yīnyuè	音乐	music
yīnyuè tīng	音乐厅	concert hall
yīnyuèhuì	音乐会	concert
yīqǐ	一起	together
yīshēng	医生	doctor
yìshù	艺术	art
yīyàng	一样	the same
yīyuàn	医院	hospital
yìzhì piàn	译制片	dubbed film
yǒu	有	have
yòubian	右边	on the right

yóucài	油菜	rape
yóujú	邮局	post-office
yóupiào	邮票	stamp
yóutiáo	油条	cruller
yǒuyì shāngdiàn	友谊商店	friendship store
yóuyǒng	游泳	swim
yóuyú	鱿鱼	squid
yòuzi	柚子	pomelo
yú	鱼	fish
yuánliàng	原谅	excuse; forgive
yuānyāng	鸳鸯	mandarin ducks
yuánzuò	原作	original
yúchì tāng	鱼翅汤	shark's fin soup
yuèbǐng	月饼	mooncake
yuēhuì	约会	date; appointment
yuèjì	月季	Chinese rose
yuèjīng	月经	menstruation
yuèjù	越剧	Shaoxing Opera
yuèjù	粤剧	Cantonese Opera
yuèpiào	月票	monthly ticket
yuèqì	乐器	musical instrument
yuèqín	月琴	4-string mandolin
yùjù	豫剧	Henan Opera
yúkuài	愉快	happy
yǔmáoqiú	羽毛球	badminton
yúndòu	芸豆	kidney bean
yúshù	榆树	elm tree
yùtou	芋头	taro
zàijiàn	再见	good-bye
zájì	杂技	acrobatics
zánmen	咱们	we
zǎo	早	early
zǎo	枣	date
zǎo'an	早安	good morning
zǎocān	早餐	breakfast

zāogāo	糟糕	bad; terrible
zǎotáng	澡堂	bathhouse
zhàcài	榨菜	hot pickled mustard tuber
zhájī	炸鸡	fried chicken
zhàn	站	station
zhàngfu	丈夫	husband
zhāngnǎo	樟脑	camphor
zhāngshù	樟树	camphor tree
zhǎnlǎnhuì	展览会	exhibition
zhànxiàn	占线	busy line (tel.)
zhǎo	找	look for
zháojí	着急	worry
zhàopiàn	照片	photo
zázhì	杂志	magazine
zhēn	针	needle
zhèn	镇	town
zhěnduàn	诊断	diagnosis
zhēng	筝	many-stringed zither
zhěngtiān	整天	all day long
zhèngzhìjú	政治局	political bureau
zhèngzhuàng	症状	symptom
zhènjìngjì	镇静剂	tranquilizer
zhēnjiǔ	针灸	acupuncture
zhēnsī	真丝	silk
zhěntou	枕头	pillow
zhēngzhū	珍珠	pearl
zhèr	这儿	here
zhǐ	纸	paper
zhīqìguǎn yán	支气管炎	bronchitis
zhǐténg yào	止疼药	pain-killer
zhòng	重	heavy
zhōngcān	中餐	Chinese meal
Zhōngguó Yínháng	中国银行	Bank of China
zhōngjiān	中间	middle

zhōnglóu	钟楼	bell tower
zhòngshǔ	中暑	sunstroke
zhōngwǔ	中午	noon; midday
zhōngxué	中学	middle school
zhōngyào	中药	traditional Chinese medicine
zhǒngzhàng	肿胀	swelling
zhōu	粥	porridge; congee
zhōumò	周末	weekend
zhù	住	live
zhùhè	祝贺	congratulate
zhùmíng	著名	famous
Zhūmùlǎngmǎ fēng	珠穆朗玛峰	Mount Qomolangma (Everest)
zhuōbù	桌布	desk cloth
zhuōzi	桌子	desk; table
zhūròu	猪肉	pork
zhùshè	注射	injection
zhúsǔn	竹笋	bamboo shoot
zhùyì	注意	pay attention to
zhùyuànchù	住院处	inpatient department
zhùzhǐ	住址	home address
zǐdiāo	紫貂	sable
zìjǐ	自己	oneself
zìmù	字幕	subtitles
zìxíng chē	自行车	bicycle
zǒu	走	walk
zuànshí	钻石	diamond
zuìhòu	最后	finally
zuò	坐	sit
zuǒbian	左边	on the left
zuòkè	作客	visit as a guest
zuótiān	昨天	yesterday
zuòwèi	座位	seat
zúqiú	足球	soccer

Appendices

1. A Table of Chinese History

夏 Xia Dynasty		c. 21-16 cent B. C.
商 Shang Dynasty		c. 16-11 cent B. C.
周 Zhou Dynasty	西周 Western Zhou	c. 11 cent B. C. -771 B. C.
	东周 Eastern Zhou	770 B. C. -256 B. C.
	春秋 Spring & Autumn Period	770 B. C. - 476 B. C.
	战国 Warring States Period	475 B. C. -221 B. C.
秦 Qin Dynasty		221 B. C. - 207 B. C.
汉 Han Dynasty	西汉 Western Han	206 B. C. - A. D. 24
	东汉 Eastern Han	25 -220
三国 Three Kingdoms (Wei, Shu, Wu)		220- 280
西晋 Western Jin Dynasty		265 - 316
东晋 Eastern Jin Dynasty		317 - 420
南北朝 Northern & Southern Dynasties		420 - 589
隋 Sui Dynasty		581 - 618
唐 Tang Dynasty		618 - 907

五代 Five Dynasties	907 - 960
宋 Song Dynasty	960–1279
辽 Liao Dynasty	916 - 1125
金 Kin Dynasty	1115 - 1234
元 Yuan Dynasty	1271–1368
明 Ming Dynasty	1368–1644
清 Qing Dynasty	1644–1911
中华民国 Republic of China	1912–1949
中华人民共和国 People's Republic of China	founded in 1949

2. Time Around the World

Beijing	12 noon		
Amsterdam	5 am	Moscow	7 am
Bangkok	11 am	New York	11 pm *
Berlin	6 am	Ottawa	11 pm *
Cairo	6 am	Paris	5 am
Chicago	10 pm *	Rio de Janeiro	1 am
Frankfurt	6 am	Rome	5 am
Hong Kong	12 noon	San Francisco	8 pm *
Honolulu	6 pm *	Sydney	2 pm
London	5 am	Tokyo	1 am
Los Angeles	8 pm *	Vancouver	8 pm *
Montreal	11 pm *	Zurich	5 am

* Refers to the preceding day.

3. Chinese Measures and Weights

In China, there are two systems of measurement—the metric and the traditional. The British or American system, though, is not used.

	Chinese Unit	Metric Unit	American Unit
AREA		6. 5 sq cm	1 sq in
		929 sq cm	1 sq ft
		0. 8 sq m	1 sq yd
		1 sq m	1,550 sq in
	1 mǔ 亩	674. 5 sq m	807 sq yd
		4,047 sq m	1 acre
	15 mǔ 亩	1 ha	2. 5 acres
		1 sq km	0. 4 sq mi
		2. 6 sq km	1 sq mi
LENGTH		1 cm	0. 4 in
		2. 5 cm	1 in
		30. 5 cm	1 ft
	1 chi 尺	33. 3 cm	13. 1 in
		91. 4 cm	1 yd
	3 chi 尺	1 m	39. 4 in
	1 li 里	0. 5 km	0. 3 mi
	2 li 里	1 km	0. 6 mi
		1. 6 km	1 mi

WEIGHT	1 qián 钱	5 g	0.2 oz
		28.4 g	1 oz
	1 liǎng 两	50 g	1.8 oz
		454 g	1 lb
	1 jin 斤	500 g	1.1 lb
	2 jin 斤	1 kg	2.2 lb
		0.9 mt	2,000 lb
	2,000 jin 斤	1 mt	2,204 lb

4. Measure Words

Measure words in Chinese are irregular and difficult to grasp. The only solution is to familiarize oneself with them by memorization and to try to use them as much as possible. The following are some of the most commonly used ones.

Measure Words	What It Modifies	Example
bǎ 把	chairs, knives scissors	sān bǎ yǐzi (3 chairs) yì bǎ dāo (a knife) wǔ bǎ jiǎnzi (5 pairs of scissors)
běn 本	books, magazines	yì běn huàcè (an art book) sì běn xiǎoshuō (4 novels)
céng 层	building floor	dì shíwǔ céng (15th floor)
cì 次	occasion	dào zhèlǐ lái guò sān cì (been here 3 times)
chǎng 场	performance	yì chǎng gēwǔ (a singing and dancing show) sān chǎng diànyǐng (3 movies)
chū 出	opera	yì chū jīngjù (a Peking opera)
dào 道	course of a meal	sān dào liáng cài (3 courses of cold dish)
duàn 段	time	hěn cháng yí duàn shíjiān

		(a long period of time)
	distance, length	hěn cháng yí duàn jùlí
		(a long distance)
duì 对	couples, pairs	sān duì fūfù (3 married couples)
		yí duì ěrhuán (a pair of
		ear rings)
fèn 份	newspapers,	yí fèn Běijīng Zhōubào (a
	portions	copy of *Beijing Review*)
	printed matters	yí fèn zhájī (a portion
		of fried chicken)
fēng 封	letters	liǎng fēng xìn (2 letters)
fú 幅	paintings	yì fú yóuhuà (an oil painting)
gè 个	most things	yí gè lí (a pear)
		liǎng gè rén (2 people)
		sān gè yuè (3 months)
		yí gè chábēi (a tea cup)
gēn 根	many things	yìgēn yáqian (a tooth pick)
		liǎng gēn shéngzi (2 lengths of rope)
		sān gēn bīnggùnr (3 popsicles)
huí 回	occasion,	zhè huí (this time)
	chapter (book)	xiě le èrshí huí (wrote 20
		chapters)
jià 架	airplanes	yí jià Bōyīn fēijī (a
		Boeing plane)
jiān 间	rooms	liǎng jiān wòshì (2 bedrooms)
jiàn 件	clothing,	yí jiàn máoyī (a sweater)
	suitcases	liù jiàn xíngli (6 suitcases)
jù 句	words, dialogue	yí jù huà (a sentence, a
		few words)
kē 棵	grass, trees	sān kē shù (3 trees)
kuài 块	money,	èr shí kuài qián (20 yuan)
	rectangular	yí kuài táng (a piece of candy)
	or square objects	yí kuài xiāngzào (a bar of soap)
		liǎng kuài miànbāo
		(2 slices of bread)

liàng 辆	vehicles	yí liàng qìchē (a bus)
		liǎng liàng zìxíngchē (2 bicycles)
pán 盘	flat objects	yì pán lùxiàng dài (a video tape)
		sān pán liáng cài (3 plates of cold food)
píng 瓶	bottles	liǎng píng píjiǔ (two bottles of beer)
		sān píng kělè (3 bottles of coke)
shuāng 双	pairs related to	yì shuāng shǒu (a pair of hands)
	hands and feet	liǎng shuāng píxié (2 pairs of leather shoes)
tiáo 条	long, linear	yì tiáo kùzi (a pair of pants)
	objects	yì tiáo jiē (a street)
		liǎng tiáo yú (2 fish)
wèi 位	people (polite)	sān wèi gùkè (3 customers)
		yí wèi zuòjiā (a writer)
yè 页	printed matter	sānshí yè (30 pages)
zhāng 张	sheets (paper,	sān zhāng piào (3 tickets)
	photos, tickets)	yì zhāng dìtú (a map)
		liǎng zhāng zhǐ (2 sheets of paper)
zhī 只	animals	yì zhī niǎo (a bird)
		sān zhī māo (3 cats)
zhī 支	writing tools	yì zhī máobǐ (a Chinese brush)
		liǎng zhī yuánzhūbǐ (2 ball-point pens)
zhǒng 种	natural group,	yì zhǒng dòngwù (a kind of animal)
	race	yì zhǒng shípǐn (a type of food)

5. Week Days

Monday	Xīngqī yī	星期一
Tuesday	Xīngqī èr	星期二
Wednesday	Xīngqī sān	星期三
Thursday	Xīngqī sì	星期四
Friday	Xīngqī wǔ	星期五
Saturday	Xīngqī liù	星期六
Sunday	Xīngqī rì	星期日

6. Months

January	Yī yuè	一月
February	Èr yuè	二月
March	Sān yuè	三月
April	Sì yuè	四月
May	Wǔ yuè	五月
June	Liù yuè	六月
July	Qī yuè	七月
August	Bā yuè	八月
September	Jiǔ yuè	九月
October	Shí yuè	十月
November	Shíyī yuè	十一月
December	Shíèr yuè	十二月

7. Figures

one	yī	一
two	èr	二
three	sān	三
four	sì	四
five	wǔ	五
six	liù	六
seven	qī	七
eight	bā	八
nine	jiǔ	九
ten	shí	十
eleven	shíyī	十一
twelve	shíèr	十二
thirteen	shísān	十三
fourteen	shísì	十四
twenty	èrshí	二十
thirty	sānshí	三十
one hundred	yìbǎi	一百
a hundred and one	yìbǎi líng yī	一百零一
a hundred and ten	yìbǎi yīshí	一百一十
a hundred and twenty-five	yìbǎi èrshíwǔ	一百二十五
a thousand	yìqiān	一千
ten thousand	yíwàn	一万
a million	yì bǎiwàn	一百万

Ordinal numbers

first	dìyī	第一
second	dìèr	第二
third	dìsān	第三
fourth	dìsì	第四
fifth	dìwǔ	第五
sixth	dìliù	第六
eleventh	dìshíyī	第十一
twenty-first	dìèrshíyī	第二十一
one hundred and	dì yìbǎi	第一百一十一
eleventh	yīshíyī	

8. Directions

east	dōng	东
south	nán	南
west	xī	西
north	běi	北
southeast	dōngnán	东南
southwest	xīnán	西南
northeast	dōngběi	东北
northwest	xīběi	西北
front	qián	前
rear	hòu	后
left	zuǒ	左
right	yòu	右
up	shàng	上
down	xià	下

9. The Chinese Horoscope

The Chinese "horoscope" is represented by twelve animals, each one being one of the Twelve Earthly Branches in Chinese astrology. The animals each represent a year in a twelve-year cycle.

Traditionally, Chinese have kept track of their age by remembering what animal sign they belong to. For many old and most traditional Chinese, they may not be able to say off hand which year they were born, but they do remember the animal sign they belong to, and from there figure out what year it was. If you want to ask a person's age indirectly, you may ask "Nǐ shǔ shénme? (What animal year do you belong to?)" The twelve animals and their corresponding years in this century are given below.

Rat 鼠 shǔ	1900,	1912,	1924,	1936,	
	1948,	1960,	1972,	1984,	1996
Ox 牛 niú	1901,	1913,	1925,	1937,	
	1949,	1961,	1973,	1985,	1997
Tiger 虎 hǔ	1902,	1914,	1926,	1938,	
	1950,	1962,	1974,	1986,	1998
Rabbit 兔 tù	1903,	1915,	1927,	1939,	
	1951,	1963,	1975,	1987,	1999
Dragon 龙 lóng	1904,	1916,	1928,	1940,	
	1952,	1964,	1976,	1988	
Snake 蛇 shé	1905,	1917,	1929,	1941,	
	1953,	1965,	1977,	1989	
Horse 马 mǎ	1906,	1918,	1930,	1942,	
	1954,	1966,	1978,	1990	
Sheep 羊 yáng	1907,	1919,	1931,	1943,	
	1955,	1967,	1979,	1991	
Monkey 猴 hóu	1908,	1920,	1932,	1944,	
	1956,	1968,	1980,	1992	
Rooster 鸡 jī	1909,	1921,	1933,	1945,	
	1957,	1969,	1981,	1993	
Dog 狗 gǒu	1910,	1922,	1934,	1946,	
	1958,	1970,	1982,	1994	
Pig 猪 zhū	1911,	1923,	1935,	1947,	
	1959,	1971,	1983,	1995	

10. Family Relations

In Chinese, there are different ways of addressing relatives on the mother and father sides.

Immediate family members

father	bàba	爸爸
mother	māma	妈妈
elder brother	gēge	哥哥
his wife	sǎosao	嫂嫂
younger brother	dìdi	弟弟
his wife	dìmèi, dìxí	弟妹，弟媳
elder sister	jiějie	姐姐
her husband	jiěfu	姐夫
younger sister	mèimèi	妹妹
her husband	mèifu	妹夫
daughter	nǚér	女儿
son-in-law	nǚxù	女婿
son	érzi	儿子
daughter-in-law	érxí	儿媳
grandson (son's son)	sūnzi	孙子
grandson (daughter's son)	wàisūnzi	外孙子
granddaughter (son's daughter)	sūnnǚ	孙女
granddaughter (daughter's daughter)	wàisūnnǚ	外孙女

Paternal relatives

grandfather	yéye	爷爷
grandmother	nǎinai	奶奶
uncle (father's elder brother)	bóbo	伯伯
his wife	bómǔ	伯母
uncle (father's younger brother)	shūshu	叔叔

his wife	shěnshen	婶婶
aunt (father's sister)	gūgu	姑姑
her husband	gūfu	姑夫
elder boy cousin	tánggē	堂哥
younger boy cousin	tángdì	堂弟
elder girl cousin	tángjiě	堂姐
younger girl cousin	tángmèi	堂妹
nephew	zhízi	侄子
niece	zhínǚ	侄女
grandnephew	zhísūn	侄孙
grandniece	zhísūnnǚ	侄孙女

Maternal relatives

grandfather	lǎoye, wàigong	姥爷，外公
grandmother	lǎolao, wàipó	姥姥，外婆
aunt (mother's sister)	yi	姨
her husband	yífu	姨夫
uncle	jiùjiu	舅舅
his wife	jiùmā	舅妈
elder boy cousin	biǎogē	表哥
younger boy cousin	biǎodì	表弟
elder girl cousin	biǎojiě	表姐
younger girl cousin	biǎomèi	表妹
nephew	wàishēng	外甥
niece	wàishēngnǚ	外甥女

11. Traditional Chinese Festivals

Chūn Jié (Spring Festival) 春节 Falling in late January or early February, it is by far the most important and celebrated festival in China. In fact, it resembles everything of the Christmas of the West. It heralds the arrival of spring and the beginning of a new year. The whole family get together for an annual reunion dinner. One of the must dishes of the rich and elaborate New Year's dinner in northern China is jiǎozi, dumplings which symbolize reunion and good luck. Tons of firecrackers are fired to chase away the ghosts and bad luck. Relatives and friends visit each other, wishing everybody good luck, a happy life, and a big fortune. The first words people say to each other after midnight are Xīnnián Hǎo! 新年好！(Happy New Year!), Wànshì Rúyì! 万事如意！(Good luck!) and Gōngxǐ Fācái 恭喜发财！(May you a fortune!).

Yuánxiāo Jié (Lantern Festival) 元宵节 On the fifteenth day of the first lunar month, falling at the end of February. The speciality for the occasion is sweet boiled dumplings made with glutinous rice flour. People hang out lanterns, do the lion dance, and shoot off firecrackers. This festival marks the traditional end of the Spring Festival. After the Lantern Festival, everything will be back to normal and a new, busy working year begins.

Qingming Jié (Pure Brightness Festival) 清明节 At the end of the second lunar month or the beginning of the third month, falling in early April. This is an occasion to remember the dead. Family members go to the tombs of the deceased to pay their respects and sǎomù (sweep the tomb). Since the festival falls in spring, people now often use the time for spring outings.

Duānwǔ Jié (Dragon Boat Festival) 端午节 On the fifth day of the fifth lunar month, falling in late May or early June. People hold dragon boat competitions and make zòngzi — a pyramid-shaped glutinous rice dumpling that is wrapped in bamboo or reed leaves. This tradition comes from the story that over 2,000 years ago Qu Yuan, a patriotic poet, was deeply grieved when his country's capital city fell to the invading enemy and drowned himself in a river. To prevent his body being eaten by fish and shrimp in the river out of respect for the poet, people made this special food to feed river creatures. Of course, now the dumplings are only a special snack eaten around the festival time.

Zhōngqiū Jié (Moon Festival) 中秋节 On the fifteenth day of the eighth lunar month, falling mostly in early September. On that day the moon is supposed to be brighter and fuller than in any other month and the moonlight is the most beautiful. In China a full moon is also symbolic of family reunion, thus that day is also known as the "day of reunion". On that day's night in the past people would burn incense to pay worship to the moon, but now every family will stay together enjoying the bright moonlight while eating the "moon cake" (a round cake stuffed with sweeted walnuts or dried fruits to symbolize family reunion).

12. Chinese Idioms

Bān mén nòng fǔ 班门弄斧

Meaning: Display or show off one's skill before an expert.

Example: Wǒ de Zhōngwén bù hǎo. Zài nǐmén miàn qián zhēn shì bān mén nòng fǔ le. (My Chinese is bad. To speak Chinese in front of you people makes me feel as if I am trying to show off.)

Yǒu bèi wú huàn 有备无患

Meaning: Preparedness averts peril.

Example: Dài shàng yījiàn máoyī, yǒu bèi wú huàn ma. (Take a sweater and you'll have nothing to worry.)

Lè bù sī Shǔ 乐不思蜀

Meaning: Enjoy oneself so much that one forgets home.

Example: Wǒ fēicháng xǐhuān zhèlǐ, jiǎnzhí shì lè bù sī Shǔ le. (I like it here so much that I almost don't want to go home.)

Mǎn zài ér guī 满载而归

Meaning: Return from a rewarding journey.

Example: Kàn, wǒ shì mǎn zài ér guī. (Check it out, I am loaded with things from this trip.)

Yí jiàn rú gù 一见如故

Meaning: Feel like old friends at the first meeting.

Example: Wǒ hé Wáng xiānsheng yìjiā yí jiàn rú gù. (Though we've just met for the first time, the Wangs and I feel as if we are old friends.)

Zǒu mǎ guān huā 走马观花

Meaning: Look at flowers while riding on horseback—gain a superficial understanding or impression through a quick observation.

Example: Zhōngguó tài dà le, nǐ zhǐnéng zǒu mǎ guān huā. (China is so big that you can only get a very superficial idea of the conditions.)

Bú dào Chángchéng fēi hǎo hàn 不到长城非好汉

Meaning: He who has not been to the Great Wall is not a true man.

Example: Wǒ yídìng yào qù Chángchéng. Nǐmén bú shì yǒu yíjù chéngyǔ, jiào "bú dào Chángchéng fēi hǎo hàn ma"? (I must go to see the Great Wall. Don't you have a saying that "He who has not been to the Great Wall is not a true man"?)

13. China's Provinces, Autonomous Regions and Municipalities

Municipalities directly under the Central Government (3)

Beijing 北京
Shanghai 上海
Tianjin 天津

Autonomous regions (5)

Guangxi Zhuang Autonomous Region 广西壮族自治区
Inner Mongolia Autonomous Region 内蒙古自治区
Ningxia Hui Autonomous Region 宁夏回族自治区
Tibet Autonomous Region 西藏自治区
Xinjiang Uygur Autonomous Region 新疆维吾尔自治区

Provinces (23)

Anhui 安徽	Jiangxi 江西
Fujian 福建	Jilin 吉林
Gansu 甘肃	Liaoning 辽宁
Guangdong 广东	Qinghai 青海
Guizhou 贵州	Shandong 山东
Hainan 海南	Shaanxi 陕西
Hebei 河北	Shanxi 山西
Henan 河南	Sichuan 四川
Heilongjiang 黑龙江	Taiwan 台湾
Hubei 湖北	Yunnan 云南
Hunan 湖南	Zhejiang 浙江
Jiangsu 江苏	

14. Common Flowers

allspice	làméi	腊梅
azalea	dùjuānhuā	杜鹃花
begonia	qiūhǎitáng	秋海棠
cactus	xiānrénzhǎng	仙人掌
camelia	shāncháhuā	山茶花
cassia	guìhuā	桂花
Chinese rose	yuèjì	月季
chrysanthemum	júhuā	菊花
cock's comb	jīguānhuā	鸡冠花
forget-me-not	wùwàngwǒcǎo	勿忘我草
fuchsia	dàoguà jīnzhōng	倒挂金钟
geranium	xiùqiú	绣球
hedge rose	qiángwēi	蔷薇
hibiscus	fúróng	芙蓉
jasmine	mòli	茉莉
lotus	héhuā	荷花
morning glory	qiānniúhua	牵牛花
narcissus	shuǐxiān	水仙
orchid	lánhuā	兰花
oleander	jiāzhútáo	夹竹桃
peony	sháoyào	芍药
touch-me-not	hánxiūcǎo	含羞草
tree peony	mǔdān	牡丹
tulip	yùjīnxiāng	郁金香
water lily	shuǐfúlián	水浮莲

15. Common Trees

aspen	báiyángshù	白杨树
banyan	róngshù	榕树
camphor	zhāngshù	樟树
Chinese parasol	wútóngshù	梧桐树
cypress	bǎishù	柏树
elm	yúshù	榆树
gingko	yínxìngshù	银杏树
lilac	dīngxiāngshù	丁香树
locust	huáishù	槐树
maple	fēngshù	枫树
mulberry	sāngshù	桑树

16. Temperatures (C) in Ten Major Chinese Cities

Month	Jan	Feb	Mar	Apr	May	Jun	Jul	Aug	Sep	Oct	Nov	Dec
Beijing	-4.6	-2.2	4.5	13.1	19.8	24	25.8	24.4	19.4	12.4	4.1	-2.7
Shanghai	3.5	4.6	8.3	14	18.8	23.3	27.8	27.7	23.6	18	12.3	6.2
Nanjing	2	3.8	8.4	14.8	19.9	24.5	28	27.8	22.7	16.9	10.5	4.4
Fuzhou	10.5	10.7	13.4	18.2	22.1	25.5	28.8	28.2	26	21.7	17.5	13.1
Jinan	-1.4	1.1	7.6	15.2	21.8	26.3	27.4	26.2	21.7	15.8	9.4	1.7
Harbin	-19.4	-15.4	-4.8	6	14.3	20	22.8	21.1	14.4	5.6	-5.7	-15.6
Xian	-1	2.1	8.1	14.1	19.1	25.2	26.6	25.5	19.4	13.7	6.6	0.7
Lanzhou	-6.9	-2.3	5.2	11.8	16.6	20.3	22.2	21	15.8	9.4	1.1	-5.5
Urumqi	-15.4	-12.1	-4	9	15.9	21.2	23.5	22	16.8	7.4	-4.2	-11.6
Guangzhou	13.3	14.4	17.9	21.9	25.6	27.2	28.4	28.1	26	21.7	19.4	13.1